Are large American corporations politically unified or divided? This question, which has important implications for the viability of American democracy, has frustrated social scientists and political commentators for decades. Despite years of increasingly sophisticated research, resolution of the issue remains as elusive as ever.

In this important new book, Mark S. Mizruchi presents and tests an original model of corporate political behavior. He argues that because the business community is characterized by both unity and conflict, the key issue is not *whether* business is unified but the *conditions* under which unity or conflict occurs.

Adopting a structural model of social action, Mizruchi examines the effects of factors such as geographic proximity, common industry membership, stock ownership, interlocking directorates, and interfirm market relations on the extent to which firms behave similarly. The model is tested with data on the campaign contributions of corporate political action committees and corporate testimony before Congress. Mizruchi finds that both organizational and social network factors contribute to similar behavior and that similar behavior increases a group's likelihood of political success.

This study demonstrates that rather than making their political decisions in a vacuum, firms are influenced by the social structures within which they are embedded. The results establish for the first time that the nature of relations between firms has real political consequences.

The Structure of Corporate Political Action will be of interest not only to social scientists but to anyone concerned with the future of American democracy.

The Structure of
Corporate Political Action

The Structure of
Corporate Political Action

*Interfirm Relations
and Their Consequences*

Mark S. Mizruchi

Harvard University Press
Cambridge, Massachusetts
London, England
1992

Library of Congress Cataloging-in-Publication Data
Mizruchi, Mark S.
    The structure of corporate political action: interfirm relations
and their consequences / Mark S. Mizruchi.
        p. cm.
    Includes bibliographical references and index.
    ISBN 0-674-84377-0 (alk. paper)
    1. Business and politics—United States. 2. Corporations—United
States—Political activity. 3. Political action committees—United
States. I. Title.
JK467.M59 1992   91-18200
322'.3'0973—dc20   CIP

For Katherine and Joshua

Contents

Preface

This book is a study of the factors that generate political unity and conflict among large American corporations. I develop a model of the conditions under which firms engage in similar political behavior. I then test the model on a sample of 57 large U.S. manufacturing firms in the early 1980s.

Most observers believe that when firms' political behavior corresponds, it is a result of their similar interests. Beyond these common interests, however, a series of economic and social ties among firms, which I call mediating mechanisms, provides a source of similar political behavior. I argue, and demonstrate, that these network factors have a greater effect on the generation of business unity than do common interests.

This study constitutes an attempt to reorient the way in which studies of corporate political behavior have been undertaken. The old debates between pluralists and elite theorists and instrumentalist and structuralist Marxists not only have ended in theoretical and empirical stalemate but have become, to use Marx's term, fetters on the furthering of knowledge in this area. The lack of progress in resolving these debates has also led to the resurgence of the "state-centered" approach to politics, in which the state is viewed as an autonomous actor with its own interests and agenda.

There is little doubt that state managers often have interests that are independent of the interests of their constituents. That state policies can be understood primarily through the internal machinations of the state bureaucracy is a point I am less willing to accept. I operate with the assumption that one cannot understand the behavior of the state without knowledge of the actions of key societal actors, and that among these actors, none is more important than big business. But to say that major corporations are key political actors is not to imply that the business community, even if unified, will automatically get what it wants from the state. The ability of business to accomplish its goals must ultimately be studied in the context of the actions of other segments of society. Although my focus here is on big business, I hope that readers who do not share my assumptions will still find value in my analyses.

A number of people and institutions have assisted me during the course of this work. It is impossible to acknowledge everyone here, but I will try. I would first like to thank my colleagues at Columbia University, where I was a faculty member during the period in which this book was written. Ron Burt, Henk Flap, Eric Leifer, Siegwart Lindenberg, Martina Morris, and Harrison White provided extensive criticisms of an earlier draft of the manuscript. I am especially grateful to Ron and Harrison for their encouragement and advice.

Many other colleagues have helped, either by reading portions of the manuscript or by providing suggestions. A partial list includes Mark Abrahamson, Howard Aldrich, Allen Barton, Peter Blau, Val Burris, Bill Domhoff, Noah Friedkin, Barry Glassner, Mark Granovetter, Tom Koenig, David Krackhardt, Emily Loose, Edwin D. Mansfield, Robert K. Merton, Alan Neustadtl, Donald Palmer, Michael Schwartz, David Sciulli, Jonathan Turner, Michael Useem, Mayer Zald, and several anonymous reviewers. I would also like to thank Michael Aronson, my editor at Harvard University Press, for his support throughout this project and Lauren M. Osborne, my copy editor at Harvard, for her herculean efforts to improve my prose.

I owe a special debt to six people who provided extensive written comments on the entire manuscript: Ron Burt, Dan Clawson, Paul DiMaggio, David Jacobs, Ephraim H. Mizruchi, and Charles Perrow. All deserve my deepest thanks. I must single out DiMaggio and Clawson in particular, Paul for his more than twenty single-spaced pages of comments and Dan for his valuable feedback on every aspect of this work. Chick Perrow provided, at a moment's notice, a second set of comments on revised drafts of three chapters. Hal Mizruchi provided comments on several versions of the manuscript.

I am grateful to the National Science Foundation, first for the initial grant that launched the project (SES-8619230) and then for the Presidential Young Investigator Award (SES-8858669) that enabled me to carry it through. The Graduate School of Arts and Sciences at Columbia provided two summer fellowships, continuing research funds, and a semester's leave, all of which contributed greatly to the completion of the book. I was also fortunate enough to have a number of extraordinary research assistants, whose work was invaluable. I would like to thank Miguel Guilarte, Shin-Kap Han, Raymond Ho, Katherine Hughes, Henry Mayorga, Jaesoon Rhee, Kambiz Sakhai, Lap-Kung Sung, Andras Szanto, Ilan Talmud, and, especially, Gwen Dordick, Helen Reid, and David Scialdone.

I would like to thank University of Chicago Press for permission to reprint portions of my article, "Similarity of political behavior among large American corporations," *American Journal of Sociology* 95:401–424, copyright © 1989 by the University of Chicago. I am also grateful to the following publishers for permission to reprint portions of previously published work: the American Sociological Association (*American Sociological Review* and *Sociological Theory*), University of North Carolina Press (*Social Forces*), University of Texas Press (*Social Science Quarterly*), and Plenum Publishing Corporation (*Sociological Forum*).

Finally, I would like to thank my wife, Katherine. The book is dedicated to her and to our son, Joshua.

The Structure of
Corporate Political Action

1 · Introduction

Sociologists who do research in the area of corporations and politics often find themselves in a quandary. On the one hand, there are the questions from those outside the specialty about why a certain issue is sociologically significant; on the other, there are the objections of political scientists who understand the significance of the issues discussed but believe they should be handled in a different way. I hope that an account of the process by which I arrived at the study presented here will demonstrate the centrality of the topic to sociologists. At the same time, I hope to convince political scientists and those in other fields that this work can contribute to theirs, even if I approach the topic differently.

The roots of this project can be traced to my role as a canvasser for the McGovern campaign during the 1972 presidential election. As a student at Washington University, I went door-to-door in white ethnic neighborhoods on the South Side of St. Louis trying to convince registered Democrats to support their party's nominee. As the results of the election demonstrated, my efforts (and those of thousands of other volunteers) clearly failed. Beyond the personal frustration, I was struck by the extent to which my working-class respondents were willing to support a candidate (Nixon) whose policies appeared to be opposed to their economic interests. The hostility to McGovern expressed by these constituents, who after all stood to benefit from McGovern's projected policy of increased taxation of corporations and the wealthy, could only be explained, I reasoned, by their internalization of attitudes that encouraged racism, chauvinism, and intolerance. The acceptance of these views appeared so complete that they were willing to vote against their own material interests. How could this happen?

Although I did not realize it at the time, the question I was asking was the now century-old one, "Why is there no widespread support for socialism in the United States?" My interest in this issue led me to take courses in sociology. In the early 1970s sociologists were still preoccupied with the distinction between the "order" and "conflict" perspectives. The order perspective was rooted in Durkheim's thought and its primary contemporary proponent was Talcott Parsons. Its fundamental assumption was that societies were stable and routinized systems of relations maintained by shared normative systems. Parsons's model stated that social norms were internalized; that is, norms became so thoroughly embedded in the personalities of social actors that they were not questioned. The conflict perspective was less explicit and its forms more varied. Such diverse thinkers as Lewis Coser, Ralf Dahrendorf, and C. Wright Mills were all at one time viewed as conflict theorists. The fundamental assumption of the conflict perspective was the idea that societies were not inherently stable but were instead characterized by disorder, conflict, and change. To the extent that there was order and stability, according to this model, it was a result of the coercion of subordinate classes by a dominant class. As Marx had stated in *The German Ideology* ([1932] 1972, p. 136), "the ideas of the ruling class are in every epoch the ruling ideas." Rather than internalizing the values of the "society," members of the subordinate class had in fact, according to this model, internalized the values of the dominant class.[1]

Both of these views had clear relevance to the question of why American workers appeared to be so conservative. If white working-class Americans were upset at protests against U.S. involvement in Vietnam or were angry about government programs to benefit blacks, the order perspective would tell us that it was because these actions were viewed as unpatriotic (criticizing the government in time of war) or socialistic (providing government assistance to people who should be expected to achieve success on their own, as the American individualistic ethos suggested). Working-class Americans refused to support McGovern, an order theorist might argue, because the values of the candidate and his supporters ran counter to the values of most Americans. In this view, the attachment of workers to values of patriotism and individualism was sufficiently strong to override even their economic interests.

---

[1] It is important to note that by no means did all Marxists agree that workers had internalized any values, let alone those of the ruling class. But this represented my own understanding at the time. For alternative views, see Gramsci (1971), Sallach (1974), and Vanneman and Cannon (1987).

The conflict perspective suggested a very different account of white workers' conservatism. In this view, the dominant class, which controlled all of the major institutions of the society including the political system, the educational system, and the media, had inculcated workers with the values of nationalism and anti-socialism. Moreover, this view suggested, the dominant class had contributed to racism by encouraging the belief that blacks could only achieve economic gains at the expense of white workers, thus turning members of the working class, who would otherwise have been economic and political allies, against one another.

In short, the order perspective suggested that workers' conservatism was a result of their internalization of values shared by the entire society while the conflict perspective suggested that workers' conservatism was a result of confusion induced by the dominant class's control of major institutions, resulting in a false consciousness and a failure to see alternatives to the present social structure.

I gradually realized that to have any hope of resolving this debate I would need to turn to the literature in political sociology. Once there I encountered another controversy, known at the time as "pluralism" versus "elite theory." Although strands of both schools of thought had existed for decades, the debate was sparked by the publication in the 1950s of two books, Floyd Hunter's *Community Power Structure* and C. Wright Mills's *The Power Elite*. Pluralists argued that power in advanced capitalist democracies such as the United States was dispersed among several different and often opposing groups, no one of which consistently dominated over time. Elite theorists argued that American society was dominated by a small group of highly integrated elites whose interests conflicted with those of the vast majority of the population.

The debate between pluralists and elite theorists closely paralleled that between order and conflict theorists. Pluralists recognized the existence of conflict, but they argued that these disputes concerned specific issues within the context of an acceptance of the general rules of the game. In addition, conflict was viewed as cutting across class and status boundaries. Thus, two workers might be almost as likely to oppose each other as they would a capitalist. Because political leaders were viewed by pluralists as accountable to their constituents, if American workers did not support socialist candidates it was because they chose not to. Thus, the pluralist model was fully consistent with the order perspective. Elite theorists provided a very different view. Although some divisions within this elite were assumed by Hunter and Mills to exist, the elites' overriding unity of interest along with their domination of the masses ensured their ability to exercise power generally unaccountable to the majority. Thus, similar to the conflict perspective, if workers did not support socialist candidates it was either because they were unable to see their "true" interests due to the inculcation of the dominant value system or because alternative candidates were simply not available. Thus, in the order and pluralist perspectives, American workers were not socialists because they did not want socialism. In the conflict and elite perspectives, American workers were not socialists because they were brainwashed, unaware of alternative perspectives, or simply unable to muster the resources to mount an effective challenge to the system.

By the time I entered graduate school in 1975, I had decided that a resolution to the pluralist-elitist debate would be necessary if the order-conflict debate was to be resolved. Like many who were attracted to graduate study in sociology, I was interested in the broad, general themes discussed in my college courses, few of which were easily convertible into empirical research projects. During my second year, however, I had the good fortune to take two seminars with Michael Schwartz, who was in the midst of a study of corporate ownership and control. What little I knew about that topic consisted of a chapter of Baran and Sweezy's *Monopoly Capital,* in which the Marxist authors argued (against other Marxists) that ownership and control had become separated in the large corporation and that firms were now run by managers. They insisted, however, that this transformation had no impact on corporate behavior. Because the idea that wealthy families and bankers controlled most large corporations struck me as anachronistic, I accepted Baran and Sweezy's argument. But I was not aware of its theoretical implications.

During that semester, Beth Mintz, one of Schwartz's students on the project, gave a presentation that demonstrated clearly the theoretical importance of the issue: the managerial revolution had been used as empirical confirmation of the existence of political pluralism. If corporations were run by bureaucrats rather than capitalists, insiders rather than outsiders, then corporations were indistinguishable from other bureaucracies and the idea of a unified capitalist class overseeing groups of corporations was a fiction. Instead, pluralism reigned as the leaders of each firm, beholden only to themselves, pursued their particularistic interests regardless of the political consequences for the class as a whole.

Mintz and Schwartz had updated the Hobson-Hilferding-Lenin theory of finance capital and argued that financial institutions, due to their control of capital, were the primary source of power, integration, and conflict resolution in the business community. To examine this thesis, they employed data on relations among firms created by overlapping board memberships, known as interlocking directorates. Using mathematical techniques from the emerging approach of network analysis, Mintz and Schwartz identified the most central firms in interlock networks based on the assumption that the most central firms (those connected to the most other firms) were also the most powerful. Their findings, based on data from the 1960s, demonstrated that banks were predominant among the most central firms. Whether this actually confirmed the finance capital argument remains unclear, but it was a striking finding nonetheless.

Schwartz and his students' ultimate aim had been to contribute to the stimulating debates over the nature of the capitalist state then occurring among Marxists. A debate had arisen during the 1970s between what were termed "instrumentalist" and "structuralist" theorists. Instrumentalists argued that the state in a capitalist society was primarily a tool of the capitalist class. Most prominent members of government were said (especially in the executive branch) to come from elite backgrounds. High levels of interaction and personnel interchange characterized corporate-state relations, and policy-making organizations that directly influenced the state represented the leading segments of the capitalist class. In short, the state was viewed as an instrument of capital. Structuralists argued that capitalists were by themselves incapable of anything other than the pursuit of their immediate interests. Because these interests often conflicted with those of other capitalists and because they were often not in the best long-run interests of the system as a whole, structuralists argued that for the system to operate in the interests of the capitalist class, it was necessary for the state to have "relative autonomy" from business. In other words, the state must do for business what business is incapable of doing for itself. Marx's discussion of the flounderings of the French bourgeoisie in *The Eighteenth Brumaire* is often presented as an example of this.

Although members of both camps either were self-identified Marxists or were closely identified with Marxist issues, the debate mirrored the pluralist-elitist debate. The key issue for both was the extent to which the elite was unified.

The debates between pluralists and elite theorists on whether the elite was unified were no less abstract than the question of whether public quiescence was voluntary or involuntary. Pluralists were quick to recognize that elites were united in their support of the general rules of the game, but they argued that within these rules conflict was typical. Elite theorists were quick to admit that conflict between elites was a frequent and normal occurrence, but they argued that the conflict over day-to-day issues was trivial compared to elites' overriding unity in support of the system and with it their social privileges. Increasingly, as with the order versus conflict theory debate, the dispute between pluralists and elite theorists became an ideological one.

Elite theorists eventually recognized that their model would have to acknowledge significant conflicts of interest within the elite. Instead of arguing simply that elites were united in their support of the system, elite theorists began to identify mechanisms that either created tendencies toward unity in the first place or created unity out of conflicts by resolving them. Intermarriage became a means by which a social elite solidified its interests. Policy-planning organizations became arenas in which disagreements were ironed out so that business could approach the state as a single unified block. Interlocking directorates assisted in the mediation of conflicts of interests among firms. It was not that conflict did not exist, but, rather, that conflict was harnessed and resolved by mechanisms indigenous to the business community.

This was an eminently reasonable argument. The obvious research strategy, then, was to demonstrate the ways in which these mechanisms in fact led to business conflict resolution. Incredibly, however, except for a small number of studies, such as those by G. William Domhoff and J. Allen Whitt, elite theorists and those sympathetic to elite theory did not do this. Instead, they plunged headfirst into what were primarily descriptive examinations of the existence of these presumed mediating mechanisms. The assumption, rarely stated but usually implicit, was that the mere demonstration that these institutions existed was sufficient to demonstrate their utility as conflict resolution mechanisms.

In fairness, pluralists had in a sense encouraged this type of analysis by denying that these institutions were common. Arnold Rose, for example, had stated (1967, p. 133) that "interlocking directorates, where they occur in the larger corporations, give them a high degree of cohesiveness." Rose was able to say this because he asserted simultaneously, without evidence, that "interlocking directorates are the exception rather than the rule" (ibid., p. 92). Statements such as these suggested that the mere demonstration of large numbers of interlocks would be sufficient to demonstrate the cohesiveness of the business community.

This challenge was taken up by several researchers, including some of those on Schwartz's project. While Mintz and Schwartz focused primarily on the role of banks within contemporary interlock networks, I focused on the structure of the network as a whole, including the density of interfirm ties, over time. I began with the premise that virtually all theorists, regardless of perspective, agreed about the structure of the American business community at the turn of the twentieth century. Where they disagreed was in what had happened since then. Managerialists (and pluralists) argued that the business community had become increasingly atomized as the multi-firm empires of powerful capitalist families gave way to bureaucratically administered organizations run by professional managers whose interests failed to extend beyond the firm's boundaries. My findings, based on an analysis of networks of 167 large firms at seven points between 1904 and 1974, suggested that managerialists were partly correct but their claims of the decomposition of capital were considerably exaggerated, especially for the period after 1935. If interlocking was an indicator of cohesiveness, as Rose had suggested, then the evidence overwhelmingly suggested that the largest American firms were indeed cohesive.

As so often happens in politically charged debates, as soon as elite theorists demonstrated the ubiquity of interlocks, pluralist critics altered the basis of their attack. Unable to deny the widespread existence of interlocks, pluralists argued instead that the existence of interlocks by itself proved nothing. Unless one could demonstrate that interlocks had actual *behavioral consequences*, the critics suggested, interlocks indicated little more than the friendship patterns of business leaders or attempts by corporate managers to respond to environmental uncertainty.

For about three years my work involved responses to this criticism. I relied for the most part on arguments that one often cannot observe the exercise of power. Despite my belief in the fundamental soundness of these arguments, the criticism persisted. The necessity of demonstrating the behavioral consequences of these interlocks became increasingly clear. Many power structure researchers had already reached this conclusion. Domhoff, for example, had emphasized the need for empirical examinations of what elites actually do. Whitt produced an empirical study that suggested the viability of a Marxist perspective while closely following pluralist methodological procedures. Persuasive as these studies were, I was convinced that until we moved beyond the case-study method, every example that demonstrated elite unity would bring forth another to demonstrate irreconcilable differences. Systematic, quantitative analysis of a large number of firms remained, in my view, a necessity. But where were the data?

An Interorganizational Model

During the period leading up to this time, I had been developing a theoretical model that synthesized components of the two main perspectives on intercorporate relations: the resource dependence and social class models. The study of interlocks had originally met opposition from managerialists who argued that interlocks are essentially meaningless because boards have little or no power and managers appoint primarily their friends to board positions. That this view ran counter to Berle and Means's original formulation, in which management was defined as the board, appeared to escape most latter-day managerialists. Organizational theorists, nevertheless, eventually developed a meaningful account of interlocks. Drawing on Selznick's classic study of the Tennessee Valley Authority, Thompson and McEwen suggested that the appointment of a representative of another firm to one's board could be viewed as a mechanism of cooptation, the absorption of potentially disruptive elements of the environment into the organization's decision-making apparatus. It took more than a decade before this notion was subjected to empirical testing, but several organizational researchers, including Jeffrey Pfeffer, Ronald Burt, Michael Allen, and Johannes Pennings, developed cooptation models of interlocking. These theorists reasoned that firms would create interlocks with firms on which they were dependent for resources or, in Burt's case, with firms that placed constraints on one's ability to realize profits. Empirical support for these arguments was mixed, but enough significant associations were found to demonstrate that interlocks were indeed meaningful phenomena.

The cooptation models went a long way toward legitimating the study of interlocking directorates, but they treated interlocks very differently than did class theorists. Yet even the class theorists had two different approaches, and it was this dichotomy that opened the way for my synthesis. The most important contemporary statement of the class model was Maurice Zeitlin's 1974 article on "Corporate Ownership and Control." Zeitlin argued that corporations must be viewed as tools used by members of a dominant class for the accumulation of capital. In other words, control emanated from outside the corporation. Interlocks were indicative of relations among members of a dominant class rather than as mechanisms by which organizations co-opt sources of environmental uncertainty. At the heart of the class structure, according to Zeitlin, was a group of closely intertwined capitalist families. Zeitlin and Richard Ratcliff were able to demonstrate this model convincingly for Chile, but evidence for the United States was less forthcoming.

The second version of the class model, best characterized by Mintz and Schwartz in *The Power Structure of American Business*, is more institutional in nature.[2] Mintz and Schwartz generally ignore the roles of families and stockowners and instead focus on the importance of financial institutions, especially banks. In other words, the corporations and their relations become the main focus. External sources of influence are important but the key external force is banks rather than capitalist families. By the time Mintz and Schwartz's book appeared in 1985, the authors had removed most of their references to the social class implications of their findings. In my 1982 work, *The American Corporate Network*, however, these implications were a key aspect of my conclusions.

One of the most interesting developments of the early twentieth century was the succession of corporate control following the deaths or retirements of the great capitalists of the period. Many of these people, such as J. P. Morgan, John D. Rockefeller, and George F. Baker, were replaced by their sons. Others, such as James Stillman, were replaced by hand-picked successors. Prior to their deaths, the fathers had established financial empires that consisted of several large, interconnected firms and a single apex, such as J. P. Morgan & Co., Standard Oil of New Jersey, and the First National Bank of New York. The sons who took over the reins of these empires had in every case less individual power than their elders had. Business histories of the period referred to J. P. Morgan as an individual, but descriptions of the

---

[2] A third version of the class model, proposed by Michael Useem in *The Inner Circle*, contains elements of both the Zeitlin and the Mintz and Schwartz versions. Useem's work is treated at several points in the book.

period after his death refer to the House of Morgan rather than to J. P. Morgan, Jr.

This transformation was evident in my data on interlocks among 167 large firms. In 1912, 27 individuals sat on six or more boards within the system. Most of these were the major capitalists of the day. By 1919 only 13 individuals sat on six or more boards; by 1935 there were only three such persons, and by 1969 there were none. This shift in importance from individuals to organizations parallels the emergence of the organization-dominated society described by James Coleman in *The Asymmetric Society*.

Yet despite the decline in importance of powerful individuals, the system of relations established by these individuals remained remarkably stable into the 1970s. The same group of New York banks that had been in the center of the network in 1912 was in the center in 1969. A disproportionate number of firms that were tied together through interlocks early in the century remained interlocked into the 1960s. I referred to this phenomenon as the "institutionalization of intercorporate relations." While not demonstrating the continued existence of a cohesive business community, the persistent density of the interlock network certainly provided the potential for its existence.

What I observed, then, were two tendencies, each of which provided partial support to one of the two models. The increasing importance of corporations with respect to the individuals who controlled them over time suggested the tenability of the resource dependence, or organizational, model. The continued existence of a cohesive system of interfirm ties suggested at least the potential tenability of the class model. Who controlled the corporation had become less relevant, I argued, than the firm's role in the structure of intercorporate relations. As I put it (in 1982), "if the Rockefellers suddenly disappeared, would the Chase Manhattan Bank slip into oblivion?"

Out of this I developed what I called an "interorganizational model of class cohesion." The argument went as follows: Class theorists believe that interfirm relations such as interlocks contribute to class cohesion. Organizational theorists argue that interfirm relations such as interlocks are organizational responses to environmental uncertainty, specifically interdependence. Several theorists recognized that there was nothing contradictory in these two notions. What I argued, in addition, was that the interdependence that according to organizational theorists served as a determinant of interfirm relations could also be a determinant of class cohesion. (The argument on which this is based, that interdependence leads to cohesion, is developed more fully in Chapter 4.) Interfirm dependence was both a direct and indirect source of class cohesion.

An Empirical Test

The conclusion to this argument brought me to the same point as my conclusion about the political consequences of interlocks: where were the data? The answer, although I did not realize it at the time, came in a 1982 discussion with Thomas Koenig about a study we were planning. Our discussion centered on how we might examine the correspondence between clusters of firms within interlock networks and clusters of the same firms based on their political campaign contributions. It took more than a year before I realized that the existence of political campaign contributions provided the means by which I could test my model of class cohesion.

The final pieces of the puzzle were my reading of Ronald Burt's work on market constraint and interlocks and the publication in 1983 of a compilation of Burt's work on the topic, which included an appendix with a large portion of his raw data. Market constraint, the extent to which members of one industry provide an obstacle to profits by members of another industry, was the measure of economic coercion for which I had been looking. This indicator, along with the campaign contribution data, provided the operationalizations for two key variables, interdependence and corporate political behavior. It thus became possible to test my argument empirically.

In this book, then, I present and test a theoretical model of business collective action. More generally, I examine the political consequences of several types of interfirm relations. My aim is to demonstrate that the social structures within which corporations are embedded affect the firms' political behavior.

The book can be roughly divided into four sections. Chapters 2 through 4 provide the substantive and theoretical core of the study. Chapter 5 provides information on data and measurement issues. Chapters 6 through 9 comprise the bulk of the empirical analyses. And Chapter 10 provides a conclusion and synthesis of theory and findings.

In Chapter 2 I examine the arguments that have been made regarding the extent to which the United States is a democracy. Included in this chapter is a discussion of the debates among political sociologists on the extent of business unity in industrialized capitalist societies. I argue that business unity must be viewed as a conditional phenomenon.

The degree to which a group is unified has been viewed by theorists of all stripes as a key determinant of its power. But what do we mean by the term unity? Chapter 3 deals with the ways in which the terms unity, cohesion, and solidarity have been defined and operationalized. I argue that a group's power is a function of the similarity of its members' behavior regardless of whether such behavior is based in cohesive within-group relations. Instead, I suggest that similarity of behavior is a function of both cohesive relations and similar positions in a social structure (even in the absence of direct communication).

In Chapter 4 I introduce a structural model of interfirm political behavior. I argue that the capitalist class of the mid-to-late twentieth century is based in the relations among corporations rather than relations among individuals. In this chapter I set forth my primary theoretical argument, that similarity of political behavior is a function of economic interdependence among firms as well as direct and indirect social network ties. This leads to a series of hypotheses that form the basis of the subsequent empirical analyses.

Chapter 5 provides a discussion of ways to empirically examine the level of business unity. I describe my use of data on corporate political action committees, which serve as my primary source, as well as methodological and statistical issues relevant to the analysis of network data. Chapters 6 and 7 contain the key empirical tests of the model, employing data on dyadic relations among a sample of large U.S. firms. Chapter 6 provides an analysis of unity and conflict in political campaign contributions. I examine the extent to which firms contribute to the same candidates, the extent to which they contribute to members of the same party and those with similar ideologies, and the extent to which pairs of firms contribute to opposing candidates in particular elections. In Chapter 7 I apply the model developed in Chapter 4 to the determinants of whether firms agree with or oppose one another in their testimony at congressional hearings. In both chapters I find that organizational and social network factors play an important role in the generation of similar political behavior among firms.

The focus of the analysis shifts in Chapter 8. Here my emphasis is on two phenomena: the extent to which members of specific industries behave in a politically similar fashion and the effects of similar behavior on the industries' relative political influence. In the first section of the chapter I examine the extent to which the leading firms in concentrated industries are more likely than their counterparts in competitive industries to engage in similar political behavior. Then, employing data on the success of industries in securing or preventing federal legislation, I examine the relation between similar political behavior and political success. I show that industries whose largest members behave similarly have high levels of political effectiveness.

In Chapter 9 I shift the level of analysis to the network as a whole. In the first part of the chapter I construct clusters of firms from five larger networks. In the second, I compute the centrality of each firm in each of the five networks. I then examine the extent to which firms with similar positions in the network as a whole engage in similar political behavior. I find that firms that are centrally located in organizational and social networks tend to be central in terms of their political behavior. In Chapter 10 I summarize the results of the study and discuss their theoretical and practical implications as well as directions for future research.

2 · Pluralism and Its Discontents

Thomas Jefferson believed that participation in politics was "ennobling," and he expressed high hopes that the democratic political system in the United States would allow citizens to achieve this ideal. But Jefferson's ideal was predicated on the existence of an agrarian society inhabited primarily by small property owners. Although Alexander Hamilton and James Madison raised concerns about the "tyranny of the majority" and argued for the need for a strong central government to keep it in check, Jefferson was equally concerned with the concentration of political power that might occur should economic power become overly concentrated. Thirty years later, Tocqueville ([1835–1840] 1945, volume 2, pp. 168–171) also raised concerns that the concentration of economic power could endanger democracy. But these fears were essentially speculative. If the democratic ideal envisioned by Jefferson had not become a reality by 1830, neither had the United States become a nation dominated by giant private corporations.

By the turn of the twentieth century things had changed considerably. The expansion of transportation and communication systems in the mid-nineteenth century, so exhaustively described by Alfred Chandler (1977), had led to the emergence of huge, vertically integrated enterprises. The operations of the robber barons of the late 1800s had led to severely restricted competition in numerous industries. The merger movement of the 1895–1904 period further consolidated economic power in a handful of enormously influential capitalists and financiers. These developments raised increasing concerns among large segments of the electorate. First Populists, then Socialists and Progressives, mounted challenges against the power of large corporations.

Despite some victories, such as the Sherman and Clayton Antitrust Acts, the movements to stem the rise of large corporations were ultimately defeated. But this did not stop the criticism. Adolf Berle and Gardiner Means's 1932 classic, *The Modern Corporation and Private Property*, reasserted concerns about concentrated economic power. The question raised in 1905 by Max Weber ("How can democracy and freedom be maintained in the long run under the dominance of advanced capitalism?" [quoted in Roth and Schluchter, 1979, p. 202]) has continued to be expressed in various forms to the present day.

But not all observers assumed that the growth of huge corporations was problematic for democracy. The strain of thought represented by Hamilton and Madison placed its faith in an informed, sensitive elite who would protect democratic institutions from "mob rule." Even Jefferson had recognized the near impossibility of Athenian direct democracy, arguing only that the electorate should play an active role in choosing its rulers. Well into the twentieth century, no longer able to deny the existence of concentrated wealth and economic power, theorists of democracy drew on this Hamiltonian legacy. The result was a perspective known as "elite pluralism." Despite continued challenges over the past half-century, it remains the most widely held argument for the democratic character of the United States.

The Changing Concept of Democracy

The history of the concept of democracy is a story of movement away from an egalitarian ideal toward elitism. In describing democracy, political theorists have typically distinguished two types: direct and representative (or republican). Direct democracy involves a system in which citizens actively participate in political decision making. Vestiges of this form remain in modern society, especially in small voluntary associations. But no existing government approaches a system of direct democracy and there is little indication that such a system has ever existed.[1]

By the time of the American Revolution, the republican concept was predominant. Schumpeter (1942, p. 250) defined this form of democracy as "that institutional arrangement for arriving at political deci-

---

[1] Even Rousseau, in *The Social Contract* (1762 [1913]), admitted that "[t]aking the term in its strictest sense, no genuine democracy has ever existed, and none ever will exist."

sions which realizes the common good by making the people itself decide issues through the election of individuals who are to assemble in order to carry out its will." Although the public is still viewed as the source of government policies, these policies are actually carried out by elected representatives. Yet by the twentieth century, this view too had become difficult to sustain. To what extent did this definition apply to any existing society?

Beyond its application to societies, questions were raised about whether democracy applied even to individual organizations. The most important of these was Michels's now classic *Political Parties.* As is well known, Michels argued that organization is essential for democracy but that democracy, whether direct or republican, is impossible in any established organization. The sources of oligarchy, according to Michels, included the inherent difficulties of administering a complex organization, the leaders' monopoly on information and means of communication, and the simultaneous "cultural superiority of the leaders" and "incompetence of the masses." It was possible to argue that the "incompetence of the masses" and the "cultural superiority of the leaders" were not inherent traits but were specific to the time and place about which Michels wrote. But it was not possible to deny the empirical power of Michels's analysis. The mass apathy and lack of leadership accountability observed by Michels were characteristic not only of the German Social Democratic Party of the early 1900s but of the governments of virtually all nominally democratic societies, including the United States. This domination of political life by a small elite left American political theorists with two choices: either admit that the United States was not democratic or redefine democracy. Not surprisingly, most chose the latter.

The first to do so was Schumpeter (1942). The prevalent idea, that the people themselves determined the issues discussed by elected officials and that these discussions resulted in the maximization of the "common good" was, according to Schumpeter, in need of a replacement that was "truer to life" (ibid., p. 269). Schumpeter's solution was both simple and brilliant. Instead of the people "choosing 'representatives' who will see to it that [their] opinion is carried out . . . [s]uppose," Schumpeter suggested, "we reverse the roles of these two elements and make the deciding of issues by the electorate secondary to the election of the men who are to do the deciding" (ibid.). As Schumpeter put it, "the democratic method is that institutional arrangement for arriving at political decisions in which individuals acquire the power to decide by means of a competitive struggle for the people's vote" (ibid.). In other words, democracy is no longer a system by which the public initiates policy and elects representatives to carry it out. Instead, democracy is a system by which the public elects representatives to *make* as well as to carry out policy (ibid., p. 282). What is it that makes such a system democratic? The single remaining thread is the "competitive struggle for the people's vote."

This definition made it possible to reconcile the empirical tendencies uncovered by Michels with the continued existence of democracy. As Lipset (1962, p. 34) put it, "Democracy in the sense of a system of decision-making in which all members or citizens play an active role in the continuous process is inherently impossible." But this, Lipset continues, does not mean that democracy *per se* is impossible. Rather (ibid., p. 36), "democracy in modern society may be viewed as involving the conflict of organized groups competing for support." While admitting that this was a far cry from the ideal of the Greek city state, Lipset argued that "it is far better than any other political system which has been devised" (ibid.; see also Lipset, 1960, p. 27).

Thus, in the arguments of Schumpeter, Lipset, and other mid-twentieth century political theorists, both nondemocratic and democratic systems are dominated by elites. What distinguishes the latter from the former is one key element: "the competitive struggle for the votes of a mainly passive electorate" (Lipset, 1962, p. 33).

Elite and Business Unity

If the United States is to be viewed as a democracy by pluralists who admit to the domination of politics by elites, it would appear to be crucial to demonstrate that the competitive struggle for votes provides the electorate with a significant set of choices. To demonstrate this, it would be necessary to show that the conflicts between segments of the elite are indicative of salient divisions and not of relatively minor disagreements over means, or simple consequences of petty personal rivalries and jealousies.

Yet this is precisely what Floyd Hunter (1953) and C. Wright Mills (1956) argued was not the case. Both authors, Hunter at the local level and Mills at the national level, claimed to have found governments dominated by unified elites. The question of what exactly is meant by unity will be discussed in Chapter 3. Before tackling that issue, it is necessary to ask, who were the elites who were being discussed? In a thorough review of major works in the elite tradition, Burton and Higley (1987a, p. 223) note that elites have generally been defined as "individuals who occupy positions of authority in large institutions" (Dye, 1983, p. 7). The elites discussed normally include not only the leaders of business and political institutions, but also members of the media, trade unions, educational, cultural, and religious institutions, and voluntary associations, including, presumably, heads of consumer and environmental lobbies.

If one defines the elite as consisting of members of such a wide range of institutions, then one is bound to find a high degree of fragmentation. Marx, to use an obvious example, placed the conflict between business and labor at the cornerstone of his analysis of society. A finding of conflict between business and labor elites is therefore exactly what a Marxist model would predict. Some scholars (Burton and Higley, 1987b) have handled this problem by distinguishing "consensual" unity from "ideological" unity. Democratic societies such as the United States are said to have consensually unified elites who "regularly take opposing ideological and policy stances in public, but . . . consistently refrain from pushing their disagreements to the point of violent conflict" (ibid., p. 296). In other words, democracy exists in countries such as the United States precisely because, despite conflicts among themselves, elites are united in support of the general rules of political life.

As creative as this solution is, it begs two questions. First, is it accurate to treat educational, religious, and labor leaders on a par with representatives of big business? Second, if the groups are not of equal power, then would the existence of unity among one of the more powerful groups pose a threat to democracy even if this group were opposed by others?

In a sense the first question is unfair, since several elite theorists have viewed the question of relative power as an empirical issue. But, as three decades of debate among sociologists and political scientists have demonstrated, this question may be impossible to answer. Does one, for example, identify a group of political controversies and then define groups as powerful based on the outcomes of these controversies, as Dahl (1961) and Polsby (1970) suggested? Does one argue that the state serves the interests of capital, as Poulantzas (1973) and other theorists, including non-Marxists such as Lindblom (1977), did?[2] Regarding the second question, the issue of the internal unity of one

---

[2] Dahl has altered his earlier position on this issue. More recently, both in a revised (1976) version of the classic Dahl and Lindblom work, *Politics, Economics, and Welfare* (originally published in 1953), and in a more recent essay (1982), Dahl has admitted that business plays a unique role in the pluralistic system. See also Manley (1983).

elite, such as business, appears to be a far more tractable yet equally significant concern.

The significance of the extent of business unity can be seen in the cases in which pluralists dealt explicitly with the issue. Based on the above conceptualization of elites, pluralists could always fall back on the argument that even if business were unified, elites were divided because other elites opposed business. To my knowledge, however, not a single pluralist who actually confronted the issue was willing to admit that business was unified.[3] The latter was a risky position to take, I would argue, precisely because a good case could be made that big business was very powerful and few pluralists were willing to deny this claim. Once business was assumed to be uniquely powerful, therefore, the only remaining strain between democracy and a corporate state was the inherent divisions within business. The chief recourse of pluralists in discussing business, then, was to argue that business itself was divided. This view became an explicit or implicit element in virtually all pluralist writings.[4]

Elite Theorists and Their Critics on Business Unity

I have already mentioned that the issue of business unity appears to be more tractable than the issue of business power. But a review of the literature on business unity reveals similar conceptual and empirical problems. The first, and best-known, post-Schumpeterian studies to raise this issue explicitly were those of Hunter (1953) and Mills (1956). A related essay by Sweezy (1970) also first appeared in the early 1950s. Hunter's power structure included professionals, government officials, and even two labor leaders, but 28 of his 40 notables were from the business community, including all of the fifteen most powerful members. Mills's power elite consisted of the leaders of business, govern-

[3] One possible exception, albeit an implicit one, is the statement by Keller (1963, pp. 82–83) that "[t]he widely accepted model of society resembling a pyramid is giving way to one with a number of pyramids, each capped by an elite."

[4] Lowi (1969, pp. 43–44) has nicely captured this pluralist argument: "Pluralists do not have to deny the Marxian proposition that there is a conflict between those who own and those who work for those who own. They need only answer by adding to Marx's the other equally intense conflicts. Exporters cannot love importers, except perhaps on the Fourth of July—and, in fact, many people may still have misgivings about the patriotism of importers. Renters cannot love owners. Borrowers cannot love lenders, nor creditors debtors, and this is particularly interesting in our day, when the biggest debtors are not the poor but the rich. Retailers cannot love wholesalers. The black middle class loves neither the black lower class nor the white sellers of middle-class housing."

ment, and the military. Here too, the power of the business leaders appeared to exceed those in the other two sectors. Sweezy's ruling class was defined almost exclusively by the ownership of capital.

All three authors argued that their elites were highly unified. This unity was viewed as primarily a result of common economic interests, common social backgrounds, and extensive social interaction, including, for Sweezy and Mills, intermarriage. Moreover, as Hunter noted, the fact that the power structure dominated the community's political life and that prominent businessmen dominated the power structure led to a political system dominated by a cohesive group of corporate elites.

Conclusions such as Hunter's provoked heated responses from pluralists (Dahl, 1958; Polsby, 1959; Wolfinger, 1960). Among their many criticisms was the complaint that neither Hunter nor Mills had actually *demonstrated* the existence of elite unity. As Wolfinger (1960) pointed out, even within the business community there were potential conflicts of interest between, for example, real-estate interests and those supporting highway development. Unless elite theorists could identify a series of important issues and show that elites were typically unified on these issues, their arguments amounted to little more than speculation.

The typical elite theorist response to criticisms of this sort by pluralists was to concede that sectors of the business community regularly split over day-to-day issues but that they were united in their general support for the system as a whole. In fact, all three authors had been quick to admit that business was not a monolithic entity, that divisions and conflict did occur. But all agreed that, in the long run, business was unified by its stake in the existing system. Sweezy put it most succinctly; while admitting that "capitalists can and do fight among themselves to further individual or group interests" (1970, p. 370), he maintained that

overshadowing all these divisions is their common interest in preserving and strengthening a system which guarantees their wealth and privileges. In the event of a real threat to the system, there are no longer class differences—only class traitors, and they are few and far between.

But these responses carried little weight with pluralists. For one thing, the idea that business elites were unified by their support of the system was so abstract as to be devoid of meaning. Consider, for example, the classical Marxist model of society. In this view, the bourgeois state was not a legitimate representative of the interests of the working class. The objective interests of the working class, therefore, called for an overthrow of the system. Existing worker support for the system could only be an example of false consciousness. By all available measures, however, the vast majority of Americans do support the existing system and do not believe that the government should be overthrown. Most Marxist theorists in the United States recognize this fact, even if they continue to believe in the illegitimacy of the state. If the working class is as united in its support for the existing state as is the capitalist class, then a demonstration that the capitalist class is unified in its support of capitalism is not very enlightening. One would have to demonstrate the existence of unity at a less abstract level (such as on actual policies) to show that business unity is a threat to democracy.

One fundamental problem with this exchange between pluralists and elite theorists is that the two sides have operated at different levels of analysis (Alford and Friedland, 1985). Pluralists described unity at the level of day-to-day political affairs. Elite theorists described unity at the level of the system as a whole. Once the distinction between levels of analysis is removed, much of the disagreement between pluralists and elite theorists disappears: both agree that business is characterized by divisions at the level of specific issues; both agree that business is unified in its support of the system. Although theoretical differences remain between the two perspectives, once the levels of analysis issue is understood, the continuing debate around whether business is primarily unified or divided is reduced to a largely ideological one.

A Shift in the Debate

Elite theorists and Marxists, both of whom I shall term "unity theorists," became increasingly aware by the late 1960s that, at least in terms of the debate on business unity, they stood at a disadvantage. The assumption that business was "ultimately" unified was too abstract. The fact that business was divided on day-to-day issues favored the pluralist model. But two intellectual developments occurred in the late 1960s and early 1970s that radically changed the nature of the debate. They were (1) the publication of works by G. William Domhoff (1967; 1970) in the United States and Ralph Miliband (1969) in Great Britain; and (2) the publication of works by Nicos Poulantzas (1973) in France and Claus Offe (1972) in Germany.

The books by Domhoff and Miliband were ostensibly attempts to build on Mills's earlier analysis. Both authors emphasized the preponderance of persons from elite backgrounds in key government positions. Both also emphasized the circulation of personnel among various elite institutions. But they added an additional, crucial, concept, which I shall call the "mediating mechanism." Sweezy, Hunter, and Mills had all noted the existence of these institutions but none had explicitly conceptualized them. Domhoff and Miliband both took the existence of conflict within the business community as their starting point. They then argued that business is able to control the state because the business community is composed of various policy-making organizations, the function of which is to resolve conflicts prior to reaching the state. In this way business enters the political arena as a unified body. Unity is not inherent within business; rather, it is socially constructed through negotiation among its leading representatives.

These mediating mechanisms could be divided into three types. The first were those that actually helped create a unity of outlook and interest. These included kinship ties (developed through intermarriage within the elite), common socialization experiences (such as attendance at the same prep schools and elite colleges), and shared membership in prominent social clubs. The second were those that had the potential to resolve conflicts between firms and sectors. These included common stock ownership of firms by other firms, joint financial ventures (such as bank loan consortia), and, more commonly, overlapping corporate board memberships (interlocking directorates). Finally, there were organizations whose explicit purpose was to advance the political goals of their members. These organizations, according to Domhoff, had as their aim the formulation and dissemination of policies that favored the long-term interests of the corporate elite. They included groups such as the Business Roundtable, the Committee for Economic Development, the Council on Foreign Relations, the Conference Board, and later in the 1970s, the Trilateral Commission. Made up of the leaders of the largest corporations and other prominent officials, these groups produced proposals that were designed to further the "national interest," which Domhoff and others interpreted to mean their class interests.

These arguments represented a considerable advance over the earlier formulations of Sweezy, Hunter, and Mills, but they contained problems as well. First, even if federal officials came disproportionately from elite backgrounds, there was no evidence that they were mere representatives of the elite once in office. As we have already seen, as long as competition among elites existed, then these officials would ultimately have to answer to the general electorate. A similar critique applied to the issue of circulation of membership among elite groups (often referred to as the "revolving door"). Simply because an official of a regulatory agency came from the industry he or she was supposed to regulate did not in itself prove that the agency was incapable of acting in the public interest, even if that meant opposing the industry. Finally, critics argued that despite the existence of policy-making organizations, other representatives of business, such as the National Association of Manufacturers, were often at odds with the groups identified by Domhoff.

These criticisms came from two sources—first, not surprisingly, pluralists, and second, interestingly, Marxists. The most telling Marxist criticism of the work represented by Domhoff and Miliband was by Poulantzas (1972). Poulantzas's review of Miliband in the *New Left Review* led to a prolonged debate between the two. Poulantzas echoed the pluralists' argument that the elite social backgrounds of government officials was insufficient proof of elite domination of the state. Departing from the pluralist argument, however, he argued that the relation between the state and business is an objective one in which the state serves the interests of business regardless of the backgrounds of state managers. Poulantzas insisted that corporate managers are concerned not with the interests of their class but only with the specific interests of their firms. Because various sectors within business have conflicting interests and because individual firms are incapable of seeing beyond their particularistic interests, business is incapable by itself of achieving political unity. As a consequence, business is incapable of acting politically as a class. The role of the state, then is to do for business what business is incapable of doing for itself: to act as arbiter and mediator, to act in the long-term interests of business as a whole. Because the long run interests of business will often conflict with the short-term interests of particular sectors, the state must have a degree of autonomy from business in order to carry out its mission. Thus, the state in capitalist society is not merely a tool of the capitalist class. It is a relatively autonomous structure with a life of its own that serves the general interests of business. The state, then, according to Poulantzas, was itself a mediating mechanism, just as the social clubs and kinship ties discussed by Miliband and Domhoff. Unlike the mechanisms described by the latter theorists, however, the state was not an internal component of the business community. It served the interests of business but it was not of business.

Poulantzas's argument led in two directions. The first was toward a view suggesting greater state autonomy. In fact, many contemporary state-centered approaches that view the state as an organization with a life of its own, independent of the interests of its constitutents, grew directly out of Poulantzas's analysis. A prototypical example is the work of Fred Block (1977; see also Block, 1987 for an overview of his subsequent work). Block argued that state managers do serve the needs of the capitalist class, but neither the managers nor the capitalists are conscious of this fact. Instead, according to Block, the state serves business because the former depends on the latter for its revenue. Interestingly, a pluralist oriented theorist, Charles Lindblom (1977), offered an almost identical argument. Other theorists, such as Skocpol (1980), rejected the idea that the state regularly serves business and argued instead that the state is an independent actor with a unique agenda.

The second view that emerged from Poulantzas's work was an emphasis on the issue of class conflict and a greater role for the working class. This view can be traced to a critique of Miliband by Isaac Balbus (1971). Balbus accused Miliband and, by implication, other elite theorists such as Mills and Domhoff, of employing a "one-class model." The focus on the elite without a simultaneous focus on the masses forced elite theorists into the conclusion that the elite never loses. Yet evidence for defeats of business during the twentieth century was abundant: the reforms of the New Deal, the institution of labor legislation, the civil rights laws, Medicare and Medicaid. If the elite dominated society and the government, how could these defeats ever occur? The traditional elite theory response to this argument was that in fact these reforms had been instituted by the elite to protect themselves against even more fundamental changes (Kolko, 1963; Domhoff, 1967; Weinstein, 1968). But even if it could be shown that the policies themselves were developed by elites in the interests of elites, this begged the question of why the elites felt it necessary to place restraints on themselves in the first place. The answer, according to Balbus (1971), Esping-Andersen, Friedland, and Wright (1976), Mintz et al. (1978), and Whitt (1982), was that the capitalist class was engaged in a continuous struggle with the working class. Although proponents of this view believed that the state was dominated by business, they also believed that business was not all powerful and that it was occasionally defeated in conflicts with the working class. The key to understanding the origins of policies, then, was to study the processes by which conflicts were resolved.[5]

The problems raised by both of these positions have yet to be resolved. Poulantzas's argument that the state operates in the interests of capital certainly fits in with a considerable amount of historical evidence but it is ultimately non-falsifiable. If the state is viewed as operating in the interests of the capitalist class, then any action that the state takes is, by definition, in the interests of capital. One possible solution to this predicament was proposed by Mintz et al. (1978). Mintz et al. argued that if the origin of policies adopted by the state could be traced to organizations that were demonstrated to be business-interest associations, then the state could be said to be controlled by business even if the policies reflected defeats for business. An example of such an event might be a situation in which industry was paralyzed by a general strike and business organizations requested the state to enact pro-labor legislation such as a shorter work week. But evidence such as this would fail to demonstrate the absence of democracy unless it could be shown that the groups requesting the legislation represented business as a whole. A Committee for Economic Development proposal that was opposed by the National Association of Manufacturers would constitute a demonstration of the very elite division viewed by pluralists as a precondition for democracy. Fortunately for elite theorists, it is not necessary to argue that the state is by definition dominated by the capitalist class. A major reason that Poulantzas found himself in this position in the first place is that he assumed that the state must play a mediating role because business itself is incapable of doing so. The argument that business has no mechanisms to ensure unity is itself empirically testable. Poulantzas asserted, without evidence, that no such mechanisms existed. But a case study by Whitt (1982) provides conclusive testimony that they do exist and that they can be politically effective.

Whitt studied five mass transit propositions that were decided by popular vote in California during the 1960s and 1970s. His analysis of the development of the Bay Area Rapid Transit System (BART) is especially informative. The need for a mass transit system in the San Francisco area had become apparent soon after the end of World War

---

[5] The parameters have changed slightly, but these issues continue to be debated. See, for example, the exchange between Amenta and Parikh and Jenkins and Brents (1991).

II. This led to the formation of the Bay Area Council, a policy-making organization made up of local business leaders. The leaders of San Francisco–based financial institutions were especially concerned about the relocation of businesses and residents to surrounding suburban areas because of their interest in maintaining property values in the central city. An efficient mass transit system, they reasoned, would enable corporations to maintain offices downtown since suburban residents would have easy access to the area. In order to build the system, two obstacles had to be overcome. First, members of the council had to reach a consensus on the type of program they would support. Second, the program had to be sold to the public, who would be asked to support a resolution to float taxpayer bonds to finance the system.

The obvious opponents of a mass transit system are those who benefit from the use of automobiles. In this case, representatives of major oil companies with offices in the Bay Area did in fact initially oppose the system. However, proponents were able to demonstrate that BART would in general not cut into the use of automobiles because it would operate on a narrow strip designed to bring people into downtown San Francisco. For the vast majority of Bay Area residents, BART would not provide an alternative to private transportation. In fact, to the extent that it eased rush hour traffic, it might even encourage greater use of private automobiles. Eventually, the Council provided virtually unanimous support for BART. In fact, support was so overwhelming that several oil companies actually contributed funds in support of the proposition.

The way in which BART was eventually passed demonstrated the political power of which a unified business community is capable. Although evidence suggested that the operation of BART would have little effect on local air pollution, pro-BART advertising stressed the environmental benefits of the system and mentioned nothing about the predicted effects on property values along the line. When studies indicated that the necessary two-thirds majority of the electorate was unlikely to support BART, Council leaders were able to pressure legislators to change the law to reduce the necessary support to 60 percent. In November, 1962, Bay Area voters passed the proposition with support of 61 percent of the electorate.

Whitt's analysis was an improvement over previous elite studies in several ways. First, by looking at actual decision making on an issue of considerable political importance, Whitt was faithful to methodological principles laid down by pluralists (see Polsby, 1970). Second, rather than seeing business as all powerful, Whitt showed, in the case of a similar proposition in the Los Angeles area that was defeated, that business does not always get its way. Third, rather than rely on assertions of business divisions, as Poulantzas had done, Whitt demonstrated, empirically, the *processes* by which business unity was achieved.

Despite the brilliance of Whitt's contribution, it too is insufficient to resolve the debate over business unity. The analysis of political processes generally depends on an intensive examination of historical case studies. By their very nature, case studies are limited in scope. The well-worn dialectic between the depth but narrowness of intensive examination of the particular versus the breadth but frequent shallowness of the quantitative analysis of the general remains a frustrating obstacle in social science inquiry (Heckathorn, 1984). On what grounds do we evaluate the generalizability of Whitt's findings? Whitt has demonstrated, in striking fashion, *how* a particular local business community was able to unify and pursue its political goals. But was this a typical case?

This problem of generalizability was noted by Pfeffer (1987). The key source of Pfeffer's argument is the classic study of protective tariff legislation by Bauer, Pool, and Dexter ([1963] 1972). The authors found, in an analysis of letters to members of Congress, that firms in industries with different interests in tariff legislation apparently made no effort to resolve their differences but instead both lobbied the state in support of their own positions. As we shall see in Chapter 7, my own analysis of corporate testimony before congressional committees confirms this view. Thirty-six cases were found between 1975 and 1987 in which the most powerful members of the same industry publicly opposed one another in their testimony. Whether business is found to be unified or divided in a particular case clearly depends on the issues selected for study.

One way around the problems inherent in historical case studies has been the quantitative analysis of the presumed mediating mechanisms. This has taken several forms. One ambitious study was conducted by Zeitlin, Ewen, and Ratcliff (1974) on Chile. Zeitlin et al. demonstrated that the simultaneous control of several corporations could be traced through kinship ties among their leading stockholders. Although individually many of the largest Chilean firms appeared to be management controlled (that is, characterized by no stockholding interest sufficient to dominate firm policy making), the authors showed that control was achieved through "a complex kinship unit in which economic interests and kinship bonds are inextricably intertwined" (1974, p. 109). The authors admitted, however, that the data necessary to replicate their analysis on the United States were unavailable. Such a replication has yet to be done.

Another frequently employed approach in recent years has been the attempt to show that officers and directors of large corporations also hold prominent positions in important policy-making, charitable, and cultural organizations. Useem (1979), for example, showed that individuals who sat on the boards of two or more corporations were more likely to sit on the boards of several types of nonprofit organizations (such as philanthropic and cultural organizations and government advisory boards) than were those who sat on only one corporate board. Ratcliff (1980) found similar patterns in a study of St. Louis business leaders.

The most commonly employed approach in the United States has been to examine networks of interlocking directorates. Several such efforts have been undertaken by federal officials during the course of the century but only since the late 1960s did social scientists begin to systematically examine them. Among the major studies of interlocks as mechanisms of business unity were those by Mariolis (1975), Sonquist and Koenig (1975), Bunting (1976a), Berkowitz et al. (1979), Koenig, Gogel, and Sonquist (1979), Koenig and Gogel (1981), Mizruchi (1982), Palmer (1983), Roy (1983), and Mintz and Schwartz (1985). A compilation of studies appeared in a special issue of *Social Science History* in 1983 edited by Domhoff. Although all of these authors called for the analysis of independent criteria to determine both the sources and consequences of interlocks, few of these studies provided such data systematically.

My own earlier study (Mizruchi, 1982) was a case in point. Most of the studies both before and after mine were based on cross-sectional data. When the vast majority of firms in the sample were found to be connected into a single large system, as Mariolis found in his analysis of 797 large U.S. firms in 1969, researchers concluded that business was unified. Setting aside for the moment the issue of the actual meaning of these connections, there was no basis on which to assess the claim that the network uncovered by Mariolis and others was unified. Was a network unified, for example, when all firms were within, say, four steps of one another? If so, Mariolis's system was not unified since "only" 91 percent of the firms could reach one another within four steps. The problem with cross-sectional discoveries of unity, then, was that such conclusions had no basis for comparison.

Sensing this problem as well as the fact that many managerialist (and pluralist) arguments were historical in nature, I compared the interlock network at seven points in time between 1904 and 1974. I also attempted to compare my quantitative findings with historical evidence from the periods under investigation. This was especially useful for the early part of the century, for which historical evidence (and consensus about that evidence) was considerable (see Mizruchi and Bunting, 1981; Mizruchi, 1982, chapter 3). In addition, my study included an analysis of the relation between interlocks and stockholding (ibid., chapters 2, 6). Nevertheless, none of these sources of additional data was as systematic as the interlock data. And although I concluded that business unity had been demonstrated and that the findings had serious implications for the viability of American democracy, I presented no evidence that these interlocks had any political consequences.

The failure to demonstrate the political consequences of interlocks became a persistent criticism of these earlier studies. Many of them suggested that interlocks played a role, but as soon as researchers attempted to demonstrate effects, they reverted to unsystematic descriptions of individual cases. By 1980, only one study existed that demonstrated a link between interlocks and corporate political behavior—Koenig's unpublished (1979) doctoral dissertation, in which he found that heavily interlocked corporations were more likely than less-interlocked firms to contribute to Richard Nixon's reelection campaign. In addition, Useem, as already noted, had demonstrated that heavily interlocked directors were disproportionately involved in important policy-making organizations. In 1980, Richard Ratcliff published a study that demonstrated that heavily interlocked banks in the St. Louis area were more likely to invest outside of the metropolitan area than were less interlocked banks. This was a creative and path-breaking study, but it dealt with bank lending activities. Such activities contained the potential for serious political repercussions to be sure, but there was still a need to examine specific political behavior resulting from interlocks.

The quantitative analysis of large corporate networks, then, contained the potential for transcending the limitations of the case-study approach. But too often these studies had resulted in assertions about business unity without supporting behavioral evidence. Instead, the mere existence of the presumed mediating mechanisms was taken as proof of their effectiveness. Most researchers within this area were careful not to explicitly state these assumptions. Instead, their conclusions remained within the bounds of their data. The unwritten but spoken view among them, however, was that these data demonstrated the existence of a cohesive capitalist class.

Thus, the solution to the problem of business unity required solutions to two problems, one theoretical, the other empirical: theoretically, there was a need for generalization that moved beyond the analysis of individual cases; empirically, there was a need for systematic quantitative data on corporate political behavior to demonstrate the consequences of the extensive interlock networks that had been identified.

An Alternative

The admission by unity theorists that inherent conflicts existed within the business community paved the way for a major advance in the level of their debate with the pluralists. Rather than relying on a common interest in the preservation of capitalism as the basis of business cohesion, unity theorists shifted their focus toward the institutional mechanisms that enabled sectors of capital to resolve their conflicts. Pluralists continued to dispute the argument that these mechanisms created class cohesion (Pfeffer, 1987), but the debate became far more focused and amenable to empirical investigation.

Despite these improvements, most parties in the controversy continue to argue about whether, or the extent to which, business is unified. Much of the recent work by political scientists on corporate political action committees has stressed the lack of business unity (Malbin, 1979; Handler and Mulkern, 1982; Sabato, 1984). An important empirical investigation by sociologists (Clawson, Neustadtl, and Bearden, 1986) responded to these studies by arguing that business is primarily unified. Much of the interpretation of this evidence, of course, depends on one's definition of unity, a crucial issue which is the subject of Chapter 3. But in spite of the diversity of definitions, the basic focus of the debate is still on *whether* business is unified.

In fact, the question of business unity has been so hotly disputed for so long that the viability of the question on which it is premised has rarely been assessed. Alford and Friedland's (1985) model, which suggests that the participants in the debate emphasize different levels of analysis, captures beautifully the earlier debates over business unity but it appears to be less applicable to the more recent debates over the effectiveness of the mediating mechanisms. Pluralists and unity theorists appear to agree that these mechanisms would lead to unity if they were effective. The key question, whether they are effective, is now primarily an empirical one.

I believe that the debate over business unity, as it is currently constituted, has outlived its usefulness. Like the relations of production that, according to Marx, facilitate the development of the forces of production early in an epoch but become fetters on their development as time progresses, the debate over business unity inspired a generation of valuable research, but it has become a fetter on the further development of our understanding of the role of business in politics. The issues that spawned the debates over business unity remain as important as ever. But the question of whether business is unified has become a non-issue. For every example of unity such as those uncovered by Whitt, one can find a case of opposition such as those uncovered by Bauer, Pool and Dexter. The fact is, there are times in which business is unified and times in which it is not. There are sectors within business that typically support one another and sectors that typically oppose one another. There are periods in which the sectors that usually support one another quarrel and the sectors that usually oppose one another unite. The key question is not whether business is unified but rather when; that is, the conditions under which unity and opposition occur.

Useem (1984), in an extraordinary study, comes very close to this position. The problem with discussions of business unity, Useem argues (ibid., pp. 9–12), is that researchers focused on different components of the business community. Those who argued that business was unified, according to Useem, looked primarily at the largest firms, which they saw as relatively unified. Those who argued that business was divided have focused on small business or both small and large firms. Since, in Useem's view, the vast majority of the business community is politically fragmented, the pluralists' contention of business disunity, based on examination of the entire system, was also generally accurate. Although Useem therefore concedes that business as a whole is generally fragmented politically, he argues that there exists among the leaders of the largest firms an "inner circle" whose multiple board memberships enable them to view the world in terms of the long-term interests of business as a whole, a worldview Useem terms "classwide rationality." Useem comes very close to the position I advocate here. He notes, for example, that "in their own limited and specific fashions, both [pluralist and unity] descriptions are also partly true" (1984, p. 12). But Useem still views the inner circle as fundamentally unified. I believe that we need to move a step further, to recognize that even the cohesion within the inner circle is conditional.

The issue of business unity is at the core of the debate over the extent to which American society is democratic. But we are in many ways no closer to resolving this debate today than we were three decades ago. Understanding the degree of business unity, I have argued, requires a drastic reorientation of our theoretical approach to the problem.

This reorientation involves, first and foremost, a recognition that we are not going to resolve the debate over business unity to the satisfaction of all parties. Such a recognition eventually emerged among proponents of the order and conflict perspectives. Sociologists of all stripes came to recognize that the usefulness of a model depended on the issues that were being studied. The issues of when business is cohesive and when and why opposition occurs are, because of their potential impact on our democratic system, matters of considerable practical as well as theoretical importance. To contribute to the understanding of these issues, social scientists will have to move beyond descriptive models toward the development of genuine theory. Such theory begins with the formulation of falsifiable hypotheses. This requires the setting aside of abstract statements about the inherent unity of business.

My hope is that the models developed here will be applicable to more general sociological concerns, including those involving theories of collective action in both small and larger groups. To the extent that such bridges can be forged, this work will become relevant to issues even more fundamental than those treated by power structure researchers.

The main purpose of this study, then, is to identify the conditions under which political unity and opposition occur within business. To do this, I develop and test a theoretical model based on concepts from organizational and political sociology. But before the model can be presented, a crucial question must be addressed: What exactly is business unity?

3 · What is Business Unity?

The previous chapter dealt with debates about the extent to which business is unified. But I was deliberately vague on just what business unity is. There were good reasons for this. The question of what unity actually means is a difficult one that requires extensive discussion. An attempt to give this issue the attention it deserves requires a chapter in itself. Assuming that the issue of business unity is an important one, it is time to define what we mean by the term.

Pluralist theorists have argued that power in advanced capitalist societies is shared by a continuously changing array of interest groups, no one of which is consistently able to attain its goals (Riesman, 1953; Dahl, 1961; Polsby, 1970), while unity theorists have argued that power is concentrated in a relatively small group of dominant elites, who are able to achieve their goals even though they often run counter to the interests of the majority (Hunter, 1953; Mills, 1956; Domhoff, 1967). Although unity (and related terms, such as cohesion) has been widely used in elite research, in many cases the term has been either undefined or poorly operationalized. In other cases, operational definitions have been substituted for conceptual definitions. In this chapter I present brief reviews of the ways in which cohesion, solidarity, and unity have been employed in the power structure and general sociological literatures. I then suggest three points: first, cohesion is most effectively treated as an objective characteristic of a social structure rather than a set of shared normative sentiments; second, the most important phenomenon to examine in order to understand business unity is the similarity of behavior rather than the similarity of sentiment or interest; and third, the concept of structural equivalence may be as likely to capture the processes described by power structure researchers as is the concept of cohesion. The focus on similarity of behavior leads to a fourth point: unity must be distinguished from cohesion.

The Significance of Business Unity

Most pluralists have by now conceded Schumpeter's (1942) point that the mass of citizens participates little in political decision making. As Schumpeter and later pluralists reasoned, given this mass apathy, the only basis for democracy in advanced capitalist societies is the existence of conflict among elites. As long as one segment of the elite is out of power, this group can always appeal to the electorate to support changes if the public is dissatisfied with the current state of affairs. But the issue of elite unity is important for another reason. As Dahl (1958, p. 465) put it, "The actual *political effectiveness* of a group is a function of its potential for control *and* its potential for unity." In other words, the business community, despite its potential for power due to its huge accumulation of resources, will be a politically powerful actor only to the extent that it is capable of mobilizing as a politically unified force.

Two problems present themselves here: First, what do we mean by "unity?" Second, what do we mean by "political effectiveness?" The bulk of this chapter deals with the first question. The second question, concerning the conceptualization of power, will be treated in the remainder of the chapter.

Cohesion, Unity, and Solidarity

A search of the literature on both sides of the debate over business unity reveals a startling fact: the term has rarely been defined by anyone (on either side of the debate) within this area. In his review of influential works from both the unity and pluralist perspectives, Useem (1984, pp. 9–12) notes the use of the terms *unity, integration, homogeneity, solidarity, consolidation, social cohesion,* and *political cohesion,* which are believed by some authors to be both the cause and/or consequence of *common interests, common purposes, feelings of community,* a *distinct identity,* and *self-sufficient autonomy.* Yet the meaning of these terms, especially in the works in which they appeared, has rarely been specified. Instead, their meaning has been assumed to be self-evident. Moreover, the terms tend to be used interchangeably. But what exactly do the terms mean?

In an effort to sort out their meaning, I begin by making no distinctions among cohesion, solidarity, and unity. As the argument proceeds, I introduce a distinction between cohesion and unity. I begin with the power structure literature.

Cohesion and Solidarity in the Power Structure Literature

Although Schumpeter (1942) argued that the basis for democracy in advanced capitalist societies was competition among elites, he was not specific about the origins of this competition or the form it would take. Hunter (1953) found that although there were subgroups within Atlanta's power structure, the larger structure was "held together by common interests, mutual obligations, money, habit, delegated responsibilities, and in some cases by coercion and force" (1953, p. 113). Unfortunately, although Hunter provided examples of the ways in which conflict was avoided (1953, pp. 111–112), he did not develop a concept of group cohesion.

A more elaborate series of points was presented by Mills in *The Power Elite* (1956). According to Mills (1956, p. 11), "[t]he elite . . . feel themselves to be, and are felt by others to be, the inner circle of 'upper social classes.' They form a more or less compact social and psychological entity; they have become self-conscious members of a social class." Here Mills argues that the power elite is cohesive because its members self-consciously view themselves as part of a particular social class. Moreover, "[b]ehind such psychological and social unity as we may find, are the structure and mechanics of those institutional hierarchies over which the [power elite] now preside . . . If they have many interconnections and points of coinciding interest, then their elites tend to form a coherent kind of grouping" (1956, p. 19). But this is not all, for "[t]he unity of the power elite . . . does not rest solely on psychological similarity and social intermingling, nor entirely on structural coincidences of commanding positions and interests. At times, it is the unity of a more explicit co-ordination" (ibid.). For Mills, then, elite cohesion is based on both social-psychological similarities as a result of similar backgrounds and commonality of interest as a result of overlaps in elite institutions. More recent analysts, including Domhoff (1970, pp. 75–99; 1974, pp. 88–90) and Useem (1984, p. 63) have developed implicit or explicit definitions along these lines. Useem (ibid.) provides as good a definition as any:

Social cohesion implies that the inner circle is truly a circle: acquaintanceship networks are dense, mutual trust and obligation are widespread, and a common sense of identity and culture prevail. All these features are embodied and reinforced in a variety of social institutions, ranging from clubs to intermarriage. While social cohesion is not a necessary precondition for mobilization, it is a powerful facilitator.

Critics of Hunter and Mills did not dispute their concepts of cohesion. Indeed, Dahl (1961, p. 226) defined solidarity[1] as "the capacity of a member of one segment of society to evoke support from others who identify him as like themselves because of similarities in occupation, social standing, religion, ethnic origin, or racial stock." And Arnold Rose, a prominent pluralist theorist, agreed with Mills that "[i]nterlocking directorates, where they occur in the larger corporations, give them a high degree of cohesiveness" (1967, p. 133). Where Dahl, Rose, and other pluralists disagreed was in the assumption that such social cohesion and institutional interlocking were widespread. As Rose (1967, p. 89) pointed out, "Power elites interlock only temporarily and on limited types of issues." This view was echoed by Dahl (1982, pp. 34–35), who argued that "rulers are rarely a solidary group."

The difficulty with all of these studies is that there is still an absence of clarity on the meaning of cohesion and how it can be measured. To a great extent this problem is a result of the fact that two different types of definitions and indicators have been employed. Useem's definition and list of indicators displays both of these properties. On the one hand, according to Useem, cohesion is characterized by mutual trust and obligation and a common sense of identity and culture (a subjective component). On the other hand, acquaintanceship networks are dense, and the common identity and culture are reinforced by institutions such as clubs and intermarriage (an objective component). This is as clear and comprehensive a description of the concept of cohesion as appears in this literature. The difficulty for the study of the political power of the corporate elite is in understanding exactly how social cohesion translates into political cohesion and how the latter is to be operationalized. Useem's point that social cohesion is a sufficient but not a necessary component of political cohesion is a crucial one, to which we shall return shortly. First, however, we shall take a brief detour into the classical and contemporary social science literature on cohesion.

---

[1] Although the terms could be treated as distinct concepts, cohesion and solidarity are often used interchangeably.

Cohesion and Solidarity in the Sociological Literature

Cohesion is one of the most fundamental concepts in sociology. Many of the classic issues in the field, from Marx's analysis of class consciousness and the conditions for successful revolution to Durkheim's thesis in *The Division of Labor*, revolve around this concept. In addition to its role in general theory, this concept has figured prominently in the areas of social movements in sociology (Fireman and Gamson, 1979; Jenkins, 1983), conflict resolution in political science (Stein, 1976), and group performance in social psychology (Markovsky and Lawler, 1988). A work by Hechter (1987), which has generated considerable controversy within sociology, is devoted exclusively to the concept.

Rather than providing an exhaustive review of this massive literature, I focus on a few key works to demonstrate the ways in which cohesion and solidarity have been defined. I have employed the terms cohesion and solidarity interchangeably; in fact, only one work of which I know, a study by Markovsky and Lawler (1988), explicitly distinguishes the two terms. Political scientists and social psychologists appear to prefer the term cohesion, while sociologists, especially social movement theorists, appear to favor the term solidarity (see the listing under solidarity in the index to Blau, 1977, p. 303).

For Durkheim ([1893] 1933, p. 64), social solidarity arises "because a certain number of states of consciousness are common to all members of society."[2] Simmel ([1922] 1955, p. 17) referred to "unity" as "the consensus and concord of interacting individuals, as against their discords, separations, and disharmonies. But we also call 'unity' the total group-synthesis of persons, energies, and forms, that is, the ultimate wholeness of that group, a wholeness which covers both strictly-speaking unitary relations and dualistic relations." And Parsons (1951, p. 96) defined group solidarity as the "commonness of the value-orientation patterns of the participants in a system of social interaction."

---

[2] For Durkheim, as for many sociologists, it is often difficult to distinguish definitions of solidarity from descriptions of its causes or consequences. The quote from *The Division of Labor* cited here is as close as Durkheim comes to defining the term. Yet social solidarity is said to "arise because" of certain conditions, implying that he is presenting not a definition but a source of solidarity. In other cases, solidarity is difficult to distinguish from its consequences. In an otherwise exemplary discussion, Moore (1979, p. 689) suggests that "a cohesive ruling group" is one that acts "in concert to further common interests." Here it is unclear whether "acting in concert" is the definition of cohesion or a consequence of it.

Interestingly, for Durkheim, the concept of solidarity was not amenable to empirical analysis. As he put it ([1893] 1933, p. 24), "social
solidarity is a wholly moral phenomenon which by itself is not amenable to exact observation and especially not to measurement."
Rather, "[i]t . . . can only be thoroughly known through its social effects" (ibid., p. 27). The problem with this view, for our purposes, is
that unless the concept can be specified *a priori*, cohesion can always
be assumed to have been operative (Hechter, 1987, p. 23).[3] Political
scientists studying conflict resolution have tended to define cohesion
operationally through responses to questionnaires whose purpose is to
tap feelings of identification with a group. But serious questions can
be raised about the extent to which common responses to question-
naire items actually provide an indicator of cohesion (Sylvan and
Glassner, 1985). This led one prominent scholar in this field to lament
that "there is nowhere adequate discussion of the term [cohesion's]
lack of proper definition" (Stein, 1976, p. 146).

In general, then, cohesion has been defined in two ways. By far the
most common is the subjective definition (cohesion as a phenomenon
of shared sentiments), exhibited by Durkheim, Parsons, and most social movement and conflict resolution theorists. More recently, an
objective definition (cohesion as a phenomenon of a group's social
structure) based in part on Simmel's definition, has become prominent. Of course, many authors employ both aspects simultaneously,
but for the sake of discussion, they are worth separating. The two
concepts are based on different views of the nature of social order.[4]

Cohesion as a Subjective Concept

In the subjective view, cohesion is a function of group members' feelings of identification with the group, in particular, their feeling that
their personal interests are bound up with the interests of the group.
In fact, the idea behind this definition is precisely that social order

---

[3] This point is elaborated in the following section.

[4] Hechter (1987) provides an excellent summary of these different views. My only
criticism of his review is that his discussion of the structural approach is limited to only
one of its variants. Hechter (ibid., p. 27) correctly points out that "collective action
often fails to occur despite interest homogeneity." He ignores the fact, however, that
other structural impediments, such as the absence of communication networks, might
play a role in preventing the emergence of solidarity. In fact, Hechter's own rational
choice model actually contains important structural components (see especially pages
46–52).

within a group is maintained because group members' sentiments override any feelings they might have as individuals that run counter to the interests of the group. This view is evident in the definitions of Durkheim, Parsons, and, to a lesser extent, Simmel. The main assumption underlying this model is that groups are maintained by shared normative systems that direct and constrain the feelings and behavior of the group's members. There are, however, two possible readings of this view. In the classic normative model, solidarity is maintained because individuals have been socialized into accepting the norms of the group (Durkheim, [1895] 1966, p. 2). That is, the norms have been *internalized* (Parsons, 1951, pp. 201–248). Once this occurs, the prospect of individuals viewing their own interests and those of the group as one and the same is unproblematic.[5]

What is striking about this view (especially in light of the supposedly deterministic models of Durkheim and later Parsons) is that it is based on the assumption that solidarity within a group constitutes an essentially voluntary phenomenon. It is important to be clear about what is meant by this. Normative theorists would undoubtedly deny that they are positing social behavior based on voluntarism, since they argue that social behavior is conditioned by society. Yet if one views norms as internalized and sees internalized norms as a basis for behavior, then this behavior is in fact voluntary. Perhaps it was not learned voluntarily, but once it is internalized, people no longer need social pressures to force them to behave according to society's (or the group's) norms.[6]

There is, however, a model consistent with Durkheim's discussion of egoistic suicide that is not dependent on the existence of internalized norms. This is the view that group pressure can ensure conforming behavior even in situations in which individuals do not share the sentiments of the group. Conforming behavior in such a context depends on the system of social relations within which an individual's behavior is embedded (Granovetter, 1985). As Hechter (1987, p. 20) has pointed out, for normative theorists, group pressure of this nature would not be sufficient to maintain social order. Some kind of inter-

---

[5] Both Durkheim and Parsons were aware, of course, that the process of internalization of norms was not always a smooth one. See Durkheim ([1897] 1951, pp. 246–258) and Parsons (1951, pp. 234–235, 243, also chap. VII).

[6] Criticisms of the view being discussed have a long history. Probably the most famous is Dennis Wrong's (1961) paper on the "oversocialized" conception of human behavior. More recently, Granovetter (1985) has taken up this theme.

nalization of norms appears to be necessary. The important point for our purposes is that group pressure can ensure behavior that conforms to group norms even if the norms are not internalized.

If behavior in accordance with group norms need not be externally enforced, there is an implied assumption that power relations between and among individuals are relatively equal. That is, it is not necessary for one person to use his or her superior power to coerce desired behavior out of others, because people in general will voluntarily behave in accordance with group norms. Once we believe that conformity of behavior can be coerced, however, then solidarity or cohesion need no longer be based on internalization of norms or on shared sentiments. This does not mean that cohesion must be forcibly enforced by those with more power over those with less power. If we view a collection of other group members as exerting such coercion then we need not specify power differentials among individuals within the group. But it is cohesion enforced by pressure nonetheless.

If the model of cohesion as a subjective phenomenon depends on the idea that norms are internalized, then it limits the scope of the concept by limiting the frequency of cases in which the phenomenon occurs. As I shall argue below, the consequences of various types of group behavior may be similar regardless of whether the behavior was voluntary or coerced. This suggests the possibility that solidarity or cohesion is more usefully described as an objective group phenomenon.

Cohesion as an Objective Concept

The idea that cohesion can be viewed as an objective, observable phenomenon independent of the sentiments of individuals is far less common among sociologists than is the subjective view. An explicit example is presented by Blau, who defines cohesion as the density of within-group relations, where density is defined as the number of actual relations between group members divided by the number of possible relations (see also Kadushin, 1968; Alba and Moore, 1983; Burt, 1983a, p. 266).[7] Exactly what constitutes the relations within the group is an open question. Certainly relations based on normative sentiment play a role, but so, for example, can similar economic in-

---

[7] This is expressed mathematically as $R / [N(N-1) / 2]$, where R equals the number of actual relations and N equals the size of the group.

terests. In another formulation, Hechter (1987, p. 18) defines group solidarity as "the average proportion of each member's private resources contributed to collective ends." Although this definition is not formulated in terms of social relations, solidarity is defined in such a way that it can be measured objectively.[8]

What is especially valuable about Blau's concept is that the key issue is the density of relations within a social structure. That is, even if relations are based on sentiments, cohesion cannot be identified by aggregating positive feelings among members of a group and calling the group cohesive if the members share positive feelings. Rather, cohesion is explicitly defined in terms of the social structure of the group, in this case, the density of within-group relations.

Even at the dyadic level, the level at which many network analysts begin when they discuss cohesion (Burt's definition [1983a] applies to the dyadic level although he uses it primarily at the clique level), this definition still views cohesion as a social relation rather than as a common feeling held by two individuals. Since sociologists dating back to Durkheim have assumed solidarity or cohesion to be a property of social structure rather than a property of aggregations of individuals, the objective definition proposed by Blau and employed by other structural sociologists may in fact be more faithful to the classical meaning of the term. I shall therefore employ an objective definition of cohesion in this study. Drawing on Blau, I define cohesion as the density of ties within a social structure. A dyadic (two-actor) relation will be cohesive to the extent that the tie is characterized by strong, intense relations (Granovetter, 1973; Burt, 1983a).

An additional advantage of an objective definition of cohesion is that it leaves open the possibility that cohesion is an involuntary as well as a voluntary phenomenon. In other words, it allows us to consider the possibility that cohesion can be coerced, that it can be enforced among the powerless by the powerful, that it can exist even when members of a group share neither the same sentiments nor the same interests. As Williams (1970, p. 583) pointed out, there is a "wide

---

[8] As noted above, Markovsky and Lawler (1988) distinguish cohesion from solidarity. "A set of actors is cohesive to the degree that it has high reachability" (1988, p. 11), that is, the distance of social ties among the group's members is relatively small. "A solidary group is a set of actors with high reachability and unity of structure" (1988, p. 12), that is, an absence of subgroups. Although Markovsky and Lawler ultimately conceive of these ties as emotionally based, their definition is a social structural one, which allows for the possibility that such ties are based on objective relations.

range within which an important degree of cohesion . . . can be maintained by coercion, the effective threat of the few over the many." Not all cohesion, he noted, "rests on consensus or voluntary participation" (see also Sciulli, 1991, chap. 2). In fact, in a small group experiment, Cook and Emerson (1978) showed that powerful members of a group could use their power to maintain conditions of cohesion.

A problem presents itself here, however. In Williams's example, cohesion is viewed as "coordinated activity." Cook and Emerson too operationalized the concept in terms of behavior. This focus is useful because behavior is directly observable and therefore lends itself more readily to objective assessment. On the other hand, there is no assurance that the existence of relations, even strong, intense ones, among members of a group will lead them to behave similarly. One would expect a correlation to exist, but it is useful to separate the two. Let us distinguish cohesion, the density of ties within a group, from unity, the extent to which a group's members behave similarly. A focus on the similarity of behavior is ultimately the most feasible way to study the link between cohesion and power.

Similarity of Behavior

Let us return to our earlier point. Why does it matter whether the capitalist class is cohesive? Because we assume that cohesion increases a group's *power*. As we noted above, according to Dahl, a group's political effectiveness is a function of its potential for control and its potential for unity. But why does cohesion increase power? The implicit assumption in these works is that cohesion increases power because it increases the likelihood that a group will act in a common fashion, that is, its members will *behave similarly*. Cohesion, defined either subjectively or objectively, may increase the likelihood that members of a group will behave similarly, but there is no necessary connection between the two. On the other hand, it is possible for different actors with no apparent direct social relation to behave similarly.

Let us consider an example. Assume that two firms with very different interests both contributed funds to the campaign of Rep. Dan Rostenkowski (D-Illinois). As Chairman of the House Ways and Means Committee, Rostenkowski plays a major role in tax legislation. If we assume that candidates who receive large amounts of funds have a greater likelihood of winning an election than do candidates who receive little funding, then the motives that precipitated the contributions to Rostenkowski are irrelevant to the outcome of the election, at least to the extent that campaign funds influence the outcome. In other words, the objective consequences of the two firms' similar behavior (Rostenkowski's increased likelihood of reelection) operate *as if* the firms shared the same interests, even if their interests were in fact opposed (Merton, 1936). Occasions on which radical feminists and right-wing fundamentalists lobbied for anti-pornography legislation provide another example. Although these two groups oppose one another on most issues and oppose pornography for different reasons, their similar behavior enabled both groups to exert more power than either would have when acting alone.

This does not mean that those with opposing interests are as likely as those with similar interests to engage in similar behavior. The extent to which common interests and common behavior correspond is an empirical question. But commonality of interests (or beliefs) is not a necessary condition for the existence of similar behavior and once two actors behave similarly, the motives precipitating their behavior become irrelevant to its consequences.

Thus, whether it is defined subjectively or objectively, similarity of behavior can occur without the existence of cohesion. Given this possibility, if we want to understand a group's power, it is essential to identify alternative sources of similar behavior.[9]

Structural Equivalence

It is possible that similarity of behavior is a function not only of cohesion but also of similar structural position. Let us consider another example.

In the late 1960s, Saul P. Steinberg was the head of Leasco, a computer leasing firm. Steinberg at the time was an up-and-coming takeover artist. In 1968 he decided to issue an offer to take over Chemical Bank, one of the six major New York money market banks. Steinberg's

[9] The focus in this discussion on behavioral manifestations of power is not meant to imply that power is exercised only if it can be empirically observed. As many authors have argued, the most effective exercise of power is often precisely that which cannot be observed (Lukes, 1974). My point is that to the extent that we study the behavioral aspects of power, a group whose members behave similarly will be in a position to exercise greater power than a group whose members behave dissimilarly. This matter is taken up in the discussion of power below.

offer promised a return of more than 50 percent to Chemical's stock-holders. At the time the plan was announced, Leasco stock was selling for $140 per share. Once the plan became known, Leasco's institutional stockholders began "dumping" their stock. Within two weeks, Leasco's stock had declined to $106 per share, thus ending the bid.

Several accounts of what precipitated the stock dumping have been presented (Business Week, 1970; Mintz and Schwartz, 1985; Glasberg, 1989). The most plausible scenario is that in an attempt to protect Chemical, whose stock they also held, from an unscrupulous "up-start," the other major New York banks, in tandem, decided to simultaneously sell their Leasco stock. If true, this example of similar behavior would be a consequence of inter-bank cohesion.

On the other hand, it is possible to imagine another account of this incident. Bank trust departments are expected to make sound and wise investments. The head of a major bank trust department might have determined that Steinberg was erratic and that Leasco was therefore a risky investment, thus leading to a decision to sell. It is certainly possible that the heads of several bank trust departments simultaneously *and unilaterally* decided to sell their Leasco stock.[10]

Whether these decisions were reached independently or through communication is unclear. It is unlikely that there was no communication among the banks. The point, however, is that even if there had been no communication, the outcome, whether anticipated or unanticipated by the banks, might very well have been the same. The question, then, is what is there about these banks that led to their similar behavior and enabled it to have the consequences that it had? My argument is that it is their common relation to Leasco, that is, their "structural equivalence."

Structurally equivalent actors are those with identical relations with other actors in the social structure (Lorrain and White, 1971; White, Boorman, and Breiger, 1976; Burt, 1987a). Thus, in a fifty-person group, two people are structurally equivalent if they both know the same five other people and do not know the remaining people (the assumption of perfect equivalence is usually relaxed in empirical ap-

---

[10] At least two other interpretations are possible. One, suggested to me by Professor Richard Lempert of the University of Michigan Law School, is that since most of Leasco's institutional stockholders also held stock in Chemical, they may have been concerned about the antitrust implications of Leasco buying Chemical. Second, individual bank trust departments, anticipating decisions by their competitors to sell their Leasco stock, may have rushed to sell theirs in order to recoup the maximum market value for it.

plications). Although those who know the same others are likely to know one another, direct relations are not necessary for two actors to be structurally equivalent.[11]

In several studies, Burt (1983a; 1987a; Galaskiewicz and Burt, 1991) has shown that structural equivalence is a stronger predictor of adoption of medical innovations, corporate philanthropy, and even the similarity of attitudes than is cohesion (which he defined, as noted above, as the presence of "strong, intense relations"). It is not necessary for my argument that structural equivalence be a stronger predictor of similar behavior than is cohesion. The key point is that factors other than cohesion can lead to similar behavior. Nevertheless, as we shall see in Chapter 6, in many cases my own data on the determinants of similar corporate political behavior are consistent with Burt's findings.

Why would structural equivalence be a stronger predictor of similar political behavior than would cohesion? There are at least two possible explanations. One possibility is drawn from Simmel's ([1917] 1950) discussion of dyads and triads. In Simmel's view, strong relations between members of dyads do not occur in a vacuum. Instead, it is precisely their common relations with third persons that help members of a dyad define what they have in common with one another. In this argument, similar behavior between two actors is assumed to result from their cohesion, but cohesion is viewed as an outcome of common relations with other members of the system.

Similarly, in his earlier work, Burt (1983a, pp. 271–272) suggested that common influence by other parties was one consequence of structural equivalence. Structural equivalence could thus be viewed as an expanded, systemic form of cohesion, in which actors with cohesive relations to the same other actors were more likely to be cohesive with one another (what network analysts refer to as "transitive" relations) because they were subject to a wide scope of common influence. More recently, however, Burt (1987a, pp. 1291–1294; see especially his footnote 4) has argued that structurally equivalent actors are as likely to

---

[11] The process by which similarly situated actors unilaterally engage in the same behavior, described here in terms of structural equivalence, resembles what Siegwart Lindenberg (1989) has called "individualized collective action." Lindenberg's argument is based on the assumption that individual actors have what he calls "social production functions." Such actors may engage in similar behavior which "is likely to have aggregate effects that are similar to or even more effective than group collective action" (ibid., p. 57).

have competitive relations as they are to have cohesive relations with one another. In this model, because structurally equivalent actors are joint occupants of positions in a social structure, they are substitutable elements of those positions. As a result, structurally equivalent actors behave similarly because they do not want to jeopardize their relations with third parties. Thus, if an occupant of a position engages in a new form of behavior, other occupants of that position are likely to quickly follow suit. This argument is supported by Burt's (1987a) findings in his reanalysis of data from the classic Coleman, Katz, and Menzel (1966) study of the adoption of medical innovations. It is also consistent with the hypothetical example, presented above, of competing firms both making contributions to Rostenkowski's campaign. In such a case, neither firm would want to jeopardize its relation with a powerful member of Congress.

A Model of Power

The preceding discussion can be summarized as follows: To the extent that cohesion plays an important role in the generation of corporate power, it is a result of its effect on the similarity of corporate political behavior. But the similarity of corporate political behavior is determined by structural equivalence as well as by cohesion. In fact, structural equivalence may play as strong a role in the prediction of similar behavior as does cohesion. Thus, it is not necessary to demonstrate the existence of business cohesion in order to demonstrate that the corporate community, in the aggregate, is a powerful and unified force. Useem (1984, p. 63) has stated that "[w]hile social cohesion is not a necessary precondition for mobilization, it is a powerful facilitator." The same could be said of intercorporate cohesion. But structural equivalence may play an equally strong (or even stronger) role in the mobilization of business. To the extent that it does, cohesion is a sufficient, but not necessary, condition for the unity of corporate political action.[12]

This discussion suggests a model such as that presented in Figure

[12] To what extent are the impacts of the similar behavior produced by cohesion and structural equivalence equal? The assumption in much of the power structure literature is that similar behavior resulting from cohesion is more effective, since it is more likely to be based on explicit coordination (but see Mintz and Schwartz, 1985, chap. 1). This appears to be a plausible argument but whether cohesion-based similar behavior is more effective than non-cohesion–based similarity is ultimately an empirical issue. There may be cases in which the unanticipated consequences of political action are as significant as the anticipated consequences (Sciulli, 1991, chap. 2; Lindenberg, 1989).

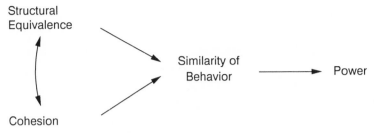

Figure 3.1. Sources of corporate political power

3.1. Given a certain level of resources, power is viewed as a function of the similarity of behavior. Similarity of behavior is viewed as a function of both cohesion and structural equivalence. If we assume that similarity of behavior is an important requisite of power, then it can be argued that although cohesion plays a role in corporate power, structural equivalence plays a role as well.[13]

But What is Power?

It hardly needs to be mentioned that the concept of power has been the subject of intense debate for decades. Several definitions and indicators have been proposed. All have received extensive criticism. The reader may be relieved to learn that it is not my purpose here to provide a comprehensive discussion of the concept or to argue for the superiority of a particular view. My assessment is that one's definition of power should be tailored to the specific needs of one's investigation. I shall provide a brief discussion of the topic only to make my own use of the term understood.

Most sociologists and political scientists have employed a variant of Max Weber's definition. Weber, as is well known, defined power ([1947] 1964, p. 152) as "the probability that one actor within a social

---

[13] Poulantzas (1973) argued that the power of the capitalist class is greater when government officials are drawn primarily from non-elite backgrounds, since this provides the appearance of an open system governed by common people. Similarly, one might argue that an apparently divided capitalist class might be more powerful than an apparently unified one, since the appearance of a non-monolithic elite would be less likely to provoke the wrath of the working class. Because this argument assumes that the control of ideology is an important source of power, however, it is flawed even on its own terms. As long as the general public does not have clear, readily available information on elite operations, it is likely to have little knowledge of the extent to which elites are unified or divided. Under these conditions, the public impression of elite cohesion is irrelevant to the elites' power, and a unified elite should be more powerful.

relationship will be in a position to carry out his own will despite resistance." In Dahl's adaptation (1957, pp. 202–203), "A has power over B to the extent that he can get B to do something that B would not otherwise do." For pluralists, who have been the primary proponents of this definition, power can only be studied by the observation of overt conflict between actors. To study political power, therefore, an examination of concrete issues is necessary. In such cases, the more powerful actor is defined as the one whose preferences regularly prevail.

Interestingly, nowhere in Dahl's definition of power is there a requirement that overt conflict occur for power to be exercised (a point that has been lost by critics and supporters alike). Covert manipulation, for example, is by definition a process of subtly coercing adversaries into actions that they would not otherwise take. Rather, it was Dahl's methodological dictum about the need to study the outcomes of concrete issues that provided the chief source of criticism.

The first such criticism appeared in a now-classic article by Bachrach and Baratz (1962). Bachrach and Baratz argued that the focus on decisions ignores situations in which pressure from elites ensures that certain issues never reach the public arena. Although they agree that Dahl's definition is useful as far as it goes, Bachrach and Baratz believe that an extension is necessary. As they put it in a subsequent work (1970, p. 8), "to the extent that a person or group, consciously or unconsciously, creates or reinforces barriers to the public airing of policy conflicts, that person or group has power" (see Crenson, 1971, for a widely acclaimed empirical study within this framework).

Although Bachrach and Baratz's concept of power implies a different methodological approach (the study of non-decisions as well as decisions), their definition is actually fully compatible with Dahl's. The ability to prevent issues from reaching the public may include the ability of one actor to achieve his or her will over the objections of another. This similarity led Lukes (1974) to advocate a third approach to the definition of power. In Lukes's view (1974, p. 23), not only can A "exercise power over B by getting him to do what he does not want to do, but he also exercises power over him by influencing, shaping, or determining his very wants." Actor A is said to exercise power over B "when A affects B in a manner contrary to B's interests" (ibid., p. 34). Because those upon whom power is exercised are frequently viewed as acting in ways contrary to their interests, this concept stands or falls on whether it is possible to define peoples' true interests. Since most pluralists (and many non-pluralists) reject the notion that it is possible to determine actors' objective interests, Lukes's model has been sharply criticized (Wrong, [1979] 1988, pp. 184–196; Clegg, 1989, chap. 5).

An alternative definition has been presented by Wrong. Drawing on Bertrand Russell, Wrong ([1979] 1988, p. 2) defines power as "the capacity of some persons to produce intended and foreseen effects on others." An advantage of this view is that it encompasses situations in which power is exercised without resistance by subordinates yet does not depend on the notion of the objective interests of the latter. Despite the attractiveness of this definition, however, the focus on intended and foreseen effects is too narrow for my purposes.

My concern is the behavior of members of a collectivity, the population of large American corporations. This behavior can be the result of conscious, goal-directed activity, as in the case of the Bay Area Council organizing to secure financing for the BART system. Or it can be the aggregate impact of several individual actions, as in the alternative interpretation of the Leasco-Chemical Bank episode described earlier. An exclusive focus on the intended and foreseen effects of collective action among elites, rightly or wrongly, conjures up images of the powerful conspiring to "put one over" on the populace. This view is precisely what I want to avoid. Regardless of the extent of organized capitalist activities, *much of the power exercised by business is an inadvertent consequence of firms' standard operating procedures.*

Conspiracy Theories

At the same time, the role of conscious collective action by business must be acknowledged as a legitimate area of inquiry. As Wrong notes ([1979] 1988, p. 143), a considerable amount of research on power structures has been accused of adhering to a conspiracy theory. Rather than simply dismiss this criticism as a cheap shot, I prefer to confront it directly. Such a task is complicated by the fact that critics rarely define what a conspiracy theory entails. I shall define a conspiracy theory as an account that is based on the notion that outcomes of events favorable to elites must have been planned by those elites. The criticism, then, is that conspiracy theorists ignore the possible unanticipated consequences of social action. In other words, conspiracy theorists are assumed to infer motives from outcomes. An example of a conspiracy theory would be the suggestion that the bombing of Pearl Harbor was deliberately provoked by the American elite to justify U.S. entry into World War II. Another would be that the white backlash to affirmative action was the result of successful planning by the ruling class, which hoped to use affirmative action to encourage racial divisions within the working class.

It is not difficult to see the problems with such after-the-fact arguments. For one thing, any outcome that appears to support the interests of the elite can be labeled the result of a conspiracy. Even outcomes that do not appear to be in the interests of the elite can, by skillful and circuitous argumentation, be shown to actually support elite interests. The passing of campaign finance laws that limited the amount wealthy individuals could spend in their own behalf, for example, appeared to be in opposition to the interests of the elite. Koenig (1987), however, noted that these laws made it increasingly difficult for office-seekers outside the political mainstream to mount strong campaigns. A conspiracy theorist might argue, based on this outcome, that the original purpose of the law must have been to exclude political outsiders. But this account is accurate only if one can demonstrate that the exclusion of political outsiders was the primary motivation behind the laws. The problem with conspiracy theory, then, is that it is based on the assumption that the outcomes of action by elites are usually (1) anticipated and (2) successful.

The appellation of a conspiracy theory certainly applies to the writings of various far-left and, especially, far-right political groups. The John Birch Society's claim that water flouridation was a Communist plot is a good example. But one would be hard-pressed to find a similar example in recent power structure scholarship. Whatever their problems, none of the works cited in Chapter 2 could be fairly accused of adhering to a conspiracy theory. Carefully planned campaigns managed by elites do occur and they often are successful. Whitt's (1982) example of the planning, dissemination of propaganda, and eventual passage of the proposition supporting the BART system is a case in point. What distinguishes Whitt's account from a conspiracy theory, however, is the care with which Whitt presents *a priori*, falsifiable hypotheses. He was thus able to demonstrate that, despite careful coordination and planning, the elites do not always get their way. As Whitt showed, an attempt by Los Angeles elites to build a system similar to BART failed because it was rejected by the voters. Moreover, as we saw in the case of Leasco and Chemical Bank, it is possible for the powerful to exercise their power in unanticipated as well as anticipated ways. Simply by virtue of their structural positions, the actions of the powerful can have a major impact on other actors in the system. Even if there had been no communication among the banks in the Leasco case, the aggregate impact of their similar actions would have been sufficient to undermine Leasco's bid for Chemical.

In short, useful as it is, a definition of power based on intended and foreseen effects is inappropriate for my purposes. My aims are (1) to emphasize the extent to which the exercise of power leads to unanticipated as well as anticipated consequences and (2) to stress the fact that the aggregate impact of the behavior of powerful actors can be substantial even in the absence of direct communication among them. I define power, then, as *the ability to affect the behavior of others, whether or not such behavior is intended or foreseen.*[14]

One final point is worth noting. My focus in this book is on the behavioral aspects of power. But this is a strategic decision, not an epistemological one. As I pointed out in the Introduction, my theoretical sympathies lie with those who argue that power is systemic and typically unobservable. I agree with Lukes that it is at least at times possible to identify actors' objective interests and that those with little power frequently act in opposition to those interests without realizing it. I do believe, however, that a focus on behavior is a legitimate component of the study of power and one for which conventional empirical techniques are well suited. For better or worse, the vast majority of social scientists in the United States (if not the West in general) are wedded to an empiricist methodology. To the extent that my theoretical aims can be accomplished with traditional em-

[14] Wrong seriously considers, but then rejects, a definition of power similar to mine. His main rationale for defining power only in terms of foreseen and intended effects is that if power is defined in terms of the unintended effects on the behavior of others, then all human actions involve the exercise of power since all human actions affect others. Thus the concept loses its analytical usefulness. Although Wrong is persuasive, he fails to consider a key point. Even if all human actions involve the exercise of power, it is still true that actions by some people have far greater effects on the behavior of others than do actions by other people. The amount of power resulting from human actions can thus be viewed as highly variable. Based on this criterion, for example, the power of large corporations is likely to far exceed that of a typical person, even though the actions of both will affect the behavior of others. It is true that unintended consequences of action can be unfavorable even to powerful actors. Revelations about General Motors spying on Ralph Nader during the 1960s, for example, probably made it easier to pass legislation that GM opposed. These cases may be exceptions, however, since one does not know how often similarly covert actions led to successful results.

pirical techniques, there seems to be little justification for abandoning them.

In research on corporate power, phenomena that we conceptualize as cohesion, unity, solidarity, and the like are important primarily because of their impact on the ability of a group (such as the business community) to behave in a politically effective fashion. Politically effective behavior, I have argued, is likely to be behavior that is similar. We are interested in cohesion therefore because of its effect on the production of politically similar behavior. It is useful to distinguish *unity*, by which I mean similar behavior, from *cohesion*, by which I mean the density of ties within a social structure. Once we insert the linking concept of similar behavior between cohesion and power, we are able to examine alternative concepts such as structural equivalence as determinants of behavioral similarity. Such a development is useful for two reasons. First, it gives us a powerful set of tools to predict the conditions under which corporate political power will be exercised. Second, it enables us to demonstrate the ways in which the collective action of powerful actors can have important consequences without the existence of any communication among them.

I have also argued that although both subjective and objective definitions of cohesion are possible, an objective definition may be more widely applicable. An objective definition enables us to avoid the often untenable assumption that similar motives produce similar behavior and that different motives produce different behavior. An objective definition of cohesion also enables us to focus on the social structures within which actors are embedded. Because subjective concepts are based ultimately in sentiments, which, as Durkheim pointed out, cannot be observed, it is almost impossible to examine social structure using a normative definition of the term. Yet it is the focus on the social structure that enables us to employ concepts such as structural equivalence, which, as we have seen, may play an important role in the generation of similar behavior. It is my position that a social structural approach to the similarity of behavior will allow us to better understand the nature of relations within the capitalist class and thus between the capitalist class and the rest of society. It will also provide a more general blueprint for research on the consequences of purposive social action.

4 · A Structural Model of Corporate Political Behavior

In the previous chapter I argued that cohesion is best treated as an objective characteristic of a social structure rather than as a set of shared normative sentiments among individuals. I also suggested that the similarity of behavior was the key concept for understanding corporate political unity. In this chapter I build on these arguments to develop a structural model of corporate political behavior. The chapter contains three sections. In the first section I briefly lay out the principles of the structural perspective, distinguishing it from its two primary alternatives. In the second section I provide the substantive and historical background for the model presented here. This section includes a discussion of the managerialist thesis and historical developments in the American business community during the twentieth century. Finally, I describe my model and propose a series of hypotheses based on it.

Normative, Utilitarian, and Structural Models

The distinction between cohesion as an objective characteristic of a social structure and cohesion as a set of shared normative sentiments is rooted in two different approaches to studying social phenomena, approaches which I shall term, following several authors (Blau, 1977; Burt, 1982; Granovetter, 1985; Hechter, 1987), the normative and structural. The normative model is important for our purposes here because of its emphasis on what sociologists call the non-contractual elements in contract or, more generally, the non-economic elements of economic behavior.

The focus on the non-market elements of economic behavior was the primary basis of Durkheim's critique of the utilitarianism of classical economics. In classical economics, individual actors are viewed as utility maximizers who, through rational calculation and assessment of alternatives, attempt to maximize benefits and minimize costs. The sources of an individual's preferences are viewed as beyond the scope of the model. Each actor is viewed as reaching his or her decisions independently.

Sociologists since Durkheim have been critical of this notion because it ignores the "impulsive forces, such as affinity of blood, attachment to the same soil, ancestral worship, community of habits" that bring people together (Durkheim, [1893] 1933, p. 278). Etzioni (1988) and Zelizer (1988) have offered extensive critiques of conventional economics from similar, although somewhat more developed, perspectives (see Polanyi, 1944; Parsons and Smelser, 1957 for classic treatments). For several decades after Durkheim, sociology in the West was dominated by the normative perspective. The primary alternative was the structural model, which was influenced first by Simmel and later by Marx. In the 1960s, however, the dominance of the normative perspective began to recede. There were several reasons for this decline, some purely scholarly and others political. But sociology came to be dominated increasingly by a more rationalistic perspective. In the study of social movements, for example, the social-psychological "collective behavior" models, with their emphasis on the spontaneous aspects of crowd behavior, were replaced by resource mobilization models that viewed social movements as attempts by rational actors to address legitimate grievances (Zald and McCarthy, 1979). The widespread social turmoil during the decade as well as the increasingly publicized abuses of power by government officials suggested to many that the emphasis on value consensus and normatively guided behavior was an inadequate model of society. At the same time, growing scholarly concern was raised over the inability of normative models to yield falsifiable, empirically testable hypotheses (Hechter, 1987). Survey research came under attack for its failure to demonstrate a link between attitudes and behavior (Deutscher, 1973).

Several alternative perspectives emerged in response to these problems. One of the later approaches to take hold, but also one with among the longest lasting influence, was what has come to be termed "structural sociology."[1] There are two general versions of structural sociology. The first, which is also frequently referred to as "network

---

[1] For good overviews of structural sociology, see Berkowitz (1982), Burt (1982), and Wellman (1988).

analysis," is the relational approach characterized by the work of Harrison White. The second is what I call the "distributional" approach, characterized by the work of Peter Blau (Blau, 1977; Blau and Schwartz, 1984).[2] The relational form of structural analysis, which is my focus here, begins with the assumption that the content of social life can only be understood by an examination of the structures of social relations within which people interact. In contrast to the normative view, "the stuff of social action is . . . to be discovered in the network of interstices that exist outside of the normative constructs and the attribute breakdowns of our everyday categories" (White, Boorman, and Breiger, 1976, p. 733). The distributional approach shares this assumption. As Blau (1977, p. x) put it, structural sociology is based on the idea that "the structures of objective social positions among which people are distributed exert more fundamental influences on social life than do cultural values and norms."

Structural sociology contains no built-in assumptions about micro-level motives. Most structural sociologists believe, however, that human actors can be assumed to be at least intendedly rational (Burt, 1982; Granovetter, 1985). In Granovetter's words (ibid., p. 506),

> [w]hile the assumption of rational action must always be problematic, it is a good working hypothesis that should not easily be abandoned . . . What looks to the analyst like nonrational behavior may be quite sensible when situational constraints . . . are fully appreciated.

Where structural sociologists differ from utilitarian theorists is in their explicit emphasis on social structure. That is, structural sociologists aim to decipher the specific elements of social structure that constrain human behavior.

The structural approach that I employ shares features with both the utilitarian and normative approaches. As with the utilitarian approach, I assume that actors are rational. Unlike the utilitarian approach, however, I emphasize that the decisions taken by actors are limited by social structural constraints, such as the actions of peers. As with the normative approach, my approach emphasizes that human decision making is affected by the actions of others. Unlike this

---

[2] Burt distinguishes the relational approach to structural analysis from what he calls the "positional" approach, and he views White's work and his own as examples of the latter. I shall make use of this distinction in later chapters, although I will not use Burt's terms. I refer to White's work as relational in the present context because he defines social structure in terms of relations among social actors rather than, as Blau does, in terms of distributions of attributes among actors. See Fararo and Skvoretz (1987) for an attempt to synthesize the two approaches.

approach, no assumption is made that actors internalize the norms that influence their behavior.

A persistent criticism of the utilitarian approach is that it fails to account for the origin of preferences. Proponents of the normative approach, for example, argue that the origin of preferences must be sought in the cultural values that characterize and distinguish various societies. The structural approach is capable of accounting for the origin of a specific actor's preferences by examining the preferences of those with whom an actor has contact or views as a reference group (Burt, 1982, chap. 5). As with the utilitarian approach, however, the structural approach fails to account for the specific content of the preferences held by one's peers or reference group. The most common response to this problem by proponents of the utilitarian approach is to acknowledge that it is not a part of its analytical system. This response has also been employed by some structural sociologists, one of whom (Wellman, 1988, p. 33) has suggested that "accounting for individual motives is a job better left to psychologists."

Because my concern is to understand the conditions under which corporations engage in similar and opposing political behavior rather than to analyze the content of the behavior, I shall operate with similar assumptions in this study. It is not necessary for me to account for the origins of why, for example, most firms support Republicans as opposed to Democrats. Fortunately, the latter has been extensively researched. Explaining the origins of the cultural values conducive to capitalism is an enormously difficult task, as the longstanding debate over Weber's *Protestant Ethic* thesis demonstrates. For my purposes, the existence of a capitalist system dominated by large corporations that seek, in various ways, to create an optimal political environment for themselves is assumed.

The model that I propose below, then, is based on the position that corporations can be viewed as rational actors that operate in accordance with their perceived interests. These interests, however, can be affected by the social structural constraints that the firms face. The presence or absence of such constraints, therefore, affects the extent to which business unity occurs. My aim in the remainder of this chapter is to develop a model that identifies these constraints.

The Model: Some Assumptions

Based on the approach described in the previous section, I begin with the assumption that the firm is a rational actor that operates under a system of constraints. These constraints are both "economic" (pertaining to the firm's production and distribution processes and relations with customers, suppliers, and distributors) and "social" (pertaining to the firm's administrative and ownership structures).[3] As a rational actor, the firm can be said to possess a set of interests. Although conflicts occur within firms at all levels, for my purposes here I shall identify the firm's interests as the interests of those who control the firm, where control is defined as the ability to determine the firm's long-term policies (Kotz, 1978). Firms pursue their interests both individually and collectively. As I argued in Chapter 3, if several firms engage in the same behavior, the consequences may be the same regardless of whether conscious collective goals were pursued. Nevertheless, there may be benefits to conscious collective action. Firms realize this and it is one reason they belong to trade associations and organizations such as the Business Roundtable. But groups of firms acting unilaterally can sometimes have the same impact. Thus, conscious collective action is not a necessary condition for the realization of firm goals and/or the exercise of firm influence.

As in the resource dependence model (Pfeffer and Salancik, 1978), I assume that corporations are under constant pressure to reduce environmental uncertainty. The reduction of environmental uncertainty may involve attempts to directly influence their environments. Because no firm can influence all aspects of its environment at all times, it must emphasize those areas that it considers most salient. One area that is increasingly of concern to corporate leaders is the firm's relation with the state. The attempt to influence political officials is thus an important mechanism for reducing environmental uncertainty.

The community of firms can be identified as a class of actors with certain common as well as opposing interests. Similar behavior may flow from these common interests, but it may also occur as a result of other factors. Given similar sets of political interests, firms might be expected to behave similarly. There is no assurance of this, however. First, firms could have different levels of resources; those with limited resources could fail to act in a given situation even if they would otherwise be inclined to support a particular action. Second, as long as

---

[3] As Granovetter (1985) and others have emphasized, even relations between customers and suppliers are often more than simply "economic." Recurring transactions between the same parties frequently result in feelings of friendship and trust that represent a far cry from the opportunistic market relations described by Williamson (1975). See Axelrod (1984, chap. 9; also Mizruchi and Schwartz, 1987). See Baker (1984) and Leifer and White (1987) for examples of social structural models of markets.

a firm stands to benefit from the outcome of group political action, "free riding" may present itself as an option (Olson, 1965). If a few politically active members of an industry lobby successfully for protective tariffs, the entire industry may benefit even though most firms did not participate in the political process. In many cases, failure to act has its costs, however. Reprisals can be taken by more powerful participants. And the benefits gained by political action are not always open to non-participants.

The assumption that firms act according to their interests is feasible, then, only if two points are acknowledged. First, it is sometimes in the firm's interest not to act, as in the case of free riding. Second, and more fundamental, possible actions that would be contrary to one's interests must be specified. Otherwise, the view that a firm behaves according to its interests is tautological. Imagine, for example, that a sales manager ("John") is invited to lunch by his boss ("Pat"). Pat asks John to choose the type of restaurant they will attend. John prefers to eat at a steak house but he knows that Pat dislikes traditional American cuisine and prefers something more exotic, such as Thai food. John's initial desire is to eat steak. Knowing that this choice will alienate his boss, however, he suggests that they eat Thai food, even though he dislikes Thai food. Is the decision to eat Thai food in John's interest? Clearly it is, since it will placate his boss. On the other hand, by placating his boss, John chooses to eat food that he dislikes. By assuming that John's decision to eat Thai food is in accordance with his interests, I am invoking what economists call the principle of "revealed preferences," which states that actors' interests can only be inferred from their behavior (Laumann and Knoke, 1987, p. 318; Coleman, 1990, pp. 340, 933; see Elster and Hylland, 1986; Cook and Levi, 1990 for cross-disciplinary treatments). This assumption is useful as a starting point. From my perspective, however, the more interesting issue is the fact that the anticipated pressure from Pat caused John to alter his behavior.

I assume, then, that firms act according to their interests, but my chief concern is the social structural factors that alter their behavior, including pressures that counteract the tendency to free ride. In fact, it is more accurate to say that my concern is with the factors that lead firms (plural) to behave similarly. Because my topic is business unity, my focus is not on the behavior of individual firms but rather on the behavior of collectivities of firms.

I begin by positing four general conditions under which similar behavior can be expected to occur. They include:

1. similar objective interests, such as membership in an industry that is about to have its regulations strengthened, or proximity of geographic locale;
2. direct pressure, or anticipation of possible repercussions, by powerful customers, suppliers, stockholders, or other outside interests;
3. social pressure to conform from those with whom one has contact; formation of similar interests through contact with similar others (Lazarsfeld and Merton, 1954);
4. mimicry of others' behavior under conditions of uncertainty (DiMaggio and Powell, 1983); for example, mimicry of peers' behavior due to competition with substitutable role partners for favor of occupants of other roles (Burt, 1982).

I alluded at the beginning of this section to two types of constraints, economic and social. The four conditions listed above all encompass one or both of these types. The distinction is sometimes blurred, since, as I suggested earlier, economic constraints are often social in nature.

In addition to the economic-social distinction, which is based on the content of the constraint, we can also distinguish "relational" and "positional" constraints, based on differences in form. Relational constraints involve direct influence, frequently by communication, between actors. Positional constraints involve decisions influenced by observing the behavior of similarly situated others, without the existence of direct communication. Conditions 2 and 3 are examples of relational constraints while condition 4 is a positional constraint. Condition 1 is also, in some cases, a positional constraint.

Organization, Class, or Both?

As we saw in Chapter 2, class theorists have posited a number of what I call "mediating mechanisms" that are presumed to facilitate business unity. These factors include kinship and social ties, policy-making organizations, interlocking corporate directorates, financial institutions, and an "inner circle" of business leaders whose outlooks transcend their individual firms.

One factor that has received little explicit attention is the role of economic interdependence. To be sure, pluralists and class theorists alike have mentioned economic sources of political conflict. But, although some theorists have hinted at economic sources of unity (Baran and Sweezy, 1966; Herman, 1981; Whitt, 1982; Useem, 1984;

Jacobs, 1988), no one has explicitly built economic interdependence into his or her model. Those coming closest to doing so are Mintz and Schwartz (1985), who focus on the power of financial institutions to resolve interindustry disputes.

The role of interdependence in business unity is particularly important because it is an issue on which the class model and a major organizational approach, the resource dependence model, converge. In the following section I develop a model of similarity of political behavior among firms based on a synthesis of the resource dependence and social class models of intercorporate relations. The section begins with a discussion of an historical analysis of interfirm relations between the early twentieth century and the mid-1970s. I then present a synthesis of the two models and derive a series of testable propositions from them. These propositions form the basis of the empirical analyses that begin in Chapter 6.

Historical Background: The Growing Importance of Organizations as Actors

One point about which pluralist, elite, and class theorists agree is that at the turn of the twentieth century, the United States was characterized by "the unilateral supremacy of corporate economic power" (Kornhauser, 1968, p. 41). The disagreements revolve around the changes that have occurred since that time. Elite and class theorists have argued that power has become more concentrated. Pluralists have argued that power has become more dispersed. An important component of both positions is their differing views on the relation between corporations and the individuals who control them.

In 1932, Adolf Berle and Gardiner Means published their now-classic *The Modern Corporation and Private Property* (Berle and Means, [1932] 1968), in which they argued that the increasing dispersal of corporate stock during the first three decades of the century resulted in the separation of ownership from control. Their followers viewed the consequences of this separation as far reaching (Riesman, 1953; Parsons and Smelser, 1957; Dahrendorf, 1959; Bell, 1960; Dahl, 1970). As Dahrendorf (1959) put it, the fact that those who owned no longer controlled and those who controlled no longer owned led to the "decomposition" of the capitalist class. Instead of a cohesive sector of society, the capitalist class had become, in Dahrendorf's (1959, p. 47) words, a "plurality of partly agreed, partly competing, and partly simply different groups." Echoing this theme, Bell (1960, p. 42) argued that the separation of ownership from control destroyed the system of private property in the means of production on which capitalism rested. Pluralists have used this argument to suggest that ownership of capital is increasingly irrelevant in understanding modern society (Parsons, 1960). Instead, those who operate individual firms are viewed as bureaucrats whose interests are those of their firm rather than those of the capitalist class as a whole (Mizruchi, 1982, chapter 1).

This assertion has been vigorously challenged, especially since the 1974 publication of Maurice Zeitlin's essay, "Corporate Ownership and Control." Zeitlin and many other researchers have challenged the empirical basis of the separation of ownership from control argument. Others (for example, Baran and Sweezy, 1966; Miliband, 1969) accepted the empirical fact of the managerialist thesis but argued that this separation has had little effect on the class character of the corporation or society as a whole.

The managerialist thesis and the debates that have revolved around it form the basis for the theoretical model examined in this book. To trace the development of the model, I present a brief historical sketch on the nature of relations among large American corporations.[4]

The Institutionalization of Intercorporate Relations

At the turn of the twentieth century, the American economy was dominated by a small number of powerful individuals, most of whom were financiers. Industrial corporations, with a few exceptions such as Standard Oil, were still relatively small and powerless. Railroads had been nearly bankrupted by the depression of 1893 and had been reorganized by investment bankers. The growth of individual corporations, particularly the formation of U.S. Steel and International Har-

[4] More recently, the managerialist thesis has been challenged from two additional fronts, one theoretical, the other empirical. Theoretically, a model from economics known as "agency theory" (Alchian and Demsetz, 1972; Jensen and Meckling, 1976; see Perrow, 1986, pp. 224–236 for a review), which focuses on the monitoring costs that managers pose for stockholders, has gained an increasing number of adherents. Empirically, the wave of takeovers during the 1980s, which left managers increasingly vulnerable to stockholders, led some observers to hail the "revolt of the owners" (Useem, 1989). One must exercise care not to exaggerate the extent of these hostile takeovers, however. The evidence that ownership and control have once again become fused is far from clear.

vester by J. P. Morgan, was dependent also on infusions of capital from investment bankers (for discussions of the period, see Corey, 1930; Josephson, 1934; Allen, 1935; Sobel, 1965; Carosso, 1970).

Observers of the period agree on two things: the power of financial institutions in relation to nonfinancials; and the power of a small number of individual capitalists, especially those who controlled those financial institutions and with them large sums of capital on which nonfinancial firms were dependent. J. P. Morgan was the best known and most powerful of this group, but George F. Baker, James Stillman, and Jacob Schiff were also major figures. Among non-financier capitalists, only John D. Rockefeller and Edward H. Harriman rivaled the others in influence and neither of the two was able to operate without alliances with financiers, Rockefeller with Stillman and Harriman with Schiff.

In a study of interlocking directorates among 167 large U.S. firms between 1904 and 1974 (Mizruchi, 1982), I found that the nature of power in the business world during the early part of the century was reflected in the network of interlocking directorates. Among 166 firms in 1904, 154 formed a completely connected graph. Among the 25 most central[5] firms in that network, 14 (56 percent) were financial institutions, even though only 25 percent of the firms in the network were financials. In 1912, 17 (68 percent) of the 25 most central firms were financials.

In addition to the preponderance of financial institutions among the most central corporations, the data also revealed the presence of a relatively large number of individuals, 24 in 1904 and 27 in 1912, who sat on the boards of six or more corporations in the network (Mizruchi, 1982).

By 1919, after the last of the great "robber barons" had died or retired, the character of the system had changed considerably and these changes continued into the 1930s. Although the great majority of corporations remained tied into a single network and financial institutions remained the most central group (though not as central as in previous years), the density of the network declined considerably and the number of individuals with six or more board seats dropped sharply (see Table 4.1).

The changes between 1912 and 1935 illustrated in Table 4.1 indicate

[5] Although it has been operationalized in numerous ways (Freeman, 1979; Mizruchi, Mariolis, Schwartz, and Mintz, 1986), centrality as used in that study was defined primarily by the ability to reach the largest number of other firms in the smallest number of steps.

Table 4.1 Characteristics of the U.S. corporate network, 1912–1935

Characteristic	1912	1919	1935
A. connected firms	140	143	145
B. density	7.6	5.6	4.0
C. three-step reach	81.9	85.5	80.7
D. financial presence	68.0	32.0	48.0
E. interlocked individuals	27	14	3
F. density (- E above)	3.9	4.0	3.7

Key: **A**, number of firms among all 167 in network that form a single, continuous graph; **B**, proportion of possible connections in which a tie exists; **C**, percent of corporations that can be reached within three steps of the most central corporation; **D**, proportion of financial institutions among the 25 most central firms in the network; **E**, number of individuals who sit on six or more boards among the 167; **F**, density of the network when those with six or more board seats are removed from the calculation.

that the system changed from one dominated by a small number of individuals to one dominated by the structures of intercorporate relations that those individuals had established, a process that I referred to as the "institutionalization of intercorporate relations." The number of connected corporations and the distances among them (reach) did not change from 1912 to 1935. The density declined sharply, however, as did the number of individuals who sat on six or more boards. When those individuals who sat on six or more boards were removed from all three networks, the densities in all three years were virtually identical.

These findings suggest that although the importance of individual capitalists declined, the structure of relations among large corporations that they had established remained (Corey, 1930). They suggest that corporations changed from tools of individuals to institutions with "lives of their own," over and above the individuals who participate in them.

It needs to be emphasized that I am not saying that powerful individual capitalists no longer exist or that they play no role in the functioning of the system. In fact, during the latter part of the 1980s, the role of "corporate raiders" reached epic proportions (as captured in the movie *Wall Street*). When viewed in historical perspective, however, things appear somewhat different. First, the individuals who make careers out of buying and selling large blocks of stock and in general manipulating corporations for their own ends were much more likely in recent years to be viewed as outsiders, protagonists in the battle against the faceless Wall Street "establishment" (Josephson, 1972), than were similar individuals in the early part of the century. Second, many of the spectacular mergers and takeovers of the late 1980s were instituted by corporations with the sometimes active support of financial institutions, rather than by individual "raiders." Finally, the individuals who do sit on several major boards and who play a major role in both corporate and political policy making (Useem's "inner circle"), though obviously influential, do not have the power that the great financiers and capitalists of the early twentieth century enjoyed.

The change in the nature of intercorporate relations in the early twentieth century United States suggests two things, both of which inform the model that I develop in this chapter. On the one hand, the decline in the number of heavily interlocked individuals suggests the increased importance of corporations relative to individuals, a theme argued by Coleman (1982) and given supporting evidence by Burt (1975). On the other hand, the continued connectivity of the interlock network among firms suggests at least the possibility of a continued level of interfirm cohesion. Historical evidence about the development of interfirm relations, therefore, reveals support for components of both the organizational and the class models. First, it suggests that we focus on corporations rather than individuals. Second, it suggests that we identify, and emphasize, the relations among firms. Both points suggest the need for an approach that takes both the organizational and class models into account. In the following sections, I present a model based on a synthesis of the organizational and class models of intercorporate relations.

The Organizational Model

The approach most closely identified with the organizational model of intercorporate relations is the resource dependence model. The roots of the resource dependence model go at least as far back as Selznick's (1949) classic study of the Tennessee Valley Authority and can be found in the works of Emerson (1962), Blau (1964), Thompson (1967), and many others (Yuchtman and Seashore, 1967; Zald, 1970; Allen, 1974; Jacobs, 1974; Aldrich and Pfeffer, 1976; Pennings, 1980). It has received its most comprehensive treatment, however, by Pfeffer and Salancik (1978; see also Pfeffer, 1987). The most important tenet of this perspective is that organizations exist in environments that are potentially turbulent and always problematic, and that the ways in which organizations deal with that environment have a major impact on their internal workings and external effectiveness. In this view, an organization's power in relation to its environment is a function of its ability to gain access to resources which are controlled by other organizations. Conversely, an organization's power in relation to its environment is a function of its control over resources that are deemed crucial by other organizations. An organization's relation with its environment becomes a process of managing and limiting uncertainty, including working out stable and predictable relations with other organizations.

A considerable amount of empirical research in the resource dependence tradition has involved an analysis of interlocking directorates as a mechanism of cooptation (absorption of potentially disruptive elements into the organization's formal decision-making structure). Thompson and McEwen (1958) spoke of a nonfinancial firm's acceptance on its board of representatives from banks to which it was seriously indebted, and numerous subsequent investigators have looked at corporate interlocks from this perspective (Dooley, 1969; Allen, 1974; Bunting, 1976b; Pfeffer and Salancik, 1978; Pennings, 1980; Carrington, 1981; Burt, 1983a; Richardson, 1987; Ziegler, 1987; Mizruchi and Stearns, 1988). Although the evidence has been far from unequivocal, high levels of debt have generally been found to be associated with interlocks with financial institutions, a finding that lends support to the model.

The cooptation approach to the resource dependence model is subject to certain ambiguities. It is often unclear whether an interlock involves the cooptation of firm A by firm B or the infiltration of firm B by firm A (Aldrich, 1979, p. 296; Mizruchi, 1982; 1987; Palmer, 1983; Richardson, 1987). Most cooptation theorists acknowledge that both processes occur, sometimes simultaneously (Pfeffer, 1972, p. 222; Allen, 1974, p. 401; Pfeffer and Salancik, 1978, pp. 164–165; Pennings, 1980, pp. 23–24). In addition, studies showing that most accidentally broken ties are not reconstituted with the same firms (Koenig, Gogel, and Sonquist, 1979; Ornstein, 1980; Palmer, 1983; Stearns and Mizruchi, 1986; Stokman, van der Knoop, and Wasseur, 1989) have raised questions about whether interfirm interlocks are even indicative of organizational strategies. Despite these questions, the general principle that the control of crucial resources alters the balance of power in interfirm relations appears to be a sound one.

The Social Class Model

In the social class model, corporations are viewed as mechanisms by which corporate leaders, as members of a dominant class, exercise power over the economy and over society in general (Zeitlin, 1974; Koenig, Gogel and Sonquist, 1979; Useem, 1979; 1984; Ratcliff, 1980; Koenig and Gogel, 1981; Domhoff, 1983; Palmer, 1983; Roy, 1983). In this view, the primary leaders of the business community are individuals whose interests transcend the boundaries of individual firms (Useem, 1984; Soref and Zeitlin, 1987). Although organizations may indeed establish linkages to facilitate the smooth flow of resource exchange transactions, many intercorporate linkages are viewed as reflective of attempts by business elites to develop structures for the mediation of intra-class disputes. The extent to which formal interorganizational linkages accomplish this function is a matter of some debate among social class theorists. But most agree that the linkages reflect primarily a class rather than an organizational dimension. For example, interlocking directorates are seen as being based more on social and political criteria than on the resource requirements of particular organizations. Class theorists believe that ties such as interlocks have consequences for corporate political behavior because they help to integrate further the leaders of firms into the corporate elite. As Mills (1956, p. 123) put it in a widely quoted passage, "Interlocking Directorate is no mere phrase: it points to a solid feature of the facts of business life, and to a sociological anchor of the community of interest, the unification of outlook and policy, that prevails among the propertied class."

Where interlocking directorates have been indicative of specific intercorporate relations in this perspective, they have been conceptualized as mechanisms of control. For example, early in the twentieth century, J. P. Morgan solidified his control over U.S. Steel and International Harvester by placing representatives of J. P. Morgan & Co. on the boards of the two companies. In recent years, however, most social class theorists have eschewed this interpretation, particularly in light of the studies, cited above, showing that most accidentally broken ties are not reconstituted with the same firms.

Despite considerable empirical support for many of its main tenets, the social class model contains two problems. The first is what is in my view an unnecessary emphasis on the coincidence of ownership and control. The second is an ambiguity surrounding the distinction between the definition of class and the maintenance of class privileges.

Ownership and Control

As we have seen, Berle and Means suggested that the dispersal of large blocs of stock led to the managerial control of corporations. This claim, if true, appeared to render irrelevant the Marxian emphasis on ownership of the means of production. For this reason, many Marxists rejected the empirical basis of the Berle and Means thesis (see Zeitlin, 1974; Zeitlin, Ewen, and Ratcliff, 1974 for counter-evidence). In fact, however, considerable stock dispersal had apparently taken place long before Berle and Means's study, yet this did not prevent control of corporations by the great financiers and capitalists of the period. Corey (1930) suggested that stock ownership was almost irrelevant to J. P. Morgan's control over U.S. Steel as well as other important corporations. As he put it (1930, p. 284):

> The House of Morgan and other financial masters did not own the corporations under their control. Nor was ownership necessary. Stockholders being scattered and numerous, control was easily usurped by minority interests, particularly when these interests were institutionalized in the formidable combination of the House of Morgan.

Rather than being based on the purely legal criterion of stock ownership, control was based on a complex set of institutional relations and obligations, which included

> stock ownership, voting trusts, financial pressure, interlocking of financial institutions and industrial corporations by means of interlocking directorates, and the community of control of minority interests, all dependent upon stockholders who did not participate in management, who could not easily combine to assert their ownership, and whose concern was limited to dividends (ibid.).

Stock ownership, then, may be an important element in corporate control and intercorporate relations, but its significance is likely to be limited by a host of other factors, especially those that involve relations with other corporations. In the early 1960s, for example, Howard Hughes owned 78 percent of the stock in TWA, but as a sanction for some of his previous behavior, a group of 17 financial institutions on which Hughes was dependent placed the 78 percent stock ownership into a trust fund, which they administered (Mintz and Schwartz, 1985).

This development suggests the need to look for sources of corporate control that are independent of ownership. In fact, as we shall see, a network approach does just that. Many theorists, both Marxist (Poulantzas, 1973) and non-Marxist (Dahrendorf, 1959; Parkin, 1979; Dahl, 1982), have acknowledged this need. It is crucial to reiterate, however, that the existence of capitalism or a capitalist class does not necessarily depend on the coincidence of legal ownership and control. Scott (1979), for example, has emphasized the collective nature of corporate control. This can occur when a cluster of institutional stockholders, no one of which owns more than a few percent of a firm's stock, collectively owns a substantial bloc. It can also result from constraints placed on corporations by loan consortia consisting of several dozen financial institutions (Mintz and Schwartz, 1985). As Wright (1985) argued, class must be viewed as a social as well as a legal category. As long as the system remains capitalistic (characterized by the private appropriation of the surplus and private investment decisions), whether particular organizations are identified as owner or management controlled is beside the point.

It is possible, in other words, to conceptualize a system of politically cohesive corporations in which major individual and family stockholdings play only a part. Of course, there are cases in which huge stock ownership interests give a particular family undeniable control over a corporation or several corporations. Two points should be kept in mind, however: first, even if a particular corporation is owner controlled in terms of a large stockholding, the corporation may in fact be dominated by other corporations, as Hughes's TWA was; second, the fact that most large corporations now appear to have no individual controlling stock interest and are therefore classified as management controlled loses much of its force once we consider the corporation in the context of its relations with other corporations. That is, it is possible for corporations as organizations to control or strongly influence other corporations, even if both of them appear to be management controlled at the level of the individual organization. External control of corporations can occur independent of ownership or family control.[6]

---

[6] By "control" I mean, in Kotz's (1978, chap. 2) words, the ability to affect the long-term policies of the firm. This is distinct from "managing," which involves the process

Definition versus Maintenance

The second major problem with the social class model is its failure to distinguish between the structures of class definition and those of class maintenance (or "reproduction," in Poulantzas's [1973] terms). Numerous studies (Soref, 1976; Koenig, Gogel, and Sonquist, 1979; Ratcliff, Gallagher, and Ratcliff, 1979; Domhoff, 1983; Useem, 1984; Soref and Zeitlin, 1987) have confirmed the existence of a group of heavily interlocked directors who disproportionately share elite backgrounds and who are disproportionately represented on the boards of local and national policy-making, civic, cultural, and philanthropic organizations. What none of these studies has done is to show a specific connection between kinship ties and one's position within these groups. (Zeitlin and Ratcliff [1988] provide evidence for this in Chile, but this has not yet been done for the U.S.) Although it is possible, even likely, that such connections exist, it is crucial to recognize that it is not necessary to establish any kinship connections for this argument to stand. That is, family connections among members of the inner circle are not necessary for the group to function, nor is family control of particular corporations. This was recognized by Useem (1982), who stated that "The dominant segment [of the capitalist class] is founded in the classwide economic and social relations among large corporations and their executives, not in the complex fabric of the nation's first families" (1982, p. 222; see also Zeitlin, 1976, p. 900).

In short, family control of corporations is not a necessary component for the existence of a capitalist class. Family ties may be a mechanism for maintaining class privileges, as are the social and policy-making organizations described by Domhoff and others. But kinship is not a necessary component of the definition of social class.

If one's social background is not a necessary criterion for membership in the capitalist class, on what basis does membership rest? The key step in answering this question is to depersonalize the issue. A class consists not of an aggregation of individuals but of relations among positions in a social structure. If we assume that the key economic actors in the contemporary United States are not individuals but large corporations, then the capitalist class can be defined as the

---

of decision making that takes place within the limits set by those who control (see Mizruchi, 1983b). By "influence" I mean the ability to affect the outcome of events in situations of collective action, as well as the ability to determine the conditions under which action will take place (Laumann and Pappi, 1976; Mizruchi, 1982; 1983b). Influence may or may not include the ability to control.

structure of relations among the controlling positions in major corporations. If we assume that either top management or the board of directors exercises operating control in most large firms, then the capitalist class consists of the relations among top officers and directors of large corporations. This definition is consistent with Useem's operationalization in which inner circle members are identified by their presence on several boards of directors. Although the studies cited above have found that directors of major U.S. corporations are disproportionately from elite backgrounds, one could propose that inner circle membership is as much a function of one's position within the corporate (and intercorporate) hierarchy as vice versa (Moore and Alba, 1982).

In the absence of family control of a corporation, one's rise to corporate leadership may be a function of aspects other than family background, or even social connections. This is not meant to imply that a meritocracy exists in the American business world, as many managerialists have claimed (Hacker, 1976; see Useem and Karabel, 1986 for an empirical refutation of this argument). It does suggest, however, that the structure of the corporation and of intercorporate relations in advanced capitalist societies may be said to exist independent of the social positions of its leaders. Even were the United States and other advanced capitalist societies to constitute pure meritocracies (assuming that an ideal meritocracy were possible), this might have little effect on the behavior of large corporations or on the relations among them.[7]

A Synthesis

Although the resource dependence and social class models are based in different theoretical traditions, several researchers have noted that the two models are to a considerable extent complementary (Mizruchi, 1982; 1983a; 1987; Palmer, 1983; Roy, 1983; Ornstein, 1984). Ornstein (1984, p. 230), for example, points out that the resource dependence model's view of corporate goals as serving the need for in-

---

[7] Another example that demonstrates the importance of an organizational base in the business community for participation in corporate policy making is presented by Useem (1984, p. 39). An outside director of an insurance company was not renominated to the board after the retail firm of which he had been president was acquired by another firm. As a director of the insurance company told Useem, "The president suddenly was without a job; he devoted his time to working with the local art museum, but he didn't keep up with the business community because he hadn't any base . . . His being on the board does not add anything."

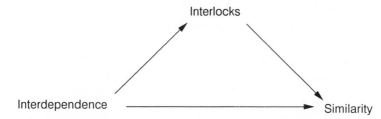

Figure 4.1. Theoretical model of similarity of political behavior

formation about the firms' economic and political environments "is not much different from the more diffuse political and ideological goals of interlocking that are emphasized in the class perspective." But though such similarities have been noted, the two views continue to be seen as separate, and competing, paradigms.

And yet the similarities are real. The facilitation of resource flows described by resource dependence theorists may in fact have the political and ideological consequences that social class theorists stress. And the political unity facilitated by interorganizational linkages, as described by social class theorists, may in fact have its basis in resource interdependencies within the business community. The idea that resource interdependence may form a basis for corporate political unity is one which, surprisingly, has never before been formally specified. The forms of cohesion and conflict mediation posited by social class theorists, including kinship and social ties, policy-making organizations, and the state, are external to the economic relations among companies, and may in fact be affected by them.[8] Thus, the class model may benefit from the incorporation of concepts developed by resource dependence theorists.

A graphic summary of the model suggested by this discussion is presented in Figure 4.1. As the resource dependence model suggests, interlocking is a function of resource dependence. As the class model suggests, similar political behavior is a function of the social ties created by interlocks. And, as my synthesis suggests, similar political behavior is also a function of resource dependence. This model enables us to decompose the effects of organizational and social network factors on the similarity of political behavior. It enables us to determine

[8] "Indeed, consensus developed within such groups as the Council of Foreign Relations is insufficient and must also be concretely developed in the relationships, for example, among General Motors, Volkswagen, and Toyota" (DiTomaso, 1980, p. 259).

the effect of interlocks on similarity of political behavior even when we control for the extent of organizational interdependence.

Combining the model of action described earlier in the chapter with the synthesis of the organizational and class models allows me to specify the major principles of a structural model of interfirm relations:

1. The fundamental units of analysis for understanding business behavior are the relations among corporations, as distinct from relations among individuals or kinship groups.
2. Whether corporations are management controlled or owner controlled is secondary to their positions in interfirm economic and social networks.
3. The power of firms with respect to other firms is a function of control over resources that are deemed necessary by other firms.
4. Corporations are subject to economic pressures from customers and suppliers and social pressures from within the business community, both of which may have political repercussions.
5. The views of corporate officials are influenced both by those with whom they have contact and by those whom they view as peers. Even if they appear to be acting voluntarily and unilaterally, corporations normally take into account how their peers and key trading partners will view their decisions.
6. Similarity of behavior among members of a collectivity contributes to the power of that collectivity.

To recap, the similarity of political behavior among firms is a function of four factors: (a) similarity of interests among firms; (b) the threat, actual or potential, of direct pressure by key customers, suppliers, or other outside interests; (c) social pressures and communication across firm boundaries; and (d) conformity induced by observation of the behavior of others in similar positions. In the following section, I draw on these principles to develop hypotheses to predict the similarity of political behavior among firms.

Sources of Business Unity

Do the mediating mechanisms posited by class theorists actually facilitate political unity among firms? Do social network factors affect similarity of behavior beyond the convergence of interests that might occur even in the absence of network ties? Is a politically unified group actually more powerful? My aim in the remainder of this work is to examine these questions empirically. In this section I identify specific variables that I expect to yield business political unity.

These variables can be divided into two general types, which I shall term *network* variables and *interest* variables. I began this chapter with the assumption that firms acted rationally in accordance with their interests. I also suggested that these interests could be modified by social structural forces. The identification of a set of common interests among firms as determinants of political unity would be useful in its own right. Theoretically, however, most students of political behavior take as given the view that actors operate in accordance with their interests. The role of modified interests or, more specifically, modified behavior as a result of social structural variables, is an area for which there is surprisingly little theoretical attention or supporting evidence, at least in the area of corporate political behavior. My task here is to identify a series of indicators of similarity of interests and then combine them with network variables. The goal is to determine the extent to which social structures and, by implication, mediating mechanisms, matter in corporate political behavior.

I have referred to four general sources of similar behavior. All but one of the four involve network variables. I shall describe the network variables first. Hypotheses for the interests variables follow.

Market Constraint as a Form of Cohesion

I shall begin with a key component of the model in Figure 4.1: the idea that economic interdependence is a source of similar political behavior. I have described the historical changes that led to this idea. But on what theoretical basis does this point rest?

Arguments supporting the notion that economic interdependence facilitates political unity go back to Durkheim, who argued, in *The Division of Labor in Society* ([1893] 1933), that interdependence was the basis of social order in modern societies. In more recent formulations, several scholars have suggested that the dependence of one actor on another gives the latter power over the former (Emerson, 1962; Blau, 1964; Coleman, 1974; Jacobs, 1974; Cook, 1977; Pfeffer and Salancik, 1978; Marsden, 1981; 1983; Burt, 1982; Cook et al., 1983). Implicit in these views is the notion that power can be used to maintain solidarity under conditions favorable to the powerful actor, even if the two actors have otherwise conflicting interests.

The idea that interdependence generates unity is far from universally shared, however. In Lowi's (1969) discussion of types of conflict among firms (quoted in Chapter 2), many cleavages involved relations between interdependent sectors, such as wholesalers and retailers. Galbraith (1952) viewed relations between interdependent customers and suppliers as a major source of "countervailing power." In the area of international relations, Keohane and Nye (1977) argued that interdependence among nations serves as a deterrent to war, but this view has generated considerable controversy (Milner, 1988).

How might interdependence be a source of conflict? Consider the auto and steel industries. Firms in these industries are clearly dependent on one another. The steel industry depends on sales to the auto companies and the auto industry depends on purchases from the steel companies. Nevertheless, it is easy to imagine how the two industries could be opposed on political issues that affect their operations. The steel industry, for example, may support tariffs on imported steel, in order to protect its market and maintain its prices. The auto companies, on the other hand, may prefer free trade in steel so they can purchase steel at lower rates. In the absence of additional forces, what one industry supports is likely to be opposed by the other.

However, it is also necessary to consider the options that members of the two industries have when selling or purchasing each others' products. The auto industry is relatively concentrated, so members of the steel industry have few alternative firms within the auto industry with which to transact. This situation indicates that the auto industry exerts more economic leverage over the steel industry than would a relatively competitive industry such as computer manufacturing. Steel too is relatively concentrated (although not as concentrated as auto manufacturing). This indicates that the steel industry exerts more leverage over the auto industry than would a competitive industry such as lumber and wood products.

The issue of leverage and interdependence concerns what may be the key concept in this book: the notion of *market constraint*. This term was used by Burt (1983a) to account for the extent to which dependence is affected by the absence of alternatives. *Market constraint is the extent to which members of one industry impose limits on the ability of members of another industry to realize profits.* The constraint of industry A over industry B is a function of two factors:

(1) the dependence of industry B on industry A for sales and/or purchases; and (2) the concentration of industry B. The oil industry, for example, does only a small amount of its business with the tobacco industry. Although the tobacco industry is highly concentrated, it therefore exercises little constraint over the oil industry. The paper industry does a substantial amount of its business with the printing and publishing industry. Because the printing and publishing industry is relatively competitive, however, it exerts less constraint over the paper industry than does the chemical industry, which does less total business with paper but is more concentrated. Constraint is highest in situations like auto and steel, in which both industries are concentrated and large transactions are made.[9]

I suggest that the existence of constraint in an interdependence relation facilitates similar political behavior among firms. Just as John decided to eat lunch at a Thai restaurant to avoid the potential wrath of his boss, a firm that is constrained by another may feel pressured to conform to what it sees as the constraining firm's wishes. Thus, the exercise of economic leverage may lead to similar behavior even if the firms' interests otherwise conflict. A similar point has been made by DiMaggio and Powell (1983, p. 154):

> [T]he greater the dependence of an organization on another organization, the more similar it will become to that organization in structure, climate, and behavioral focus . . . [T]he greater the centralization of organization A's resource supply, the greater the extent to which organization A will change isomorphically to resemble the organizations on which it depends for resources.

Similarly, Fligstein (1990, pp. 5–7) has suggested that less powerful organizations tend to support the dominant firms in their organizational fields, which may include suppliers and distributors. Whitt (1982) has described a case in which several San Francisco banks that had originally supported a statewide mass transit proposal reversed their position. This appeared to be due to the anticipation of pressure from oil companies on which the banks were dependent for business. Findings from an earlier study (Mizruchi and Koenig, 1986) support this notion. In an analysis of relations among the largest members of 14 major industries, Koenig and I found that the level of constraint

---

[9] Burt has employed this model to demonstrate that more concentrated industries maintain higher profit margins. See Scherer (1980) for a related argument by an industrial organization economist.

between industries was positively related to the similarity of their political behavior.[10]

One problem with this discussion is that I have failed to distinguish situations in which dependence is roughly equal (or symmetric) from those in which one party is clearly dominant. I have suggested that a firm that exercises market constraint over another firm can coerce conformity. But what of situations in which both firms exercise constraint over one another? Does this reciprocal dependence of two firms cancel out the leverage of each? My argument is that it does not. The level of symmetry in a constraint relation should make no difference in the level of pressure toward conformity. When members of two concentrated industries are highly dependent on one another, neither has a large number of alternatives and both have a stake in maintaining a smooth relationship. As Emerson (1962, pp. 33–34) put it:

> If the power of A over B is confronted by equal opposing power of B over A, is power then neutralized or cancelled out? We suggest that in such a balanced condition, power is in no way removed from the relationship. A pattern of 'dominance' might not emerge in the interaction among these actors, but that does not imply that power is inoperative in either or both directions . . . [B]alance does not neutralize power, for each party may continue to exert profound influence over the other. It might even be meaningful to talk about the parties being controlled by the relation itself.

---

[10] The results of that study suggested that controlling for constraint, the volume of transactions between industries will be negatively related to the similarity of political behavior. We interpreted this finding as an indication that in the absence of constraint, two interdependent firms would tend toward opposing (or different) political positions, a finding consistent with the pluralist argument. Two problems associated with this finding have led me to delete this variable from the present study. First, although there are several examples of interdependent industries that might have opposing political interests, there are many other examples in which interdependent industries have similar interests (for example, American auto makers and auto parts suppliers would probably both support import restrictions on foreign cars) or in which industries that transact little or no business (for example, chemicals and tourism) might have opposing interests. Second, in the current study, based on far more extensive and reliable data, I found that volume of transactions was a positive predictor of similarity. This occurs, I would suggest, because volume of transactions is indicative of similar substantive processes as those encompassed by the concept of constraint. When volume of transactions was added to the analysis, its effect was positive and the effects of the other variables remained virtually identical. Because I do not see the variable as adding substantively to the processes captured by the concept of market constraint, and because the two variables are confounded (volume of transactions is part of the definition of constraint), I have omitted volume of transactions from the analysis.

The processes that generate similar behavior will be different in the asymmetric and symmetric cases. If firm A's constraint over B is one-way, then B is expected to conform to A's wishes. If A and B exercise roughly equal levels of constraint, then the similar behavior could result from at least three different processes: A forces B to conform, B forces A to conform, or they reach a mutually acceptable position. What is important to note, however, is that regardless of the different methods by which the decisions are reached, the *consequence* of the constraint relation is similarity of behavior.

This discussion suggests that we can expect to find a positive association between constraint and behavioral similarity regardless of whether the constraint is mutual or one-way. It also suggests that the level of asymmetry in constraint relations should have no effect on the degree to which firms behave similarly. This leads to the following hypotheses:

H1: The greater the level of constraint among firms, the greater the similarity of political behavior.
H2: The asymmetry of constraint among firms has no effect on the similarity of political behavior.
H3: The asymmetry of constraint among firms has no effect on the strength of the relations in H1 above.

Ownership and Directorate Networks

Of the four sources of similar behavior described above, two involve social communication or pressure or the emulation of peers. These variables are indicative of various types of social network ties among firms. The most commonly employed indicator of social network ties among firms is interlocking directorates.

As we have seen, class theorists have assumed that interlocking directorates are an important source of corporate unity. Interlocks may involve strategic responses to organizational interdependence, including market constraint relations (as in Figure 4.1). They may also reflect friendship ties among firm CEOs. But whether they originate primarily as organizational or social relations, their consequence is the communication of information. As Useem (1982, p. 211) put it, "the unplanned consequence of . . . interlocking directorates is the formation of a communication network that inevitably helps a segment of the corporate elite identify its members' shared political interests." This notion should apply not only to direct ties between firms but also to their indirect ties, that is, situations in which two firms interlock with the same third firm. The latter is important because it provides the two firms with a common source of what Useem (1984) has called "business scan," the ability to acquire diffuse information about developments across a broad range of sectors. Because the boards of financial institutions, especially commercial banks, are most likely to include representatives of several major industries, business scan will most likely be achieved through membership on financial boards. Mintz and Schwartz (1985) have also argued that major commercial banks play an important role in resolving or preventing disputes across sectors because of their role in the allocation of scarce capital funds. In a pilot study for this project (Mizruchi and Koenig, 1988), Koenig and I found a strong positive association between indirect interlocks through major banks and the similarity of corporate political behavior. Therefore, it will be worthwhile to examine the number of cases in which firms share directors with the same bank, as well as with one another.

Common stock ownership by financial institutions in the same companies is another potential source of corporate political unity. The prevalence of institutional stockholding has increased considerably since World War II to the point that institutional investors are now the largest stockholders of major U.S. corporations. Although only a minority of *Fortune* 500 corporations have more than five percent of their stock owned by a single bank (Kotz, 1978), the existence of sizable blocs of stock held by groups of financial institutions is far greater (Corporate Data Exchange, 1981). Considerable controversy exists over the extent to which the banks that own corporate stock actually use the holdings to wield influence over corporate policy. Herman (1981) argues that not only does this rarely occur, but if a bank is dissatisfied with management's policy, it typically invokes the "Wall Street Rule." That is, it sells its stock rather than intervening in the firm's affairs. Mintz and Schwartz (1985) agree that institutional investors do not typically dictate policy to management. They argue, however, that the Wall Street Rule is not a neutral form of exit (Hirschman, 1970) but rather a form of punishment known more appropriately as "stock dumping." In Mintz and Schwartz's view, the knowledge that institutional investors could dump their stock serves as a significant threat to most managers. If the latter is the case, we might expect firms whose stock is owned by the same financial institutions to take pains to curry favor with and avoid alienating their institutional stockholders. If institutional stockholding has an effect on corporate political behavior, firms with similar stockholders should behave similarly. Results from an earlier study (Mizruchi and Koenig, 1988) revealed a positive association between the number of banks that held stock in members of a particular industry and the similarity of political behavior within that industry.[11]

This discussion suggests the following hypotheses:

H4 and H5: The number of interlocking directorates, both direct and indirect, among firms is directly related to the similarity of their political behavior.

H6: The number of financial institutions that hold stock in the same firms is directly related to the similarity of political behavior among the firms.

Indicators of Common Interests

The prevalent view among students of corporate political behavior is that firms act in accordance with their interests. This dictum is subject to modification as we move to more concrete descriptions of behavior. But applied to the behavior of collectivities of firms, whether acting individually or as members of a group, similar political behavior among firms is, in this view, a function of their similar interests.

I have argued that this view ignores the social structural forces that constrain the behavior of firms. Instead, I suggest, it is their relations with other firms that determine both how firms perceive their interests and the ways they act upon them. It is possible, however, that knowledge of firms' interests, independent of their network relations, is sufficient to explain their political behavior. The burden is on me to demonstrate that network factors matter, above and beyond what could be gleaned from an analysis of common interests. In order to determine the effect of network variables on the similarity of political behavior among firms, therefore, it is necessary to control for common interest variables that have been identified by theorists of corporate political behavior.

The most obvious example of similar political interests is member-

[11] Direct stockholding relations and joint ventures between firms are also worthwhile areas of study. Both phenomena, however, occurred too infrequently to play a meaningful role in the analysis.

ship in the same industry or industries. Others include common geographic locale and similar interests toward labor, government regulation, and defense spending. In this section I develop hypotheses to examine the extent to which similar types of interests lead to similar political behavior.

Industry and Geographic Location

Members of particular industries compete economically, although the extent of this competition varies across industries. Nevertheless, most observers of corporate political behavior, including pluralists, have assumed that members of the same industry have at least some basis for similar political behavior. The extent to which similarity of political behavior varies across industries is examined in Chapter 8. The issue here is whether members of the same industry are more likely to behave similarly than are members of different industries. There are at least two reasons to believe that this would be the case. First, and most important, government policies frequently affect entire industries. In fact, many of the arguments about the political interests of labor intensive and regulated firms as well as defense contractors are based on the assumption of industry-specific interests (see, for example, Ferguson and Rogers, 1986). Second, firms in the same industries are generally in structurally equivalent positions in terms of their interdependence with other industries. Based on the logic of structural equivalence discussed in the previous chapter, we would expect firms subject to similar economic constraints to behave similarly politically. DiMaggio and Powell (1983) suggest that firms will often attempt to mimic those whom they view as peers. In the business world, a firm's peers are frequently the other members of the firm's primary industry (Fligstein, 1990, pp. 5–7). This latter point suggests that membership in the same industry contains a social structural as well as a pure interest component. In the empirical analyses, especially those in Chapter 8, I attempt to untangle the effects of social structural aspects of industry membership. For now, both the interest and social structural arguments suggest the same hypothesis:

H7: Firms in the same primary industry will exhibit greater similarity of political behavior than firms in different primary industries.

Most large manufacturing corporations are involved in several industries. Although it is possible to clearly identify a firm's primary industry in most cases, there is increasing overlap among firms in the secondary industries in which they operate. The same logic that was employed for the previous hypothesis suggests the following:

H8: The greater the number of common industries in which firms produce, the greater their similarity of political behavior.

By suggesting that firms within the same industries are more likely to engage in similar political behavior than firms in different industries, I am not suggesting that similar behavior is unlikely to occur across industries. On the contrary, the hypothesized effects of market constraint and the other network variables assume the existence of cross-industry unity. Nor am I suggesting that conflict does not occur among members of the same industries. Other things being equal, however, I expect membership in the same industries to be a source of corporate political unity.

Although most studies of corporate networks in the United States have found them to be national in scope, considerable clustering along regional lines has also been observed (Dooley, 1969; Levine, 1972; Allen, 1978; Mizruchi, 1982). It is well understood that regional interests play an important role in national politics. Some researchers have argued that elites in different locales compete with one another (Molotch, 1976; Friedland and Palmer, 1984; Logan and Molotch, 1987). There are at least two reasons to suspect that firms located in the same geographic areas might engage in similar political behavior. First, some issues might be of specific concern to firms in particular areas. Second, even members of a specific industry may be divided along geographic lines. Chemical firms in the Northeast that are forced to comply with certain environmental regulations, for example, might favor the extension of such regulations to members of their industry in other parts of the country (Ferguson and Rogers, 1986).[12] Thus, we would expect firms with headquarters in the same state to be more likely to engage in similar political behavior than firms with headquarters in different states. Most large manufacturing corporations have plants in two or more states. Although Useem (1984) found that most corporate philanthropic activities were concentrated in their headquarters locales, it is plausible to assume that firms with

[12] In a study of the coal industry, Bowman (1989) demonstrated that in the early part of the century operators of unionized mines in Northern states supported the efforts of workers to unionize mines in Southern states.

plant locations in the same states might have a source of political similarity beyond that resulting from common headquarters locations.

This discussion suggests the following hypothesis:

H9: The greater the geographic proximity among firms in terms of corporate headquarters and plant locations, the greater their similarity of political behavior.

As with Hypotheses 6 and 7, the hypothesis on geographic proximity contains a potential social network component. Palmer, Friedland, and Singh (1986), for example, treat headquarters proximity as an indicator of common interests. They also note, however, that officials of major firms in close proximity are more likely to interact, both professionally and socially, than are officials of more distant firms. This suggests that the social interaction among firms in the same locale might generate similar political behavior independent of their common geographic interests. Because it is almost impossible to separate the effects of common interests and social interaction with this variable alone, however, I shall focus my attention on interlocking directorates as an indicator of social network ties.

Political-Economic Factors

Membership in the same industries and geographic proximity are two variables that are likely to be indicative of common interests among firms. In recent years, researchers have identified several other, more specific, sources of common interests. Potential sources of cleavage within the business community include capital intensive versus labor intensive firms, firms in heavily regulated industries versus those in less regulated industries, firms with heavy dependence on military contracts versus those with little or no dependence, and firms with foreign interests versus those with primarily domestic interests (Ferguson and Rogers, 1986; Burris, 1987; Clawson and Neustadtl, 1989). Researchers have theorized that capital intensive firms will be less anti-union than labor intensive firms; that firms in regulated industries will be more sensitive to regulatory legislation than will firms in less-regulated industries; and that firms with significant foreign interests and dependence on military contracts will favor high levels of defense spending. Several researchers have found, in studies of political campaign contributions, for example, that defense contractors have a strong tendency to direct their political campaign contributions to Democrats, especially incumbent Democrats (see Handler and Mulkern, 1982; Burris, 1987; Clawson and Neustadtl, 1989). Burris and Clawson and Neustadtl also found that firms in industries that came under regulation after World War II were more likely to support Republican candidates than were firms in industries that had been regulated since early in the century.

Because the focus of my argument is on the factors that determine the similarity of political behavior among firms, the hypotheses derived from the model presented above all assume that the phenomena are relational; that is, a relation (such as market constraint or interlocking) is hypothesized to predict another relation (similar political behavior). The political-economic variables of the present discussion describe firm-specific characteristics: a firm's level of capital intensity, whether it is in a regulated industry, whether it is a defense contractor, and the extent of its foreign interests. In order to examine these factors within the relational framework of my argument, it is necessary to express them in relational terms. This can be done by thinking of firms as grouped together based on whether (or the extent to which) they share characteristics on these variables. In other words, I hypothesize that firms that share similar interests in labor, regulation, defense, and foreign investment will be more likely to engage in similar political behavior than will firms that do not share the same interests. Specifically:

H10: The more similar the level of capital intensity among firms, the more similar their political behavior.

H11: Firms with common interests in government regulation have a higher level of similarity of political behavior than do firms without common interests in regulation.

H12: Firms with common interests in military spending and common interests in foreign investment have a higher level of similarity of political behavior than do firms without common interests in military spending or foreign investment.

To reiterate, my interest is not in the effects of firm characteristics *per se* but rather the extent to which particular types of interfirm relations affect the similarity of interfirm behavior. Because my primary theoretical focus is on the network variables summarized in Hypotheses 1 through 6, the interest variables of Hypotheses 7 through 12 are treated here primarily as control variables rather than as components of the theoretical model. My aim is to ensure that the observed effects of the variables in Hypotheses 1–6 are not artifacts of simple firm interests. Operationalizations of all variables are described in the following chapter.

In this chapter I have developed a model of corporate political action based on the assumption that firms are rational actors operating under a system of social structural constraints. My purpose has been to identify a group of constraints that increase the probability that firms will engage in similar political behavior. The perspective that emerges here, based on a synthesis of the organizational and social class models of intercorporate relations, is grounded in historical developments in industrial capitalism during the past century. Although many large corporations in the United States remain under the control of individual or family interests, when viewed historically, organizations rather than individuals must be seen as the key political actors in contemporary American society (Coleman, 1982; Laumann and Knoke, 1987; Mizruchi, 1987). To the extent that individuals in the business community are important politically, it is as representatives of organizations.

But the leaders of large corporations are capable of acting collectively as a class, and even when these activities are not coordinated, their consequences can be substantial. The transition from individual and family capitalism to a more bureaucratic, organizational form in no way suggests that business has become less of a political force. Business political power is likely to be greatest, however, when its members behave similarly. To understand the conditions under which similar political behavior occurs is therefore of paramount importance.

The model developed in this chapter specifies several conditions under which similar behavior can be expected to occur. It is time now to evaluate the empirical viability of the model. The following chapter discusses the use of data on corporate political behavior as well as the indicators of the network variables proposed as sources of behavioral similarity. The empirical test of the model begins in Chapter 6.

5 · Political Action Committees and Corporate Political Behavior

In Chapter 3 I argued that similarity of behavior is an important component of the political effectiveness of a collectivity. In Chapter 4 I developed several hypotheses designed to predict the similarity of political behavior. But to what specific type of behavior does this apply and how is it to be measured? I suggested in Chapter 2 that case studies of firm behavior, although valuable, will never enable us to resolve general questions about the conditions under which business unity occurs. On the other hand, systematic, quantitative data on corporate political behavior have until recently been scarce.

The degree to which unity and conflict occur within business depends not only on the content of an issue but also on its specificity. As issues become more general, the level of consensus increases. Thus, the vast majority of Americans believe in the legitimacy of the existing political system. As issues become more concrete, however, the likelihood of opposition increases. Political actors often agree on general goals but differ on the means for achieving them. How can this problem be addressed empirically?

My focus is on what I shall call *expressions of interest.* An expression of interest is a choice taken by an actor that constitutes or reflects the actor's preference. At a general level, this expression could include actions designed to protect one's class privileges, such as support for a local charitable organization. At a specific level, expressions of interest involve particular events related to the resolution of more general issues (Laumann and Knoke, 1987, p. 107). I shall focus on what I call, borrowing from Merton (1949), "middle-range" expressions of interest. Middle-range expressions of interest involve subjects of political contention that are specific enough to provide a legitimate basis for opposition but general enough to reflect the larger agenda of political actors. At a middle-range level, expressions of interest could be directed toward a particular policy (such as protective tariff legislation) or toward the election or appointment of favored personnel. In this study I employ both of these types of expressions of interest: contributions to candidates for public office and positions taken on areas of proposed legislation, as expressed in testimony before congressional committees. In the following sections I describe my use of political campaign contributions. The analysis of corporate positions on proposed legislation is discussed in Chapter 7. Before beginning this discussion, however, one key issue must be addressed: the level of analysis at which I approach the study of business unity.

A Dyadic Approach

Corporate political unity is usually perceived as a characteristic of a national or local business community at a particular point in time. It follows that to study business unity, one should treat business as a collectivity of firms. This is not my approach here, however. Rather, I focus, at least initially, on *dyads*, or pairs of firms. The move from discussions of business as a whole to an analysis of dyads would seem to require a considerable leap of logic. In fact, however, the dyadic approach is fully consistent with my argument in the preceding chapters.

I have suggested that business unity must be viewed as a conditional phenomenon. That is, unity is more likely to occur under some conditions than under others. I hypothesized that similar political behavior will increase in the presence of various network ties. But how do we examine the effects of these network ties?

If business as a whole, or big business, is our unit of analysis, then the obvious approach is to draw a sample of firms and examine the network that the firms create. We could then compare this network with other networks. We could focus on industries, sectors, or even nations (if such data were available), or we could focus on a population of firms over time. A longitudinal approach, in particular, would enable us to examine the effects of changing historical conditions on business unity. All of these group-level approaches have the advantage of maintaining a focus on business as a collectivity of actors. But they share one major disadvantage: they prevent us from being able to identify direct connections between variables.

Consider, for example, the relation between the similarity of political behavior and director interlocks. Suppose that we hypothesize that a business community with many interlocks will have a higher level of behavioral similarity than will one with few interlocks. The problem with this approach is that by measuring ties at the group level, we lose information. We do not know whether the interlocks within the group are between the firms whose political behavior is most similar. We know only that both phenomena occur somewhere in the group.

At the dyadic level, on the other hand, we know specifically whether one type of tie (such as an interlock) corresponds to another (such as similarity of political behavior). No information is lost because there is no aggregation process. An analysis of dyads, therefore provides the most direct test of hypotheses based on relational data (Laumann and Marsden, 1982).

This approach does have its limitations. One problem, noted by Simmel ([1917] 1950), is that the character of a dyad can be affected by the larger social structure within which it is embedded. A firm's dependence on another may change markedly if a third firm is available to provide the same resource at comparable cost. This suggests the need to ensure that dyads are not viewed in isolation from larger social structures.

A second, and perhaps more important, limitation of a focus on dyads is the danger of what sociologists call the atomistic fallacy: in this case, drawing inferences about the unity of the population as a whole based on information about the unity of individual dyads. The extent to which various group structures emerge from specific dyadic relations has been the focus of considerable attention (Cartwright and Harary, 1956; Davis, 1963; Holland and Leinhardt, 1970; Chase, 1980). Although patterns have been discovered between the character of dyadic relations and the structures of larger groups, there is no guarantee that a given set of dyadic relations will produce a particular group structure. For example, it is possible for a network to contain internally cohesive subgroups (with tightly connected dyadic relations) that are distinct from (and opposed to) one another. The networks observed in this study are not divided into hostile camps. But there is no assurance that in general, the existence of unified dyads will generate a unified global structure.

If one cannot draw system-level inferences from dyadic-level data, does this not raise serious questions about the use of dyads to study business unity? The answer is a resounding no. To see why this is the case, recall that my key argument is that the entire question of "is business unified?" is no longer a viable one. Rather, business unity must be seen as a conditional phenomenon. Business unity can vary not only across time and nation, but also across sector, industry, and firm. This means that unity need not be a property of the system as a whole. It can be a property of groups, or even pairs, of firms. The question is, "Where does unity occur and what accounts for it?" When this point is taken into account, the advantage of dyads, in particular the specificity with which the effects of relational variables can be assessed, becomes apparent. Relations at the dyadic level are not the whole story of business unity, to be sure. But they are a very important part of it.

What happens at the dyadic level, of course, may be affected by higher-level processes. I shall incorporate these factors within the dyadic analysis. In Chapter 8 I move to the industry level of analysis and in Chapter 9 I move to the system level. In Chapter 10 I return to the issue of system and dyad in light of the study's findings. I begin, however, by examining the question, "If business unity is conditional, where and under what conditions is it likely to occur?"

Political Action Committees and Large Corporations

As I have already noted, my analysis of middle-range expressions of interest focuses first on political campaign contributions by large American corporations. An important development from a social scientific as well as policy point of view was the Federal Election Campaign Act of 1971. This act allowed corporations to establish political action committees (PACs), which, although legally distinct organizations, were in fact funded by the firms. As part of the new law, PAC contributions to political candidates were required to be filed with the Federal Election Commission. Data on all such contributions are available to the public.

The first political action committees were established by labor unions in the 1940s. Although political contributions by major capitalists date back to the nineteenth century (Sabato, 1984), the first business PACs did not emerge until the 1960s. Prior to the early 1970s, accurate data on corporate contributions were generally unavailable. Because it was unclear whether corporations doing business with the government could legally contribute, few major firms established PACs. Instead, contributions were funneled through executives, business partners, and other difficult-to-trace routes (Alexander, 1976; Allen and Broyles, 1989). The 1971 campaign act contained no restrictions on to whom firms could give contributions, but it did limit PAC giving to $5,000 per candidate per election.

The typical corporate PAC raises its funds through appeals to the firm's salaried managers and stockholders. In some cases appeals are made to rank-and-file employees, although these appeals are limited by law to two per year. Contributions to the PAC by individual managers are sometimes earmarked for specific candidates. Most PACs, however, attempt to discourage earmarking since earmarked choices can run counter to those of the committee. In a detailed study of 71 corporate PACs, Handler and Mulkern (1982) found that in only 11 was the CEO a member of the PAC. In most cases, however, the CEO was heavily involved, both as the major contributor and in the selection of the committee itself. In 31 of the 40 PACs for which Handler and Mulkern had such information, *all* members of the committee were appointed by the CEO.

Social scientists, muckraking journalists, and politicians themselves wasted no time in making use of PAC contribution data. Political scientists in particular have conducted numerous studies of the behavior of corporate PACs. Economists, business scholars, and, more recently, sociologists have also become involved.

Social scientists studying corporate PACs have been concerned primarily with four issues: (1) the determinants of whether corporations form PACs and, if so, the size of their expenditures (Masters and Baysinger, 1985; Masters and Keim, 1985; Boies, 1989); (2) the determinants of PAC political strategies (Malbin, 1979; Herndon, 1982; Rothenberg and Roldan, 1983; Eismeier and Pollock, 1984; Gopoian, 1984; Sorauf, 1984; Maitland and Park, 1985; Clawson, Neustadtl, and Bearden, 1986; Burris, 1987; Clawson and Neustadtl, 1989; (3) the effect of PAC contributions on the outcomes of elections (Jacobson, 1980; 1984; 1990; Herndon, 1982; Green and Krasno, 1988; 1990); and (4) the effect of PAC contributions on the voting behavior of legislators (Chappel, 1982; Esty and Caves, 1983; Jones and Keiser, 1987; Grenzke, 1989; Wright, 1989). Several authors have focused on two or more of these topics (Epstein, 1979; 1984; Malbin, 1979; Budde, 1980; Alexander, 1981; 1983; Handler and Mulkern, 1982; Etzioni, 1984; Sabato, 1984; Eismeier and Pollock, 1988).

Sociologists have been less concerned with detailed analysis of PACs *per se* and more concerned with employing PAC data to examine theories about the extent of integration within the business community and the effects of corporate network structures on business political activity. Koenig (1979), for example, found that corporations that were central in networks of interlocking directorates were more likely than peripheral firms to contribute to Richard Nixon's 1972 reelection campaign. Ratcliff, Gallagher, and Jaffee (1980) found that positions of CEOs in a local social network influenced their contribution patterns to statewide campaigns in Missouri. Clawson et al. (1986) found that corporate PACs rarely come into direct opposition in individual congressional races (see also Neustadtl and Clawson, 1988; Clawson and Neustadtl, 1989). And Burris (1987) found different contribution patterns between Sunbelt and non-Sunbelt firms as well as between heavily regulated and less regulated firms.

Most of the data on corporate political behavior employed to test the theory developed in this book are drawn from the contribution patterns of corporate political action committees. Some of the data come from corporate testimony before Congress. Because my aim and my application differ from those of most social scientists who have employed PAC data, it is important to discuss the meaning of these data and the ways in which I employ them. In order to do this, it is first necessary to describe my units of analysis.

Units of Analysis

Whether we deal with the system, subgroup, or dyadic level, the issue of business political unity assumes a unit of analysis that transcends the individual firm. In particular, to speak of business unity implies that the business community as a whole is the focus of the analysis. My primary interest is not business as a whole, but rather the largest corporations, those that historically have had the greatest political impact. This does not mean that small business is politically insignificant or that the entire business community can be understood without taking small business into account. I define big business as my unit of study because it is they who have the greatest impact on the economy and, to the extent that business influences it, society as a whole. In 1985, the largest 200 manufacturing firms in the United States accounted for 61 percent of all manufacturing assets (United States Bureau of the Census, 1986). Thousands of bankruptcies occur every year in the United States, but when a Lockheed or Chrysler is threatened with bankruptcy it becomes a major political issue. Thus, although the study of the political behavior of small business is an important one and one in which we are sorely in need of research, my focus here is on the political behavior of big business.

Because I am interested in charting the political behavior of the largest American corporations, I have defined my universe for sampling as the *Fortune* 500 industrial corporations. Ideally, one would prefer to examine firms in several sectors. I have elected to focus on manufacturing corporations to ensure the comparability of data across industries. The sample is designed to be representative of the widest possible range of industries within the 500. Therefore, instead of sampling randomly from the entire list of firms (which would tend to overrepresent industries such as the oil industry), I selected, for each of the twenty major manufacturing industries in the U.S. Census Bureau's Standard Industrial Classification scheme, the three largest firms whose primary operations were in those industries, according to *Fortune*, in 1980 (based on the May 1981 listing). For the few cases in which one of the three largest firms did not have a PAC in 1980, I included the next largest firm that had a PAC. Because a small number of the twenty industries did not have three firms among the 500, the final sample consisted of 57 firms, which yielded a sample of 1,596 interfirm dyads. A list of the firms is presented in Table A.1 in the Appendix at the end of the book.[1]

---

[1] For the purposes of the input-output census, the 20 two-digit manufacturing industries are classified into 51 different markets. Some two-digit industries therefore have firms that operate in different markets in the two-digit I-O table. This was the case in five of my industries: stone, clay, and glass; machinery, except electrical; electric and electronic equipment; transportation equipment; and instruments and related products. In two of these industries (stone, clay, and glass and transportation equipment), more than three firms were selected (the "Big Three" automobile firms and defense contractors such as United Technologies and McDonnell-Douglas were members of the transportation equipment industry). Four firms were also selected in two other industries (paper and allied products and primary metals) in which one of the firms' primary industries was the subject of uncertainty (the firms were assigned to different primary industries by *Fortune* and *Standard and Poor's*). Market transaction patterns among different markets within the same two-digit industries were virtually identical. Three industries (furniture and fixtures, leather and leather products, and miscellaneous manufacturing) had no *Fortune* 500 firms with PACs whose primary operations were in those industries. By excluding from the study firms that did not have a PAC, I could be accused of "sampling on the dependent variable" (Berk, 1983). Only a few firms were affected, however. Had I included these firms, all similarity of political behavior scores involving their campaign contributions would have been set to zero. Preliminary analysis indicated that inclusion of these firms would have yielded stronger results, especially for the effect of market constraint. This suggests that the results reported below are based on conservative estimates.

Data on congressional contributions have appeared biannually since 1976, but only since 1978 are the data considered reliable (Clawson and Neustadtl, 1989). Nineteen eighty is a particularly good year for this analysis because it was an election with an unusual degree of corporate support for challengers. This suggests that whatever opposition occurs among firms should be at its highest in this election. Replications of studies based on 1980 data by Clawson and Su (1990) reveal an increase in support for incumbents in the post-1980 period but no general changes in the sources of among-firm variation over time.[2]

PAC Contributions as an Indicator of Business Unity

The primary dependent variable in this study is the similarity of political behavior among firms. Several operationalizations of this variable are employed. The main one, however, is the extent to which two firms in a dyad contributed to the same congressional candidates in the 1979–80 election cycle. This measure is designed to tap one aspect of corporate political unity. It is not the only measure that can be employed. In fact, several variations of it are examined at various points in this book.

Clearly, there are other aspects to corporate political behavior than a firm's contributions to electoral campaigns. Nevertheless, the overwhelming consensus of the literature in this area is that regardless of the effect of PACs on the outcome of elections or on the voting behavior of individual legislators, corporate CEOs view PAC contributions as an important aspect of the firm's overall political strategy (Handler and Mulkern, 1982, pp. 61, 72–78; Sabato, 1984, pp. 34–35, 49; Useem, 1984, pp. 139–141; Clawson and Neustadtl, 1990).[3]

---

[2] Studies of the effects of structural variables on the contribution patterns of particular firms have revealed considerable consistency across years (Maitland and Pak, 1987; Clawson and Su, 1990; also compare the findings in Burris, 1987, with those in Clawson and Neustadtl, 1989). One of my pilot studies based on 1980 data (Mizruchi and Koenig, 1986) was also successfully replicated with 1982 data by Burris (private communication). Because systematic data on corporate PAC contributions have been available only since the late 1970s, it will be several more years before statistically reliable longitudinal analysis at the system level is possible. In terms of comparative data, although such data are readily available for director interlocks (Stokman, Ziegler, and Scott, 1985), no comparable source exists for political campaign contributions.

[3] The extent to which PAC contributions influence elections and congressional voting are the subjects of considerable controversy. They appear most likely to affect the

I believe that the extent of common campaign contributions is a valid indicator of *one behavioral aspect* of corporate political unity, provided that certain factors are taken into account. This issue, however, is an important and complex one, worthy of extensive discussion, especially since one of the aims of this study is to increase our understanding of the relation between common behavior and political integration. It especially deserves extensive discussion because of the potential for misunderstanding that may occur about the purposes of this study.

First, it is important to reiterate that my unit of analysis is *not* the individual firm, but rather the *relation* between pairs of firms. Social scientists have paid extensive attention to the political behavior of individual firms, and the volume of this research is increasing rapidly. I am concerned here with factors that determine the behavior of individual PACs primarily to the extent that such factors could potentially render spurious the observed associations between the relational variables that are the subject of the study. This does not mean that I will not make use of the previous research on PACs, but only that the aims and emphases of this study differ from most of the previous work.

Second, it is necessary to emphasize that the issue of the similarity of corporate political behavior is logically independent of the content of the behavior (Blau, 1982, p. 276). The debate over business unity is concerned primarily with the social structure of interfirm relations. For the purposes of this study, whether individual firms support Democrats or Republicans is secondary to whether groups of firms support the same types of candidates. Thus, my aim is not to examine which firms tend to contribute to Republicans or incumbents or liberals (although I do present these data). These issues have been the subject of extensive investigations by sociologists and political scientists (see Ferguson and Rogers, 1986; Burris, 1987; Clawson and Neustadtl, 1989). Rather, my aim is to examine the determinants of when particular pairs of companies contribute to the same candidates or, in other analyses, candidates of the same party or ideology.

To what extent can common contributions be used as an indicator

---

outcome of elections in cases in which large amounts are given to challengers facing vulnerable incumbents. They are most likely to affect congressional votes on specialized issues which receive little publicity. It is important to reiterate that for my purposes, it is not necessary to demonstrate that PAC contributions influence congressional voting or the outcomes of elections. My concern is with PAC contributions as expressions of a firm's political interests.

of business political unity? Several problems present themselves. First, some firms that share similar interests contribute to different candidates of the same party or to different candidates who share similar positions. The extent to which contributions to candidates of the same party or ideology operate as a substitute for contributions to the same individuals is an important empirical question that I will address in Chapter 6. Evidence on this point suggests, however, that, within limits, the ideology of the candidate plays a relatively small role in the selection of candidates to support. For one thing, many corporations engage in "pragmatic" strategies, in which the ideology of the candidate is less important than the role that the incumbent legislator plays in legislation of interest to the firm. This role is often independent of the legislator's vote on the final bill. As a PAC official told Clawson and Neustadtl (1990, pp. 8–9):

> We are not big on voting records . . . because frequently the final vote on a particular bill isn't really important . . . Probably what's more important is what's thrashed out internally in some of the important committees in Congress. And it doesn't much matter how people vote afterwards. It's what they argued for or tried to get done or stopped from happening, getting done, in those interpersonal discussions that take place.[4]

Even among more ideologically oriented PACs, contributions will flow primarily to candidates who are viewed as having a chance to win. Therefore, corporate PAC money rarely flows to conservative Republican challengers in heavily Democratic districts with powerful incumbent legislators.

An extensive review of the literature indicates that most PACs make their decisions based on a general view that support of particular *individuals* is in the company's general interest.[5] The feeling that a member of Congress might perform special favors for the firm is certainly one motive, but most research on PAC contributions suggests that it is not the overriding factor in the majority of cases (see Handler and Mulkern, 1982, p. 61; Sabato, 1984, p. 49; Clawson and Neustadtl, 1990). Being "good for the company," of course, includes support of commensurate positions on policy matters that concern the company.

---

[4] These sentiments were echoed by several other officials interviewed by Clawson and Neustadtl.

[5] Professor Thomas Koenig, with whom I worked on an earlier study, has confirmed this view based on his interviews with PAC officials.

Since some candidates who share a firm's view on important issues receive the firm's contributions while others do not, however, additional factors are involved. Reasons for supporting a particular candidate may include the individual's honesty and integrity, accessibility, and leadership qualities, as well as his or her power and effectiveness (Useem, 1984, pp. 139–141).

In short, to assume that business political unity can best be measured in terms of the similarity of party or ideology of candidates who receive support may be unwarranted because these factors may not be the predominant ones influencing a firm's decision to contribute to a particular candidate. I shall address this issue empirically in Chapter 6.

Potentially Spurious Effects

Political scientists have suggested three main factors that could potentially render the similarity of campaign contributions spurious as an indicator of unity. These are: (1) the degree of common activism between pairs of firms; that is, the extent to which both firms contribute to large numbers of candidates; (2) political strategies that lead even opposing firms to contribute to the same candidates; and (3) the political environment within which firms operate, in particular, whether there are closely contested elections that draw a disproportionate amount of attention.

Before pursuing these issues, one crucial point must be noted. Whether any of these factors, especially the latter two, could possibly render my analysis spurious is doubtful. The reason is that common activism, common political strategies, and common tendencies to channel contributions to candidates in close elections are all aspects of the dependent variable. In other words, *they are components of the very political behavior that I am attempting to explain.* Nevertheless, to dispel any doubts that such variables might confound my findings, I shall discuss each of them in turn.

Common Activism

Not all corporations have political action committees. However, the vast majority of the largest firms (80 of the 100 largest and 150 of the 200 largest industrials) had formed PACs by 1980. Because this study focuses on the largest firms, there were few firms meeting the selection criteria that did not have PACs. Corporations that do have PACs vary in the number of candidates to whom they contribute (Masters and Baysinger, 1985). Two firms that contribute to many candidates will, *ceteris paribus*, have a higher level of common contributions than two firms that contribute to few candidates.

For example, consider four firms: U.S. Steel, which contributed to 192 candidates; International Paper (170); Louisiana-Pacific (56); and National Gypsum (33). Let us assume for the moment that there were 1,000 candidates who were possible recipients of campaign contributions. Given their numbers of contributions, the random probability of U.S. Steel and International Paper jointly contributing to a particular candidate is .192 × .170, or .0327. This means that, based on the assumption of randomness, the expected number of common contributions between U.S. Steel and International Paper would be 32.7. The probability of a common contribution between Louisiana-Pacific and National Gypsum, on the other hand, is only .056 × .033, or .0018, meaning that the expected number of common contributions between these two firms is only 1.8.

One way to handle this problem is to employ a measure of common political behavior that is independent of the number of contributions made by the two firms. I have done this in previously published work (see, for example, Mizruchi and Koenig, 1986; Mizruchi, 1989). But is this necessary?

The vast majority of the firms from which my sample was drawn contributed substantial amounts in the 1980 federal elections. The average firm within my data set made more than $60,000 in contributions, enough to make contributions of more than $100 in every congressional race in the United States. Therefore, among these firms, the decision to focus contributions on a limited number of races was a political decision, not a result of a shortage of funds (Neustadtl and Clawson, 1988, p. 177). Weyerhaeuser, for example, spent more than $123,000 on 117 candidates while Time, Inc. distributed less than half as much money ($55,000) among 152 candidates. Given these figures, one might argue that controlling for the number of contributions is superfluous. Unfortunately, simply because a firm could contribute smaller amounts to a larger number of candidates does not mean that its level of resources does not affect its decision making. Empirically, it is virtually impossible to separate the effects of common activism (where two firms contribute to a large number of individuals) from common decisions to contribute to specific candidates. For this reason, I have controlled for the level of activism in this study. I should note, however, that in an earlier study (Mizruchi and Koenig, 1986, p. 485), I found that measures that did not control for the level of activism yielded results similar to those that included such controls. The main difference was that results based on controlling for activism were more conservative.

Details of the measure of similar political behavior controlling for activism are provided later in this chapter.

Common Political Strategies

Students of PAC behavior have identified two broad strategies used by corporate PACs. Handler and Mulkern (1982) have referred to these as "pragmatic" and "ideological" strategies. Pragmatic PACs tend to be concerned primarily with the short-term interests of the firm and tend to give to incumbents who are in positions of influence over matters affecting the firm, regardless of the ideology or party of the legislator. Thus, pragmatic PACs have often been found to give as much to Democrats as to Republicans. Ideological PACs, which first emerged as a major force in the 1978 elections (Malbin, 1979; Handler and Mulkern, 1982), are more concerned with changing the character of Congress in a pro-business direction, even if it means ignoring the short-term interests of the firm. They are thus more willing to support challengers if they believe that the challenger has a chance of winning.[6] An example of a pragmatic PAC among my 57 firms is Rockwell International, a producer of military hardware. Among the 95 candidates to whom Rockwell contributed in the 1980 elections, 53 percent were Democrats (compared to about 36 percent for all 57 firms) and 31 percent were either liberal or labor Democrats.[7] The prototypical ideological PAC was Dart and Kraft, whose president, the late Justin Dart, was a militant conservative who at one point circulated a letter to officers of all corporate PACs urging them to support pro-business challengers. In 1980, Dart and Kraft made only 6.7 percent of its 132 contributions to Democrats, most of whom were conservatives. Eighty-five percent of Dart and Kraft's contributions went to conservative Republicans.

Researchers have identified five general factors associated with the

[6] Eismeier and Pollock (1988, pp. 27–30) have distinguished among what they call *accommodationists, partisans,* and *adversaries.* Accommodationists closely resemble pragmatists while partisans and adversaries closely resemble ideological firms.

[7] See Chapter 6 for an explanation of the ideological categories and Table A.1 in the Appendix at the end of the book for a distribution of contributions by each firm.

degree to which corporate PACs exhibit pragmatic or ideological behavior (Malbin, 1979; Handler and Mulkern, 1982; Herndon, 1982;
Eismeier and Pollock, 1984; Sabato, 1984; Maitland and Park, 1985).
These include the size of the PAC (smaller PACs tend to be more
pragmatic), the existence of Washington representatives (pragmatic
PACs are more likely to have Washington representatives), the degree
of diversification of the parent corporation (more diversified firms
tend to be more ideological), the primary sector in which the firm
operates (industrial firms tend to be more ideological than average,
except for defense contractors), and the regulatory environment facing
the firm (industries that have been regulated for decades tend to be
more pragmatic, while those that have recently come under regulation
tend to be more ideological). Most of these factors are functions of the
industries in which the firms operate. Since the extent to which two
firms operate in the same industries is one of the variables in the
model, a major portion of the convergence in contribution patterns
based on common pragmatic or ideological strategies will be subsumed under this variable.

To examine the extent to which common pragmatic strategies affected the similarity of firm contribution patterns, I estimated the
regression equations presented in the following chapter with a control
for pragmatic strategies. Degree of pragmatism was defined, following
Clawson et al. (1986), as the proportion of contributions going to
incumbents. The absolute value of the difference in these proportions
was calculated for each dyad. For example, American Can made 52.2
percent of its contributions to incumbents and International Paper
made 73.5 percent of its contributions to incumbents. The difference
was 21.3 percent. Because Clawson et al. found a $-.9$ correlation
between pragmatic strategy and ideological strategy (the terms were
defined independently), simultaneous inclusion of both factors was
not feasible. The results revealed, not surprisingly, that the lower the
difference in pragmatic strategy, the greater the similarity of contributions. That is, if both firms gave to similar proportions of incumbents, they tended to contribute to the same candidates (and vice
versa). The inclusion of this variable in the analyses presented in
Chapter 6, however, had virtually no effect on the magnitudes of the
other coefficients.

As I have already noted, a firm's political strategy can be viewed as
a component of the dependent variable, since two firms that engage in
the same strategies will, by definition, be more likely to contribute to

the same candidates. Nevertheless, even if the inclusion of this variable in the model could theoretically render the model spurious, this is not the case empirically. Controlling for differences in pragmatic strategies had no effect on the strength of the theoretically specified variables described in the following chapter.

Political Environment (Close Elections)

Many firms, especially ideological firms or pragmatic firms with limited resources, tend to contribute disproportionately to candidates in close elections, where they believe the contributions can affect the outcome of the election (Jacobson, 1980; 1984; Herndon, 1982). This might lead various firms' contributions to converge partly on this basis. As with the effect of pragmatic versus ideological strategies, common contributions to close elections is actually an element of the similarity of political behavior I am attempting to explain. Nevertheless, to be absolutely certain that this variable could not render my results spurious, I examined whether removing the variation attributable to this factor altered the effects of the variables in the model analyzed in Chapter 6. The extent to which common contributions to candidates in close elections affects convergence of behavior was operationalized, following Maitland and Park (1985), as the proportion of contributions made to candidates involved in races in which the election was decided by 10 percent or less.[8] The absolute value of the difference in these proportions was calculated for each dyad. For example, Armco Steel made 45.2 percent of its contributions to candidates in close elections and Johns Manville made 22.0 percent of its contributions to candidates in close elections. The difference was 23.2 percent. As with common pragmatism, the results based on the analyses presented in the following chapter show that similarity in the strategy of giving to candidates in close races was also significantly related to the similarity of contributions. As with similarity of pragmatism, however, the inclusion of this variable into the analyses presented in Chapter 6 had no effect on the results.

Thus, even when common activism, common pragmatic strategies,

---

[8] This operationalization is subject to a logical fallacy, since the outcome of the election (a margin of less than ten percent) succeeded the contributions. The use of this measure assumes that contributors had prior knowledge indicating the likelihood of a close result. In most cases, given the accuracy of polling data, this is probably a reasonable assumption.

and common contributions to close elections are taken into account, the effects of the variables in the model presented in this study were found to be unchanged.[9]

Two Common Misconceptions About PACs

Finally, I would like to discuss two widely held misconceptions about the behavior of corporate PACs. Many sociologists and political scientists believe that corporate PACs frequently contribute to both candidates in an election in order to "hedge their bets." News reports during the 1970s about representatives of foreign governments contributing to both sides during presidential and congressional races did much to foster this belief. If contributions by PACs to both sides in a race were common, then analyses based on common contributions between pairs of firms might be misleading. In such a case, common support by two firms for one candidate would ignore the existence of one or both firms' simultaneous support for the candidate's opponent. In fact, however, such "split-giving" is rare and is frowned upon in the PAC community (Handler and Mulkern, 1982, p. 84; Rothenberg and Roldan, 1983, p. 10; Sabato, 1984, p. 88). In an earlier study (Mizruchi and Koenig, 1986) it was found that common gifts to two or more candidates in a given election occurred in fewer than two percent of all contributions. Moreover, many apparent cases of split-giving actually involve contributions to a losing candidate in a primary followed by a contribution to a different candidate in the general election (Handler

---

[9] Some students of corporate political behavior have argued that firms with conflicting interests sometimes contribute to the same candidates as a means of competing for access. I have already argued that, even if two firms have opposing interests, the objective consequences of their similar behavior operate as if they shared the same interests. Most of the literature on corporate PACs suggests that contributions to the same candidates are generally indicative of shared rather than conflicting interests. Reasons for this include the fact that members of particular industries, which generally share political interests even though they compete economically, tend to have similar contribution patterns (virtually all studies find that industry is a significant predictor of contribution patterns); and the fact that businesses, even those that otherwise pursue widely different political strategies, rarely come into direct opposition in particular races (Clawson et al., 1986). Corporate PAC officials themselves admit that they share political interests with their economic competitors. As one PAC officer (among many expressing a similar view) told Neustadtl, Scott, and Clawson (1991, pp. 225–226), "We are major competitors with a company called [NAME] . . . We hate each other but I have a very good relationship with them down here and often we work together on the Hill for certain bills." Based on interviews with corporate PAC and party officials, Sabato (1984, p. 49) concluded that "both the interests *and* the research information . . . of two different PACs must coincide before both will contribute to the same candidate."

and Mulkern, 1982, p. 85). In the 1980 race for the House seat in Texas's eighth district, for example, three firms (Dow Chemical, Exxon, and Georgia-Pacific) made contributions to primary opponents of the incumbent Representative, liberal Democrat Bob Eckhardt. After Eckhardt won the primary, all three firms contributed to his general election opponent, Republican Jack Fields (the eventual winner). Although the multiple contributions by the same firms within the same race would appear to be examples of split-giving, in fact the contributions represented a consistent strategy of attempting to unseat Eckhardt.[10] The issue of split-giving was handled in the Mizruchi and Koenig study by removing all cases of split-giving from the data file. This modification made virtually no difference in the results. Therefore, there was no need to repeat the procedure here.

A second common misconception is that a firm's Washington office plays a primary role in the candidate selection process and that contributions made by PACs that are not based on the advice of Washington offices are a poor guide to a firm's political strategy. In actuality, although firms with Washington offices do tend to be more pragmatically oriented (whether the existence of the office is the cause or consequence of such pragmatism is unclear), Sabato (1984, p. 38) found that in only two percent of corporate PACs were decisions regarding to whom to contribute made primarily by the Washington staff. Instead, the great majority of decisions (86 percent), regardless of whether the PAC was pragmatically or ideologically oriented, were made by the PAC's board and/or the CEO. In an additional eleven percent of the cases, decisions were made jointly by the PAC board and the Washington staff.

The fact that contribution decisions are rarely made by the Washington staff in no way implies that PAC contribution patterns are a poor guide to a firm's political strategy. As I have already noted, the overwhelming consensus of the voluminous political science literature is that PAC behavior is an important element in a firm's overall political strategy.

Operationalization and Measurement of Variables

In this section I describe in detail the measurement, operationalization, and data sources of my primary indicator of similar political

[10] As the chairman of one oil company PAC put it, "We would've given to any name on the ballot against [Eckhardt]" (quoted in Sabato, 1984, p. 129).

behavior and the exogenous variables employed in the study. Following that I discuss some of the statistical issues that arise in dealing with the dyadic data on which much of my analysis rests. Much of this discussion is necessarily technical in nature. (Readers who prefer to avoid discussions of measurement and technical details might prefer to skip these sections and refer back to them as necessary. To facilitate this, Table 5.1 presents a summary description of the variables discussed in the following paragraphs.)

Measuring Similarity of Political Behavior

The data set for the first operationalization of the dependent variable (contributions to the same candidates) was the list of all contributions to congressional candidates in the 1980 elections. Presidential campaign contributions were not included because presidential candidates

Table 5.1. Descriptions of variables and measures

Variable	Description
Similarity of behavior	Common campaign contributions, standardized by number of contributions of each firm
Geographic proximity	Headquarters location in same state (0 = no; 1 = yes)
Same primary industry	Same primary two-digit industry (0 = no; 1 = yes)
Common industries	Number of common two-digit industries, standardized by level of diversification
Market constraint	Measure of economic interdependence based on transactions and concentration
Common stockholders	Number of financial institutions that hold stock in both firms
Direct interlocks	Board of directors overlaps between firms
Indirect interlocks	Number of same banks and insurance companies with which firms interlock
Asymmetry of constraint	Ratio of larger to smaller constraint score between firms
Capital intensity	Difference in ratio of firms' assets to employees
Regulated industry	Common primary membership in regulated industry (0 = no; 1 = yes)
Defense contracts	Common recipient of defense contracts (0 = no; 1 = yes)
Common plant locations	Number of states in which both firms have plants
Foreign subsidiaries	Number of countries in which both firms have subsidiaries

are provided with public financing. To measure behavioral similarity, lists of every contribution made by each firm were compared among all 1,596 pairs. Although behavioral similarity is defined in terms of the extent to which two firms contribute to the same candidates, the number of candidates contributed to in common is partly determined, as I noted earlier, by the number of contributions made by each firm. To ensure that the degree of activism did not confound the measure of behavioral similarity, the following measure of association was employed:

$$S_{ij} = n_{ij} / (n_i n_j)^{\frac{1}{2}}$$

where S_{ij} equals similarity, n_{ij} equals the number of contributions in common, and n_i and n_j equal the number of contributions made by firms i and j respectively. This measure, which is identical to the measure of association employed in several studies of interlocking directorates (Mariolis, 1975; Mizruchi and Bunting, 1981), provides an indicator of behavioral similarity that is independent of the number of contributions by each firm.

This measure (S_{ij}) is equivalent to a Pearson product-moment correlation prior to subtracting the means in computing the sums of squares and cross-products. Thus, if the means of the observations are zero, the Pearson correlation reduces to S_{ij}. When unit means are small, S_{ij} is virtually identical to a Pearson correlation.

There is one possible situation in which S_{ij} could be biased toward firms with high numbers of contributions. Consider a case in which there is a pool of 100 candidates who could receive contributions. Imagine that firms A and B each contribute to 50 of these candidates while firms C and D each contribute to ten. If the contributions are distributed randomly, simple probability theory tells us that firms A and B will contribute to about 25 candidates in common (giving their dyad a similarity score of .5) while firms C and D will contribute to only one in common (giving their dyad a score of .1).[11] This suggests that the higher the number of contributions, the higher the similarity score, even when contributions are randomly distributed.

There are two reasons that the use of S_{ij} does not pose a problem, however. First, the above example is based on the assumption that the

[11] The joint probability of two independent events is the product of the probabilities of each event. In these examples, the probabilities are .5 × .5, which equals .25, and .1 × .1, which equals .01. With 100 candidates, the joint probabilities yield expected numbers of common contributions of 25 and 1 respectively. In the first example, S_{ij} is computed as $25 / (50 \times 50)^{1/2}$, which equals .5. In the second example, S_{ij} is $1 / (10 \times 10)^{1/2}$, which equals .1.

candidate pool is fixed. In fact, this is not the case. There is no limit on the number of candidates to whom PACs may contribute. Therefore, in the present context, the unit means are indeterminate. For practical purposes, they are approximately zero. Second, if we employ a Pearson correlation in place of S_{ij} (with means based on the 2,279 candidates registered with the Federal Election Commission), the results are virtually identical to those reported below based on S_{ij}. The two measures are almost perfectly correlated (.995). This is important because using a Pearson correlation nullifies the bias identified in the above example. In that case, both the A-B and C-D dyads would have correlations of zero. In the analysis of common contributions, in which all candidates (including those in primaries) are involved, I shall employ S_{ij} as my measure of similarity of political behavior. In the analysis of opposition between firms, in which only candidates in general elections are involved (meaning that the size of the candidate pool is fixed), I shall employ a Pearson correlation. The latter computation is described in Chapter 6. Empirically, both measures yield virtually identical results in this study.

Measurement of the Predictors

For each firm, I recorded the two-digit industry in which the firm did the most business, plus all of the two-digit industries in which it produced. For each dyad, I coded a dummy variable indicating whether the two firms had primary involvement in the same industry, as well as the number of two-digit industries in which they were both involved. The latter variable was standardized to account for both firms' degree of diversification. This was done by dividing the number of common industries by the square root of the product of the number of industries in which each firm produced (the same measure of association employed to measure the dependent variable).

Organizational studies in which interdependence is a key variable have been forced to operate at the industry level of analysis (Pfeffer and Salancik, 1978: Burt, 1983a). The reason for this is that input-output tables on business transactions are available only at the industry level. My own preliminary results (Mizruchi and Koenig, 1986) were also based on an interindustry level of analysis. Although the interindustry level of analysis has proven adequate for the studies that have employed it, a more appropriate unit of analysis for corporate political behavior is the relations among firms. Therefore, the present study will operate at the interfirm level. The measure of constraint will be adapted to this level, following studies by Galaskiewicz et al. (1985), Palmer, Friedland, and Singh (1986), and Burt (1987a).

The decision to employ interindustry input-output data at the interfirm level of analysis requires elaboration. A key issue is the level of aggregation, that is, the extent to which one can assume that the relations characteristic of an industry as a whole also characterize the industry's individual members. Although data are not available for individual firms, the Standard Industrial Classification scheme has several different levels. This enables researchers to determine the extent to which members of two or more sectors at one level display sufficiently equivalent sales and purchase relations to be grouped into the same sector at higher levels. For example, the two-digit tobacco industry contains several four-digit industries, including cigarettes, cigars, and chewing tobacco. Studies by Blin and Cohen (1977) and Kaysen and Turner (1959) have shown that several industries at the four-digit level can be grouped together without a significant loss of information (see Burt, 1983a, pp. 60–63, for a useful summary), and Burt (1983a; 1988a) has found his models empirically viable at both four-digit and two-digit levels of aggregation. These findings support the argument that members of the same industry can be considered structurally equivalent in terms of their sales and purchase relations with other industries (Burt, 1983a, pp. 9–10). There is differentiation of types of production within industries (Leifer and White, 1987), but this study minimizes these differences by focusing only on the largest firms within each industry.

Of course, the input-output table is based on relations among establishments (subunits of firms), not relations among the firms themselves. To what extent can interestablishment relations be conceptualized at the interfirm level? Burt (1983a) shows that director interlocks between members of different industries are associated with the extent to which one industry exercises market constraint over another. Since director interlocks occur not through establishments but through firms, Burt's finding actually suggests that *firms* will interlock if they produce in industries in which a constraint relation exists. That the latter tends to occur is supported by studies that show a positive association between a firm's capital dependence and its interlocks with financial institutions (Dooley, 1969; Pfeffer, 1972; Pennings, 1980; Mizruchi and Stearns, 1988). Based on this logic, I have hypothesized that pairs of firms will exhibit similar political behavior to the extent that they operate in industries in which constraint relations exist.[12]

Finally, many firms, in order to circumvent market constraints on their establishments, acquire their own establishments in the industries by which they are constrained (Williamson, 1975; Burt, 1983a, pp. 70–74). If an automobile manufacturer acquires an establishment in the auto parts industry, then the former is no longer subject to extra-industry constraint by firms that operate in the auto parts industry. The auto manufacturer, however, is now subject to whatever constraints exist on the auto parts industry and it is no longer able to exert its own constraint on that industry (Burt, 1983a, pp. 73–74; see also Granovetter, 1985 and Perrow, 1986 for further discussion of the disadvantages of hierarchies).

The foregoing suggests that the extent to which a particular firm owns establishments in industries by which its primary industries are constrained should be taken into account in measuring interfirm market constraint. This is accomplished by controlling for the number of common industries in which the two firms operate. As we shall see below, there is a strong association between interfirm market constraint and the number of common industries in which the firms produce. To ensure that the constraint and primary industry variables would remain entirely separate, intraindustry market constraint relations were coded as the mean of overall market constraint among the interindustry dyads.

As noted in Chapter 4, constraint is defined by Burt (1983a, pp. 36–60) as the dependence of one industry on another for sales and purchases, weighted by the concentration of the latter industry. Specifically, it is the proportion of industry A's total transactions that involve B, multiplied by the four-firm concentration of B (the proportion of sales in B accounted for by the four largest firms). Based on Hypotheses 1–3, I have operationalized three variables relevant to constraint: the total amount of constraint in the dyad; the symmetry of the dyadic constraint; and the interaction between the two.

As discussed earlier, data on market constraint are available only at

---

[12] Ideally, we would want to know the particular firms between which transactions take place. Nevertheless, if establishments in industry A are constrained by those in industry B, then a firm in B need not be a business partner of a firm in A in order to exercise constraint over that firm. Although the firm in A has the option of shifting its business to other firms within B, to the extent that B is concentrated, the firm in A is unlikely to achieve a more favorable deal by doing so.

the interindustry level. However, three studies (Galaskiewicz et al., 1985; Palmer, Friedland, and Singh, 1986; and Burt, 1987a) have presented operationalizations of constraint at the interfirm level. In Burt's approach, constraint relations involving the firm's primary industry are treated as approximations of that firm's constraint relations. The Galaskiewicz et al. measure is computed by listing all constraint relations between industries in which the two firms are involved and taking the median constraint score. And the Palmer et al. measure involved a summation of the number of significant constraint relations between the industries in which the firms in the dyad were involved, where significance was determined, following an earlier analysis by Burt (1983a), on the basis of the extent to which a particular constraint score exceeded the industry's mean.

I computed the Burt measure by summing, for each dyad, the amount of constraint exerted by firm j on firm i and firm i on firm j.[13] The Galaskiewicz et al. measure was computed as described above. And the Palmer et al. measure was computed by the formula $C_{ij} = (n_{ij} + n_{ji}) / (n_i n_j)^{\frac{1}{2}}$, where C_{ij} equals the constraint between i and j, n_{ij} and n_{ji} equal the number of significant constraint relations between i and j, and n_i and n_j equal the number of industries in which firms i and j operate.

There is little substantive basis on which to decide among these three measures. Each has advantages and disadvantages and each is positively associated with one another. This suggests that none of the three measures adequately captures the concept of interfirm constraint but that each of the three reflects some aspect of the underlying concept. To handle this problem, I constructed a latent variable based on extraction of the first principal component of the correlation matrix among the three measures. The loadings on the first principal component were .676, .583, and .831 respectively, with an eigenvalue of 1.488. Factor scores were employed as the measure of interfirm market constraint.

I argued in Chapter 4 that firms with high levels of market constraint will be likely to engage in similar political behavior regardless of whether the constraint was mutual or one-way. In order to test this it is necessary to examine the degree of asymmetry in the constraint relation. This was computed by taking, for each firm in the dyad, the

---

[13] "[T]he *cohesion* of a relationship can be defined as the average of [the dependence of A on B and the dependence of B on A]" (Emerson, 1962, p. 34).

ratio of the larger constraint score to the smaller one. Because zero was a possible score, a value of .001 was added to each score prior to computation. Adding a constant to a ratio variable, of course, removes the ratio character of the measure. This strategy was viewed as a necessary, if imperfect, means of handling this problem. Experimentation with several constants revealed that the value of the constant had little effect on the results.

Because the three measures of asymmetry were subject to the same conceptual issues as the three measures of constraint, a latent variable based on a linear combination of these three variables was also created. Loadings on the first principal component were .464, .789, and .776 respectively, with an eigenvalue of 1.440. Factor scores were employed as the measure of asymmetry of market constraint. Finally, because I argued in Chapter 4 that the null effect of asymmetry on similarity of behavior should be constant at all levels of constraint, I inserted a multiplicative interaction term for constraint and asymmetry. This interaction term should have no effect on the level of similarity.

Direct interlocks were computed by comparing lists of directors between the two firms in each dyad. The number of direct interlocks is the number of directors who sit on the boards of both firms. Indirect interlocks were calculated by comparing lists of directors between the two firms and each of the fifty largest commercial banks and twenty largest life insurance companies in the United States in 1980. The number of indirect interlocks is equal to the number of banks and insurance companies that have direct interlocks with both manufacturing firms in the dyad. For example, in 1980 Anne L. Armstrong and former Governor John B. Connally were directors of First City Bancorporation of Texas. Armstrong sat on the board of General Motors and Connally sat on the board of Ford. This created an indirect interlock between Ford and General Motors. In this particular case, both Armstrong and Connally were outside directors of all three boards. In other cases indirect interlocks are created by officers of the firms, including cases in which officers of two manufacturing firms sit together on the board of a third firm. Interlock researchers have debated for years about the utility of distinguishing interlocks created by officers from those created by outside directors (Mizruchi, 1982; Palmer, 1983; Mintz and Schwartz, 1985). Most researchers agree that officer interlocks are more likely to be indicative of specifically organizational ties, such as resource dependence relations, between the firms.

Both types of interlocks are seen as useful sources of information. Both types are also viewed as representative of social ties among members of the corporate elite. Since my primary aim here is to treat interlocks as social network rather than specifically organizational phenomena, I shall employ all direct and indirect interlocks without distinguishing between officer and non-officer interlocks. I should note, however, that much of the interlock research even in the organizational tradition has not differentiated the two (see, for example, Burt, 1983a).

Stockholding relations were determined through comparisons of lists of the firms' leading stockholders. The variable was operationalized as the number of institutional stockholders that held at least 0.5 percent of the stock in both firms in the dyad. Standardized measures of the interlock and stockholding variables are employed and discussed in Chapter 9.

Geographic proximity was examined for both corporate headquarters and plant locations. For headquarters, I created a dummy variable, which I coded 1 if the firms' headquarters were in the same state and 0 otherwise. For plants, I coded the number of states that included plants of both firms in the dyad. This variable was then standardized by the geometric mean (the square root of the product) of the number of states in which the two firms had plants, in the same way as the dependent variable and the Palmer et al. measure of constraint.

Based on the synthesis of the organizational and class models represented in Figure 4.1, the interlocking and stock ownership variables will be treated as intervening variables. Director interlocks have been shown to be partly determined by resource dependencies (Allen, 1974; Pfeffer and Salancik, 1978; Pennings, 1980; Burt, 1983a). In addition, interlocking is believed by some theorists (Laumann and Marsden, 1982; Burt, 1983a) to solidify an already existing resource exchange relation. Most importantly, in the social class model, interlocks are expected to play an independent role in contributing to business political unity (Ratcliff, 1980; Domhoff, 1983; Useem, 1984; Mintz and Schwartz, 1985). By including interlocking as an intervening variable, we will be able to determine the extent to which interlocking interprets or extends the impact of economic interdependence.

Similar theories on the role of intercorporate stock ownership have not been as extensively developed. Burt (1983a), however, has examined the extent to which establishments own subsidiaries in industries by which the former are constrained, and his analysis of stock ownership follows the same logic as his analysis of director interlocks (see also Berkowitz et al., 1979). Therefore, it is theoretically consistent to employ stock ownership ties as an intervening variable along with director interlocks. Stock ties may also affect whether interlocks occur, an issue examined by Kotz (1978), Mizruchi (1982), and Caswell (1984).

The full hypothesized model based on this discussion is presented in Figure 5.1. All effects are expected to be positive, except that of asymmetry of constraint (not shown in the figure) on behavioral similarity, which is expected to be zero, and that of same industry on direct interlocking, which, because of legal restrictions, is expected to be negative.

Data on campaign contributions were derived from the Federal Election Commission's 1980 tape, which includes all PAC contributions in the 1979–80 election cycle filed with the Commission. Data on directors, place of headquarters and plant locations, and on the industries in which the firms were involved, were derived from *Moody's Industrial Manual* and *Standard and Poor's Register*. *Fortune* and *Standard and Poor's* were used to identify firms' primary and secondary industries. In a few cases the *Standard and Poor's* and *Fortune* primary industry classifications differed. The results reported below were based on the *Fortune* classifications. Stock ownership data were culled from the *CDE Stock Ownership Directory* (Corporate Data Exchange, 1981). Interindustry input-output data and constraint scores from 1977 (the closest year to 1980 for which such data are available) were provided by Ronald Burt. Burt (1988a) has shown that relations between industries in the input-output table are highly stable over time.

Hypotheses 10–12 dealt with four variables: similar levels of capital

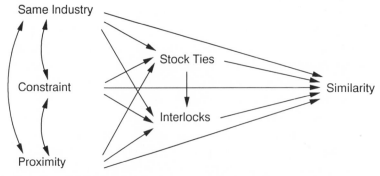

Figure 5.1. Hypothesized effects on similarity of political behavior

intensity, common subject of government regulation, common dependence on defense contracts, and common foreign interests. Dyads in which both firms received defense contracts in 1980 were coded as 1. All others were coded as 0. Data on defense contracts were provided by Dan Clawson and Alan Neustadtl. A firm's capital intensity is often operationalized as its ratio of total assets to number of employees. Since my concern is with the similarity in the firms' level of capital intensity, a difference score was employed. Because the distribution of firms' capital intensities was highly skewed, I transformed the values to logarithms (base e). The relative capital intensity between firms was computed as the absolute difference between two firms in the natural logarithm of their ratios of assets to employees. It is important to note that a low value on this measure indicates a similar level of capital intensity. Therefore, a negative effect of this variable on the political similarity score would indicate that firms with similar levels of capital intensity engage in similar political behavior.

Most of the industries that have been under federal regulation since the early part of the twentieth century are in non-manufacturing sectors. As noted in Chapter 4, it is industries that have come under regulation in more recent years that should be expected to be most hostile to government. Drawing on Clinard et al. (1979), Burris (1987) classified the following as newly regulated industries: chemicals, petroleum refining, paper and wood products, metal manufacturing, electrical equipment, motor vehicles, mining, and textiles. I employed this classification scheme here. Dyads in which both firms had their primary production in newly regulated industries were coded as 1. All other dyads were coded as 0. Common foreign interests were operationalized as the number of the same countries in which the firms had subsidiaries, standardized by the geometric mean of the number of countries in which each had subsidiaries.

Statistical Issues in the Study of Dyadic Data

The dependent variable operationalized above is interval scaled and normally distributed.[14] Therefore, ordinary least squares regression

---

[14] The measure of similarity of political behavior could be thought of as ratio scaled but this would involve the assumption that a dyad with 100 contributions in common exhibited behavior that was twice as similar as one with 50 contributions in common. I see no theoretical advantage to such an assumption. The other endogenous variables in the model can be viewed as interval scaled as well.

analysis would appear to be an appropriate technique. However, because my units of analysis are the 1,596 dyads created by relations among 57 firms, the observations are not statistically independent. Each firm will appear in 56 separate observations. This raises the possibility of autocorrelation in the regression results. There is no one agreed-upon approach to handling network autocorrelation, in which the data are cross-sectional.[15]

One notable effort has been developed by Fienberg, Meyer, and Wasserman (1985; see Galaskiewicz et al., 1985 for an application). This approach, however, involves log-linear models, which are less powerful for the interval-scaled data employed in this study. Another approach, based on spatial autocorrelation models, has been developed for use with cross-sectional data (see Ord, 1975; Cliff and Ord, 1981; Doreian, 1981; see Loftin and Ward, 1983 for an application). Dow et al. (1984) discuss three approaches to calculating regression equations with this model, one of which (iterative residual regression, or IRR) I have employed in a previous study (Mizruchi and Koenig, 1988).

IRR involves transforming the standard matrix equation for OLS regression ($Y = XB + e$) to $Y - \rho WY = (X - \rho WX)B + v$, where ρ is the autocorrelation parameter, W is an $N \times N$ matrix of overlaps among the observations, and v is an $N \times 1$ vector of randomly distributed error terms. Rho (ρ) is estimated by an iterative procedure, in which the residuals from the initial OLS equation are regressed on the residuals weighted by W (that is, $e = \rho We + v$) to obtain the first estimate of ρ. Rho is the correlation coefficient and We is an $N \times 1$ vector of transformed residuals. Rho is then inserted into the $Y - \rho WY = (X - \rho WX)B + v$ equation, which is solved using OLS regression, and ρ is reestimated from this equation's residuals. Iteration

---

[15] The "true" number of degrees of freedom in the present analysis is somewhere between the number of nodes minus one (56) and the number of dyads minus one (1,595). The extent to which the degrees of freedom approach the number of dyads depends on the level of autocorrelation. If the autocorrelation is removed, the observations can be treated as if they were independent (Hannan and Young, 1977, p. 59; Lincoln, 1984, p. 57). The data presented in this study are not based on a random sample. In fact, the data can be viewed as a population of dyads among the largest firms in several industries. In this case, the use of statistical significance tests is unnecessary. I have included significance tests for two reasons: first, as a heuristic device for interpreting the strength of relations among variables; second, because my aim is to make generalizations about "the causal processes that generated [the] data" (Blalock, 1979, p. 242). Although I use statistical significance tests as a guide, then, I do not rely exclusively on them in my substantive conclusions.

ceases when the difference between two successive values of ρ reaches an appropriately small level.

In a dyadic analysis, **W** consists of an $N \times N$ dyad by dyad matrix. That is, the cells in the matrix are dyads of dyads. **W** can be created by noting, for each pair of dyads, the number of firms in common. For example, a dyad that includes Mobil and Texaco contains no overlap with one that includes General Motors and United Technologies. The Mobil-Texaco, GM–United Technologies cell will receive a 0. A dyad that includes GM and Westinghouse, however, contains an overlap with the GM–United Technologies dyad. The cell entry for these two dyads will be 1. The result of this coding of inter-dyad overlaps is a binary matrix in which all pairs of dyads that overlap particular firms contain a one and all independent dyad pairs contain zeros. Each element in the matrix is then divided by its row sum, so that all rows sum to one.

This technique appears to be well suited to the present study. The main problem is computational. Dow et al.'s illustrations, as well as the Mizruchi and Koenig study, had sample sizes of under 100. The present study has a sample size of 1,596, meaning that **W** would have dimensions of 1,596 × 1,596. Because of the enormous amount of storage capacity that would be necessary to invert a matrix of this size, this technique is not feasible for the present analysis.[16]

An alternative is to employ least squares with dummy variables (see Hannan and Young, 1977 for a discussion of this approach with pooled cross-sectional time-series models). In this approach, dummy variables are created for 56 of the 57 firms. For each dyad, the dummies for the two firms are coded as 1 and all other dummies are coded as 0. For dyads involving the "reference" firm, only one dummy is coded as 1. With the creation of the dummy variables, the potentially autocorrelated disturbances in the equation $Y = XB + e$ are shifted out of **e** and into **X**. The remaining terms in **e** satisfy the criteria for OLS regression (Hannan and Young, 1977, pp. 64–65). Hannan and Young's simulation results suggest that LSDV yields efficient and consistent estimates.

I have employed LSDV models in three previously published analyses based on these data (Mizruchi, 1989; 1990a; 1991). The use of this technique contains two problems, however. The first problem is pri-

---

[16] The analyses presented in Chapter 8 are amenable to IRR. See the discussion therein.

marily a substantive one. LSDV models of dyadic data treat all of the variation that is unique to particular firms as a spurious effect. If a heavily interlocked firm is involved in a large number of relations with high levels of political similarity, LSDV will assume that the simultaneously high level of interlocking and similar political behavior in dyads involving this firm are substantively irrelevant. But there are few grounds for making this assumption. The fact that heavily interlocked firms are also involved in dyads high in similar political behavior is at least potentially an important substantive finding, but the logic of LSDV prevents such a finding from ever emerging. This suggests that LSDV is probably overly conservative. In statistical terms, it may lead to Type II errors.

In addition to the problem with the firm-specific effects, preliminary evidence from a simulation study by Krackhardt (1990) indicates that with spatially autocorrelated dyadic data, LSDV may fail to provide unbiased estimates. Although the data to be analyzed below do not appear to have high levels of autocorrelation, the inability to guarantee unbiased estimates does not bode well for LSDV as a general approach to dyadic data.

The key point to recognize is that the purpose of LSDV is not to remove the firm-specific effects *per se*, but rather to remove the autocorrelation due to the non-independence of the observations. Controlling for firm-specific effects is one way of removing network autocorrelation. If another technique existed that was capable of removing the autocorrelation, it might prove to be superior to LSDV. Fortunately, such a technique is available: a procedure developed by Mantel (1967) and Hubert (for example, Baker and Hubert, 1981) called quadratic assignment (QAP). Krackhardt (1987; 1988) presents illustrations relevant to the analysis of multiple network data.

QAP is a nonparametric technique that adjusts the probabilities of OLS coefficients based on the extent to which the observed relations between variables deviate from the expected relations given a certain network structure. Consider two 57 × 57 matrices, one for the similarity of political behavior and one for level of market constraint. QAP begins by producing all possible permutations of the constraint matrix (that is, rearranging the positions of the specific actors while preserving the original structure of the matrix). To give a simple example of how this works, imagine a network with three persons, A, B, and C, in which A and C both know B but not one another. This network would appear graphically as a straight line in which B was in

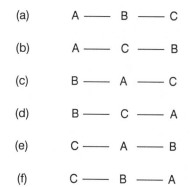

Figure 5.2. All possible permutations in a three-unit network with two ties

the center flanked by A on one side and C on the other, as indicated by panel a in Figure 5.2. The number of possible permutations in a network is $N!$, where N equals the number of nodes (persons, organizations, etc.). Because this network contains three nodes, there are six (3!) possible permutations involving the three actors with the existing straight line structure. The remaining five permutations are listed in panels b through f in Figure 5.2.

To return to the two 57 × 57 matrices for similarity of political behavior and constraint, QAP computes the coefficient for the effect of market constraint on similarity for each permutation. Because the number of possible permutations is $N!$ (in this case 57!), it is not feasible to examine all permutations in most cases. Where N equals 10, for example, there are more than 3.6 million possible permutations. Mantel (1967) developed a solution for the mean and standard deviation of all possible coefficients, provided that the distribution of coefficients is normal. Given a normal distribution, the probability of the observed coefficient can be computed from a Z-score based on its number of standard deviations from the mean. If the distribution of coefficients is not normal, however, the consequences can be severe (Krackhardt, 1987, p. 178). An alternative is to randomly sample a large number of permutations. In the analysis that follows, I randomly extracted 1,000 permutations from all 57! possible ones.[17] The probability level of the coefficient is simply the number of permutation

---

[17] I am indebted to David Krackhardt for his assistance in providing the software on which the analysis is based. Jeff Eldredge, Shin-Kap Han, and Helen Reid assisted in its implementation.

coefficients that exceed the observed coefficient, divided by the number of permutations plus one (in this case, by 1,001). In other words, a probability of .003 indicates that only three of the 1000 randomly drawn coefficients exceeded the observed coefficient. Krackhardt (1988) has shown that QAP produces unbiased estimates regardless of the degree of autocorrelation.[18]

[18] I mentioned above that I had published three articles based on LSDV analyses. Although some small differences were found when the data from those analyses were reanalyzed with QAP, the QAP results led to virtually identical substantive conclusions. Some of the differences between the LSDV and QAP results are discussed in the Appendix to Chapter 6.

6 · Political Campaign Contributions: Unity and Conflict

In Chapter 2, we saw that for pluralists, a key basis for American democracy is the existence of divisions within the business community. I argued that the issue of whether business is unified is moot, and that we should focus our efforts instead on identifying the conditions under which unity and conflict occur. In Chapter 3 I examined the concepts of unity and cohesion, arguing that (1) the primary reason for our interest in unity is that it increases a group's power and (2) a primary basis of power is similarity of behavior. In Chapter 4 I developed a structural model of similarity of political behavior among firms based on the organizational and class models of interfirm relations. In Chapter 5 I described the proliferation of corporate political action committees and the value of these data for understanding corporate political behavior.

In this and the following chapter, I test empirically the model developed in the previous chapters. In this chapter I use political action committee data to examine the determinants of contributions to the same candidates, contributions to candidates with similar ideologies and party affiliations, and business opposition (situations in which pairs of firms support opposing candidates in particular elections).

The 1980 Election

In 1932, at the height of the Great Depression, the incumbent Republican president, Herbert Hoover, was overwhelmed in his bid for reelection by Democratic challenger Franklin D. Roosevelt. In addition to their sweeping victory in the presidential election, the Democrats captured both the Senate and the House of Representatives from the Republicans. Prior to 1932, the Republicans had won three consecutive presidential elections and had controlled the Senate since 1918 and the House from 1918 through 1930. Political scientists (Key, 1955; Burnham, 1970) have developed the concept of "critical," or "realigning," elections to describe "substantial shifts in the underlying partisan distribution" (Flanigan, 1972, p. 126). The 1932 election is viewed as the prototype of the critical election.

The 1980 election was the first since 1932 in which an incumbent president was defeated in a bid for reelection. In addition, the Republicans captured control of the Senate for the first time since 1954. Although the House remained Democratic, the Democrats lost 33 seats, and with the large contingent of conservative Democrats, the Republicans in effect had a working majority. The debate over whether 1980 constituted a critical election died down considerably after the Democrats gained 26 seats in the House in the 1982 election and recaptured the Senate in 1986. But 1980 was clearly characterized by an unusual number of successful challenges to incumbents.

Although its precise impact is difficult to assess, it is probable that the extensive contributions by corporate PACs had some effect on the success of Republican challengers (Jacobson, 1984). The trend toward the ideological contribution strategies described in the previous chapter began in full force in the 1978 election cycle and picked up steam in 1980. By 1982 corporate PACs began a decade-long return to the traditional pragmatic strategy of giving to incumbents regardless of party and ideology. Because of the unusual degree of support for challengers (and the correspondingly high level of variation in firm strategies), the 1980 cycle provides an excellent laboratory for examining the sources of corporate unity and conflict.

Tests of Structural Hypotheses

The key tenet of the structural model of political behavior is that interfirm economic and social relations, both direct and indirect, serve as mediating mechanisms that contribute to similar political behavior among firms. Variables that indicate direct relations among firms are market constraint and direct interlocks. Variables that indicate indirect relations include common financial stockholders and indirect interlocks. Membership in the same primary industry provides an indicator of two firms' equivalent positions in economic exchange networks, while proximity of headquarters location (in the same state) provides an indicator of potential for communication among local business elites. Also included in the analysis, as described in Chapter

4, are three variables that measure sources of political coalescence identified by political scientists: similar levels of capital intensity, common membership in newly regulated industries, and mutual interest in defense contracts.[1]

The first analysis involves the primary indicator of similar political behavior among firms, the standardized number of contributions to the same candidates, described in the previous chapter as S_{ij}. Table 6.1 presents means, standard deviations, and correlations among the variables included in the analysis.[2] The similarity scores across the 1,596 dyads range from a low of 0, shared by ten dyads, to a high of .593, held by the General Electric-LTV dyad. The mean was .233. Since the mean number of contributions per firm was 99.3, the average dyad involved two firms with just under 100 contributions each, about 23 of which were to the same candidates. Other dyads with high levels of similarity included GE and General Motors (.591), Mobil and Texaco (.583), and General Motors and Pepsico (.557). Twenty-one dyads had scores of .500 or above.

Results of three multiple regression equations with quadratic assignment probabilities (described in Chapter 5) are presented in Table 6.2. Similarity of contribution patterns is the dependent variable in all three equations.

A Note on Interpreting the Regression Coefficients

Before discussing the results in these equations, a brief explanation is necessary. Most of the analyses presented in this and the following chapters employ multiple regression equations. Regression is a widely employed technique in the social sciences that requires no special explanation here. The quadratic assignment procedure, which adjusts the probability levels of the coefficients to account for network autocorrelation, is described in Chapter 5. Many of the equations and coefficients presented over the next several chapters may be difficult to interpret. As a guide to their interpretation, I shall focus on pairs of firms that have roughly "average" characteristics. Consider, for example, Bethlehem Steel and Monsanto Chemical. Bethlehem contributed

---

[1] Variables measuring common plant locations and common foreign subsidiaries were omitted from the analyses described in this chapter. Repeated analyses, including several in previously published work, indicated that both variables had virtually no relation with any of the dependent variables.

[2] Four endogenous variables employed in subsequent analyses are also included in this table.

Table 6.1. Means, standard deviations, and correlations among variables (N = 1596)

Variable	Mean	SD	2	3	4	5	6	7	8	9	10	11	12	13	14	15	16
1. Similarity	.233	.107	119	086	083	153	281	098	264	074	001	192	234	-347	-378	-760	140
2. Proximity	.081	.274	—	079	018	058	118	084	142	023	036	067	039	-072	-065	000	021
3. Same primary industry	.050	.218		—	358	110	045	-045	003	-089	-102	072	201	-007	-006	-036	168
4. Common industries	.174	.222			—	274	034	-036	054	-062	-235	058	195	-027	-059	-061	119
5. Market constraint[a]	.000	1.000				—	047	001	059	370	-133	048	149	-039	-043	-135	112
6. Common stockholders[b]	1.160	.665					—	060	175	164	046	069	089	078	015	-246	072
7. Direct interlocks	.048	.241						—	237	030	-012	-008	-033	-047	-032	-088	086
8. Indirect interlocks	.403	.719							—	057	-097	153	051	-088	-099	-297	129
9. Asymmetry of constraint[a]	.000	1.000								—	124	-024	013	020	-028	-102	-019
10. Capital intensity	.638	.546									—	023	079	083	-016	-055	-115
11. Regulated industries	.132	.338										—	152	-071	-071	-091	041
12. Defense contracts	.049	.216											—	029	-007	-281	095
13. Similarity of ideology[b]	.565	.170												—	797	269	-012
14. Similarity of party[b]	.170	.111													—	346	-023
15. Opposition	-.072	.054														—	-138
16. Testimony agreement	.043	.265															—

a. Factor scores
b. In logarithms (base e)

Table 6.2. Determinants of similarity of campaign contributions

Independent variable	(1)	(2)	(3)
Constant	17.554[d] (.000)	17.385[d] (.000)	17.103[c] (.003)
Proximity	1.825 (.123)	1.926 (.115)	1.674 (.156)
Same primary industry	2.733[b] (.018)	2.713[b] (.028)	1.209 (.187)
Common industries	–	0.637 (.430)	-0.326 (.453)
Market constraint	1.291[b] (.034)	1.258[b] (.037)	1.057[a] (.063)
Common stockholders	3.762[b] (.011)	3.678[b] (.015)	3.415[b] (.019)
Direct interlocks	1.553 (.141)	1.575 (.139)	2.072[a] (.072)
Indirect interlocks	2.981[d] (.001)	2.977[d] (.001)	2.647[c] (.002)
Asymmetry of constraint	0.033 (.998)	–	–
Constraint*asymmetry	-0.402 (.488)	–	–
Capital intensity	–	–	0.114 (.485)
Regulated industries	–	–	3.631[a] (.084)
Defense contracts	–	–	8.395[c] (.007)
R^2	.155	.153	.197

a. $p < .10$
b. $p < .05$
c. $p < .01$
d. $p < .001$

Note: OLS estimates with QAP probabilities. All probabilities are one-tailed except for those involving asymmetry, which are two-tailed. N=1596 in all equations. Metric coefficients are reported, with quadratic assignment probabilities in parentheses. Coefficients are multiplied by 100.

to 104 candidates in 1980, Monsanto to 96. Twenty-two of their contributions were to the same candidates, yielding a similarity score of .220. Because both firms contributed to about 100 candidates, a "ten point" (one-one hundredth) increase in their similarity score (from, say, .220 to .230) amounts to about one additional common contribution. Coefficients in the table are multiplied by 100 to facilitate this calculation.

Let us examine the coefficients in Equation 1 of Table 6.2. Bethlehem and Monsanto are not in the same primary industry. If they were, the model would predict an increase in their common contributions of about 2.7 candidates. A one-unit increase in the market constraint between the two firms would yield a predicted increase in their common contributions of about 1.3 candidates. An increase in common stockholders of one logarithm (about 2.7) would increase their predicted common contributions by about 3.8 candidates. And one additional indirect interlock would lead to about three more common contributions. If we include in our estimate the coefficients in the model that were statistically significant,[3] then a one-unit change in each of these variables would be expected to increase the number of common contributions between Bethlehem and Monsanto from 22 to about 33. If we include all of the coefficients in the model, then a one-unit change in each variable would predict an increase in the number of common contributions to almost 37. In Equation 3, with the three political-economic variables included, the impact is even stronger. If Bethlehem and Monsanto were both recipients of defense contracts, it would increase their predicted common contributions by 8.4 candidates. Were both firms' primary production in newly regulated industries, their common contributions would increase by 3.6 candidates. Overall, a one-unit change in each of the statistically significant variables in Equation 3 would yield a predicted increase in the number of common contributions between Bethlehem and Monsanto from 22 to about 43. If we include all of the coefficients in the model, then a one-unit change in each of the variables would increase the predicted number of common contributions to 46.5 candidates.

The relative strength of the variables in predicting similarity of contribution patterns is more difficult to assess because the variables are not measured in the same units. For example, a one-unit increase in market constraint means something very different from a one-unit increase in indirect interlocks. A traditional way to compare the strength of predictors is the use of standardized coefficients. This

[3] As noted in Chapter 5, because my data constitute a population, I use probability levels in this study primarily as a heuristic device. For this reason, as well as for the fact that as a nonparametric test quadratic assignment produces more conservative probability estimates than OLS regression, I shall employ a .10 level of significance rather than the more conventional .05.

approach is less useful here, however, because the strength of the effects is adjusted by the quadratic assignment procedure. The most convenient, albeit imperfect, way to assess the relative strength of the predictors is to compare the probability levels of the coefficients. The lower the probability, the stronger the effect.[4]

Results on Similarity of Contribution Patterns

Equation 1 of Table 6.2 reveals support for most of the hypotheses presented in Chapter 4. The strong effect of primary industry confirms the hypothesis that firms within an industry are likely to exhibit shared political behavior. The hypotheses on the effects of constraint were also confirmed. The market constraint factor was a significant positive predictor of similarity but the degree of asymmetry in the dyadic constraint relation had no effect. In addition, the level of asymmetry had no effect on the strength of the constraint coefficient (the interaction effect was non-significant). These findings suggest that the potential for economic coercion is associated with the similarity of political behavior but the key factor is the existence of constraint in the dyad rather than the relative balance of constraint between the two firms. This is consistent with my argument in Chapter 4 as well as Emerson's power-dependence model discussed therein.

Common stock ownership by financial institutions was also positively associated with similarity of political behavior. Although this finding is not necessarily indicative of an exercise of financial influence over the decisions of nonfinancial corporations, it is consistent with the arguments, described in Chapter 4, that financial institutions play a role in enforcing similar political behavior within the business community.

The findings on interlocking are especially noteworthy. Although

[4] The coefficients in the equations represent the mean difference between dyads at each level of the independent variable. Thus, the dyads in the same primary industry with average numbers of contributions make (in Equation 1) about 2.7 more common contributions than dyads whose firms are not in the same primary industry. The extent to which the observations fit the model is assessed with the coefficient of determination (R^2). The size of the R^2 depends on several factors, such as the amount of variation in the variables and the size of the sample, that differ greatly across analyses (as we shall see with the lower R^2s in Chapter 7 and the much higher ones in Chapters 8 and 9). There is evidence that the size of these coefficients is systematically underestimated in dyadic data (Hubert, 1987, p. 123), although the precise amount of this underestimate is difficult to discern. I shall present R^2s in the tables that follow so that the relative fit of alternative specifications of a particular model can be compared. The reader should exercise caution, however, in comparing the magnitudes of these coefficients either across analyses within this study or with those of other studies.

the level of direct interlocks between manufacturing firms is positively associated with similarity of political behavior, the effect is not statistically significant. This finding is consistent with those of Mizruchi and Koenig (1986) and Burris (1987; but see Clawson and Neustadtl, 1989). However, the effect of indirect interlocking through banks and insurance companies is strongly positive. This is consistent with the finding by Mizruchi and Koenig (1988) that the level of indirect interlocking among the largest firms within 25 industries was positively associated with the similarity of their contribution patterns.

This finding appears counterintuitive. After all, why would firms that were tied indirectly through financial institutions be more likely to behave similarly than firms that were tied directly to one another? One possibility, consistent with the Mintz and Schwartz (1985) model, is that financial institutions are able to use their economic power to achieve political goals, including the ability to dictate, overtly or covertly, the contribution strategies of certain manufacturing firms. In this view, firms that are heavily dependent on financial institutions behave in ways which they believe will win favor with (or avoid the wrath of) officials of these institutions, even in the absence of direct coercion (Whitt, 1982, p. 116). Another fully compatible explanation is based on the distinction between cohesion and structural equivalence discussed in Chapter 3 (Lorrain and White, 1971; White, Boorman, and Breiger, 1976). In a series of books and articles, Burt (1982; 1983b; 1987b) has found that structural equivalence (the extent to which pairs of units within a social structure share similar relations to other units) is a stronger predictor of the adoption of innovations than is cohesion (which Burt [1983b, p. 262] defined as "intense, mutual relations"). That is, two individuals who share equivalent positions in a social structure are more likely to exhibit the same behavior than are two individuals who share close relations with one another.

Burt's argument has relevance to the findings reported here. Firms that share a direct interlock tie have a slight tendency to contribute to the same candidates, but the effect does not differ significantly from zero. On the other hand, firms that are tied to the same third parties are significantly more likely to contribute to the same candidates. Burt argues that structurally equivalent actors are likely to have competitive relations with one another, for example, when they use "one another to evaluate their relative adequacy" (1987b, p. 1291). According to Burt (ibid.), "[t]he more similar ego's and alter's relations with other persons—i.e., the more that alter could substitute for ego in ego's role relations . . . the more likely that ego will quickly adopt any innovation perceived to make alter more attractive as the object or source of relations." This point is applicable to corporate behavior as well. In a reanalysis of data from an earlier study of corporate philanthropy (Galaskiewicz, 1985), Galaskiewicz and Burt (1991) found that structurally equivalent (as opposed to cohesive) corporate officials had similar evaluations of nonprofit organizations. Both Galaskiewicz and Useem (1984) found that corporate officers were highly sensitive to the ways in which their firms' gifts were perceived by other members of the corporate community. Whitt's (1982) findings suggest that corporate leaders may be equally sensitive to the ways in which their political contributions are perceived. Useem (private communication) has noted that CEOs appear to be concerned that others important to them view them as having "done the right thing" with regard to political contributions. And Handler and Mulkern (1982, p. 61) reported that "pressures felt by CEOs to emulate the example of peers" is a major motive influencing a firm's decision to form a PAC.[5] The findings reported here suggest that structurally equivalent firms may adapt their behavior to the perceived preferences of the same set of alters.

The results presented here do not prove the tenability of either the Mintz and Schwartz or the Burt arguments, but they are consistent with both of them. In the case of the Mintz and Schwartz model, it would be necessary to assemble direct evidence on the role of financial institutions in influencing political decision making. Such evidence is available for particular cases (see, for example, Neustadtl, Scott, and Clawson, 1991) but it is not available on a systematic basis. With reference to Burt's argument, several researchers (Alba and Moore, 1983; Friedkin, 1984) have conceptualized cohesion in terms of indirect as well as direct ties. Friedkin (private communication) has suggested that "the *objective cohesion* of two actors should increase as a function of the direct (one-step) and indirect (two-step) paths that join them." In this model, two actors might behave similarly because of influence by the same third parties. In response to this argument, Burt (1987b, p. 1293) has noted that "it seems wrong to attribute evidence of ego-alter contagion to indirect communication through shared contacts when there is no evidence when communication is direct." The fact that direct contact between firms does not influence common political behavior while common contact with the same

---

[5] Note also the similarity between this discussion and the processes described by DiMaggio and Powell (1983). See Chapter 4.

financial institutions does is consistent with Burt's argument. If one posits a special role for financial institutions, as Mintz and Schwartz do, however, then it is still possible to argue that two firms with ties to the same financial institutions are both directly influenced by the latter.

To what extent is the effect of indirect ties on common contribution patterns contingent on the presence of a direct interlock tie? To examine this, I inserted a multiplicative interaction term into the equation. The effect of this variable was virtually zero while the other coefficients and probabilities remained virtually the same. This indicates that the positive effect of indirect interlocks on similarity of political behavior is unaffected by whether or not a direct tie exists.[6]

The one variable in Equation 1 that did not perform according to expectations was geographic proximity. Although the existence of headquarters location in the same state was positively associated with contributions to the same candidates in a simple correlation, the coefficient in the regression equation approached but did not reach statistical significance. In two previously published analyses of these data (Mizruchi, 1989; 1991) using least squares with dummy variable models (see Chapter 5), I found a strong effect of common headquarters location. The finding reported here is one of three in which results using quadratic assignment differed from those using LSDV. An examination of the reasons for these differences is presented in the Appendix to this chapter.

The number of common states in which the firms had plants had a negligible effect on the similarity of their contribution patterns. This variable was deleted from the model since it had no impact on either the dependent variable or the coefficients of the other predictors. There are at least two possible interpretations of this finding. First, because top corporate officials generally live in or near the corporate headquarters city, the proximity coefficient may be a reflection of the social interaction among elites in similar locales. This is based on the assumption that social interaction is a source of similar political be-

---

[6] The positive but marginally non-significant effect of direct interlocking would appear to run counter to Useem's (1984) argument, since board ties form the basis of inner circle membership. For Useem (1984, pp. 45–48), however, interlocks were viewed as important primarily because they increased a director's "business scan," or breadth of information sources. Because indirect interlocks provide contact with a wider range of firms, these ties potentially provide even greater opportunities for business scan. Thus, the finding on the importance of indirect ties is consistent with Useem's thesis.

havior (see Palmer et al., 1986, p. 786 for a similar argument). Second, the finding may also reflect a greater concern among corporate officials with the fate of their headquarters locale than with their plant locales (Useem, 1984, p. 120; Logan and Molotch, 1987).

The results presented in Equation 1 of Table 6.2 did not include the variable for the standardized total number of common industries between two firms, which was excluded because of its partial confounding with same primary industry. Equation 2 contains the variables from Equation 1 (minus asymmetry and the constraint*asymmetry interaction term) plus the number of common industries. The insertion of this variable has little effect on the results. It is not itself a strong predictor of similarity of contribution patterns, nor does its inclusion lower the effect of being in the same primary industry or those of the other variables. This finding is the second of the three cases in which the results from the quadratic assignment procedure differ from those of the LSDV model (the standardized number of common industries had been a strong predictor of common contributions in the LSDV model). The sources of this discrepancy are also discussed in the chapter Appendix.

Equation 3 of Table 6.2 is identical to Equation 2 but also includes the three political-economic variables (similar levels of capital intensity, common membership in newly regulated industries, and common dependence on defense contracts) described in Chapter 4. The effect of difference in capital intensity is virtually zero. The effects of common interests in defense spending and regulation are both positive, however, the former strongly so. The strong finding on common dependence on military contracts corresponds to the finding, suggested by several studies of PAC contributions, that defense contractors contribute disproportionately to Democrats. Both findings are indicative of industry effects. This is evident from the fact that once they are controlled, the effect of same primary industry disappears. More important for my theoretical interests is the fact that when the three variables are controlled, the overall effects of the relational variables remain basically unchanged. Although the effect of market constraint drops slightly, that of direct interlocks increases to a point at which its probability level drops below .10. The effects of common stockholdings and indirect interlocks remain strongly positive. The effects of the economic and social network ties among firms on the similarity of their political behavior, therefore, are not accounted for by the political-economic interests of the firms. The four key network variables in Equation 3 (market constraint, common stockholdings, and direct and indirect interlocks) all have probabilities below .10 and together lead to a predicted increase of about 9.2 common contributions, from 22 to 31, between our two typical firms, Bethlehem Steel and Monsanto.[7]

An Inner Circle Effect?

Even after controlling in the dependent variable for firms' numbers of contributions, dyads containing large firms continue to have higher levels of similar behavior than do dyads containing smaller firms. This finding is substantively interesting because it accords with Useem's (1984) argument that corporate unity is highest among the largest firms. Useem argued that there exists within the business community a subset of heavily interlocked directors whose information scan enables them to develop a "classwide rationality." It is at these top levels within the corporate world, according to Useem, that business unity is most likely to occur. Following Lincoln (1984), I computed the dyadic firm size by taking the product of the *Fortune* 500 size ranks of each firm (transformed by taking the reciprocal of the square root of this figure). The effect of size was statistically significant in a positive direction when inserted into Equation 3 of Table 6.2 and added about three percent to the explained variance.[8]

To further examine this argument, I looked at two additional proxies for common inner circle ties: common membership in the Business Roundtable, an important business policy making organization (Domhoff, 1983; Maitland and Pak, 1987), and the geometric mean of the concentration of the firms' primary industries (Mizruchi and Koenig, 1988), based on Useem's notion that the largest firms in the most concentrated industries are those most likely to spawn inner

---

[7] I should reiterate that the absolute size of the increase in common contributions predicted by the model varies with the number of contributions by firms in a dyad. For a dyad containing firms that made about 200 contributions each, such as U.S. Steel (194) and Westinghouse (201), a one-unit increase in each of the four network variables would be expected to increase the number of common contributions by about 18, in this case from 89 to 107. In dyads with smaller numbers of contributions, the absolute increase will, of course, be smaller.

[8] The insertion of size into the equation also depressed the effect of market constraint to slightly below statistical significance and negated the significant effect of defense contracts. This finding renders the effect of constraint spurious, however, only if constraint is viewed as a function of size. Yet size may be viewed as a function of constraint: firms become large because of heavy involvement in transactions, and firms involved in high constraint relations are by definition central in transaction networks.

circle membership. Following a suggestion by Maitland and Pak (1987; see also Burris, 1987; Clawson and Neustadtl, 1989), I created a dummy variable for common membership in the Business Roundtable with data drawn from Green and Buchsbaum (1980). Forty of the 57 firms (70 percent) were Business Roundtable members and 49 percent of the 1,596 dyads included two firms with Business Roundtable membership. Dyads in which both firms were Business Roundtable members were more likely to contribute to the same candidates even when firm size was controlled. None of the other coefficients was affected by the insertion of this variable into the analysis. This finding suggests that common membership in a major policy-making organization is associated with similar political behavior. Causal inference is difficult here since common Business Roundtable membership could itself be an example of similar political behavior. Still, the finding, combined with that of size and those of the other network variables, lends support to the inner circle thesis. The effect of concentration is marginally significant and its inclusion did not affect the coefficients of the other variables. This finding is also consistent with the inner circle thesis, although only modestly so. The concentration effect is discussed in the Appendix to this chapter.

Indirect Effects

In Chapter 5 I presented a model in which common stockholding, direct interlocks, and indirect interlocks were hypothesized as intervening variables between market constraint and similar political behavior. The model suggested, consistent with the resource dependence model, that interlocks and stockholding relations among firms could be functions of market constraint relations. Table 6.3, which is based on the model in Figure 4.1, presents regression equations with these three variables as endogenous.

The strongest predictor of common stockholders was geographic proximity, but common primary industry was also a marginally significant predictor (Equation 1). Market constraint, although slightly positively associated with common stockholders, was not a significant predictor. The insertion of the standardized number of common industries into the equation has a downward effect on the common primary industry coefficient (Equation 2). The fact that financial institutions are more likely to invest in firms whose headquarters are in similar locales indicates either that financial institutions prefer to

Table 6.3. Determinants of stockholding and interlocking

Independent variable	(1) Stock Holders	(2) Stock Holders	(3) Direct Interlocks	(4) Indirect Interlocks
	\multicolumn{4}{c}{Dependent variable}			
Constant	1.132[d] (.000)	1.126 (.149)	0.028[a] (.098)	0.138[c] (.003)
Proximity	0.276[c] (.006)	0.277[c] (.002)	0.069[c] (.010)	0.277[c] (.003)
Same primary industry	0.096[a] (.090)	0.083 (.158)	–	-0.083 (.179)
Common industries	–	0.038 (.419)	-0.045[a] (.074)	0.178 (.133)
Market constraint	0.025 (.277)	0.023 (.278)	0.001 (.415)	0.024 (.252)
Common stockholders	–	–	0.019[a] (.061)	0.159[b] (.016)
Direct interlocks	–	–	–	0.657[d] (.001)
R^2	.016	.016	.011	.098

a. $p < .10$
b. $p < .05$
c. $p < .01$
d. $p < .001$

Note: OLS estimates with QAP probabilities. All probabilities are one-tailed. N = 1596 in all equations. Metric coefficients are reported, with quadratic assignment probabilities in parentheses.

invest in particular geographic areas or that communication among firm leaders may play a role in financial investment strategies. Market constraint has virtually no impact on common stockholdings.

The most notable finding on the determinants of direct and indirect interlocking (Equations 3 and 4) is that market constraint is unrelated to either variable. Geographic proximity, as expected, is positively associated with both types of interlocking. The null finding on the effect of market constraint is inconsistent with Burt's (1983a) results at the industry level. Burt found that industries in which constraint relations exist are more likely to have interlock ties. Attempts by Galaskiewicz et al. (1985) and Palmer et al. (1986) to replicate this finding at the firm level have been unsuccessful, although Burt's (1987a) attempt was successful. As noted in the previous chapter, the measure of constraint employed here is a composite score based on three different operationalizations. In order to see whether effects could be observed for the individual rather than the composite measures of constraint, regression equations were estimated for direct and indirect interlocks using each of the three operationalizations discussed earlier (the Galaskiewicz et al., Palmer et al., and Burt measures). The effect of constraint was zero in all but one of the six equations (not shown here). The constraint between the firm's primary industries (the Burt interfirm measure) was a significant positive predictor of indirect interlocks. Since firms within the same primary industry have a positive probability of being indirectly interlocked, this finding could be viewed as consistent with Burt's. But none of the operationalizations of market constraint had an effect on direct interlocking between firms.

The main conclusion to be drawn from the models of stockholding and interlocking relations is that although two of the three variables are significant predictors of similarity of political behavior, none appears to interpret the effects of the other exogenous variables on similarity. In other words, constraint does not affect similarity through its effect on interlocks. Rather, its effect, as well as that of interlocking, is direct. Although the null effect of constraint on interlocking is not consistent with the traditional resource dependence model, the findings on the direct effects of constraint and interlocking on similarity of behavior support both the social network model and the synthesis of the organizational and the class models presented in Chapter 4.

Ideology and Party Preference

Previous work by sociologists (including myself) using PAC data to examine corporate political unity has operationalized unity primarily in terms of contributions by firms to the same candidates. Contributions to the same candidates, however, may not be the only means by which unity is expressed. Interfirm unity may also manifest itself in contributions to similar *types* of candidates. A major reason for this is that firms with similar interests may choose to focus on a limited number of races. For example, a New York–based firm that supports Republican conservatives may decide to contribute to candidates from the Northeast, while a California-based firm with the same focus may contribute primarily to candidates from the West Coast. Members of two industries, both of whom support moderate Democrats, might contribute primarily to members of committees that serve the interests of their particular industries. In both cases, firms with similar ideological positions and/or party preferences would nevertheless contribute to different candidates. This raises two important questions. First, to what extent do firms that contribute to the same candidates also contribute to candidates of similar ideologies and party affiliations? Second, to what extent do the factors that determine contributions to the same candidates also determine contributions to similar types of candidates? To examine this issue, I turn to an analysis of the extent to which pairs of firms contribute to candidates of similar ideology and party affiliation.

Background

As far back as the classic works by Lazarsfeld, Berelson, and Gaudet (1944) and Lazarsfeld and Merton (1954), as well as those by Hunter (1953) and Mills (1956), sociologists have argued that high levels of social interaction are a source of similar attitudes and worldviews. This view has been used to argue that, by virtue of their common social backgrounds, common attendance at elite prep schools and colleges, intermarriage, and common social club memberships, elites in advanced capitalist societies come to share similar attitudes (what Lazarsfeld and Merton called "homophily"). Although the literature on this topic is vast (Perrucci and Pilisuk, 1970; Useem, 1978; 1984; Moore, 1979; Barton, 1980; 1985; Moore and Alba, 1982; Domhoff, 1983; and Whitt and Mizruchi, 1986 for recent applications), evidence that common interaction within the elite is a source of similar attitudes is far from solid.

Because many campaign contributions are given to particular individuals who appear important for the firm's interests regardless of their ideologies, the ideological pattern of a firm's contribution patterns is unlikely to be a perfect reflection of the firm's ideological position. This is especially true for firms that follow what Handler and Mulkern (1982) call "pragmatic" strategies, which generally involve giving to incumbents regardless of party or ideology. Chrysler, for example, made more than 68 percent of its contributions to Democrats in general and more than 53 percent to Democrats classified below as either liberal or pro-labor. Few observers have suggested that Chrysler's management was ideologically liberal. One could argue, however, that it was prudent politics for the firm to contribute to those who had assisted in the firm's bailout.

Operationalization of Similarity of Ideology and Party

The data set for the ideology and party variables again comes from the list of contributions to congressional candidates in the 1980 elections. In this case, because of the necessity of coding data on a candidate's ideological positions, only candidates who ran in general elections were examined.[9] Each such candidate was coded into one of seven categories based on party affiliation and descriptions of ideology provided in the *Almanac of American Politics* (Barone and Ujifusa, 1982). For incumbents, ratings from interest groups (primarily the Americans For Democratic Action and the Committee on Political Education of the AFL-CIO) on prior votes were also used. In the case of newly elected or recently defeated candidates, earlier and later volumes of the *Almanac* were examined. Initial coding was performed by graduate students and was checked and amended, if necessary, by the author. Trial codings by the three students revealed inter-rater reliabilities of at least .9. A list of the codings for all candidates is presented in Table A.2.

The seven categories were liberal Democrat, conservative Democrat, labor Democrat, moderate Democrat, moderate Republican, moderate-to-conservative Republican, and conservative Republican. Labor Democrats were defined as candidates who have strong pro-labor records but who score in the moderate range on measures of liberalism. These candidates tend to be liberal on economic issues and conservative on social and foreign policy issues. Examples are Richard Gephardt and Dan Rostenkowski. Moderate Democrats are candidates whose liberalism scores tend to approximate those of labor Democrats but who do not have strong pro-labor records. These tend to be moderate Southerners such as Dale Bumpers and Ernest Hollings. Moderate-conservative Republicans are Republicans who, unlike those such as Lowell Weicker and Charles Mathias, cannot be considered liberals but who oppose New Right policies on at least one important issue. Such candidates included Mary Buchanan, Gary Hart's 1980 senatorial race opponent, who was a supporter of the Equal Rights Amendment. A breakdown of proportions of candidates of various classifications receiving contributions from each firm is presented in Table A.1. As is evident from the table, nearly 57 percent of

---

[9] Seven incumbents who received contributions and for whom ideology data were available were defeated in primaries during 1980. These individuals were also excluded from the analysis. Because of their small number, however, their exclusion had a negligible effect on the findings.

the candidates who received contributions from the average firm were conservative Republicans; 21 percent were liberal, labor, or moderate Democrats.[10] Also listed are the bases of the two main dependent variables: proportions of contributions going to Democrats and a political ideology score, which consists of a mean based on the following assignments for each category: liberal Democrats, 7; labor Democrats, 6; moderate Democrats, 5; moderate Republicans, 4; moderate-conservative Republicans, 3; conservative Democrats, 2; and conservative Republicans, 1.[11] Eleven of the 57 firms made more than half of their contributions to Democrats, led by Chrysler at 68 percent and Philip Morris at 62 percent. Five firms made more than 90 percent of their contributions to Republicans, led by Dart and Kraft, J. P. Stevens, and National Gypsum, all at over 93 percent. Chrysler was also the most "liberal" firm, with a score of 4.585 followed by E G & G at 4.184. Blue Bell was the most conservative firm, with a score of 1.167.

For each dyad, I computed a difference score (in absolute values) for the proportion of contributions going to Democrats and Republicans and a difference score for contribution ideology. For example, Armco Steel made 11.5 percent of its contributions to Democrats while Springs Mills made 40.5 percent of its contributions to Democrats. The difference was 0.290. Armco's ideology score was 1.787 while Springs Mills' score was 2.081. The difference was 0.294. The difference scores of both variables were moderately right-skewed so they were transformed to logarithms. I added one to the value of each difference score prior to the transformation so that the lowest possible difference score would be equal to zero.

In certain cases, the value of a dependent variable computed as a difference score may be determined partly by the original values of the

[10] The percentages listed in Table A.1 are the proportion of candidates of each classification who received contributions from the firm regardless of the size of the contribution. I have treated the act of giving as more important than the size of the gift, which, as Neustadtl and Clawson (1988, p. 176) have pointed out, may depend on the firm's resources. Overall, the means weighted by the number of contributions by each firm are virtually the same as the unweighted means presented at the bottom of Table A.1.

[11] The values assigned to these categories constitute an ordinal scale with 7 as most liberal and 1 as most conservative. Moderate-conservative Republicans were coded as less conservative than conservative Democrats based on their generally higher scores on the Americans for Democratic Action liberalism index. Although, as a mean of an ordinal variable, the ideology score undoubtedly contains some measurement error, I view it as a reasonable approximation of the degree to which a firm contributed to liberals.

scores. For example, if school officials want to study the effects of a special program on children's test scores, the level of improvement for each child is likely to depend partly on the child's initial score. The ideology and party difference scores used here, however, should be scale invariant, since firms that made high proportions of their contributions to Democrats simultaneously made low proportions of contributions to Republicans. Therefore, there was no need to control for each firm's ideology score or tendency to contribute to members of a particular party. Trial analyses with these controls yielded results that were substantively identical to those presented below.

Results

Correlations between the ideology and party variables and each of the exogenous variables in the model are presented in Table 6.1. Table 6.4 presents the results of three regression equations with quadratic assignment probabilities. The models are the same as those in Table 6.2. Because the dependent variables were difference scores while our interest is in behavioral similarity, a negative coefficient indicates a positive association with similarity of behavior (except for capital intensity, which is itself a difference score). In other words, the dependent variable in Table 6.4 is the logarithm of the difference in the firms' ideology scores.

The similarity of ideological and party contributions were correlated .347 and .378 respectively with contributions to the same candidates. It is hardly surprising that firms that contribute to the same candidates are more likely to contribute to candidates of the same ideology and party. Interestingly, however, more than 80 percent of the variation in the latter two variables is unaccounted for by the former. This finding suggests that similarity of ideological and party preference are clearly distinct from preference for the same candidates. It also suggests that although the model presented above is able to predict contributions to the same candidates, its ability to predict similarity of ideological and party contributions is in no way a foregone conclusion. This suggestion is borne out in the findings in Table 6.4. In the analysis of contributions to the same candidates, four of the first six exogenous variables were significantly and positively associated with the extent of common contributions. The present findings are considerably weaker than those based on common contributions.

In Equation 1, only one of the variables that was a significant pre-

Table 6.4. Determinants of similarity of ideological contributions

Independent variable	(1)	(2)	(3)
Constant	0.527 (.221)	0.533 (.271)	0.549 (.382)
Proximity	-0.081[b] (.039)	-0.084[b] (.036)	-0.077[b] (.046)
Same primary industry	-0.002 (.479)	-0.003 (.470)	0.008 (.402)
Common industries	–	-0.027 (.349)	-0.020 (.422)
Market constraint	-0.013 (.223)	-0.010 (.285)	-0.008 (.326)
Common stockholders	0.050 (.093)	0.053 (.080)	0.057 (.054)
Direct interlocks	-0.038 (.190)	-0.038 (.197)	-0.037 (.179)
Indirect interlocks	-0.042[b] (.044)	-0.041[a] (.057)	-0.033 (.108)
Asymmetry	0.002 (.922)	–	–
Constraint*asymmetry	0.012 (.392)	–	–
Capital intensity	–	–	0.043 (.216)
Regulated industries	–	–	-0.061 (.181)
Defense contracts	–	–	0.074 (.185)
R^2	.026	.024	.033

a. $p < .10$
b. $p < .05$

Note: OLS estimates with QAP probabilities. All probabilities are one-tailed except for those involving asymmetry, which are two-tailed. N = 1596 in all equations. Metric coefficients are reported, with quadratic assignment probabilities in parentheses. Because the dependent variable is a difference score, a negative coefficient indicates a positive association with similarity of political behavior (except for capital intensity).

dictor of contributions to the same candidates (indirect interlocking) was also a significant predictor of ideological similarity. A second variable, geographic proximity of headquarters, which approached significance as a predictor of contributions to the same candidates, was significantly associated with ideological similarity. Membership in the same primary industry has no association with ideological similarity, despite the fact that members of the same industries are likely to contribute to the same candidates. The same holds true for market constraint relations (although the coefficient for market constraint is in the expected direction). Moreover, firms whose stock is owned by the same financial institutions are no more likely to contribute to candidates with similar ideologies than are firms without common stockowners, despite the fact that common stock ownership is significantly associated with contributions to the same candidates. In fact, there is a slight tendency for firms with common stockholders to contribute to candidates with different ideologies.[12]

Interpretation of the coefficients in this analysis is complicated by the logarithmic transformation of the dependent variable. One consequence of this transformation is that the effects of the independent variables on the actual, non-logged, difference scores are not linear (equal at each level). For our Bethlehem Steel-Monsanto example, a one-unit increase in indirect interlocks lowered the log of the difference score by .042. This translates to a predicted decline in the actual difference score of .078, from .889 to .811 (as noted above, a value of one was added to each difference score prior to calculating the logarithm). The decline in the difference score for Bethlehem Steel and Monsanto predicted by headquarters location in the same state was .147. The model as a whole, however, barely improves on chance prediction.

Equation 2 presents the same model with the asymmetry variables omitted and with the standardized number of common industries included. The latter variable is associated with similarity of ideological contributions but the coefficient is not statistically significant. All of the other coefficients in the model remain unaffected (although the probability of the indirect interlocks coefficient rises above .05). Equation 3 includes all of the variables from Equation 2 plus the political-economic variables (similar levels of capital intensity, common interests in regulation, and common interests in defense contracts). None of these three variables is significantly associated with similarity of ideological contributions and two of the three (capital intensity and defense contracts) are in the opposite-of-expected direction. The effect of headquarters proximity remains significant but that of indirect interlocking rises above .10. Overall, the predictive strength of these models is very small.

---

[12] This coefficient is not designated as "significant" in the table because the tests in these equations are one-tailed and the coefficient is in the opposite-of-hypothesized direction.

The fact that firms in the same industries, those with market constraint relations, and those with common stockholders are likely to give to the same individuals but are not likely to contribute to those with similar ideologies suggests that the effects of these variables on common contributions operate primarily in a pragmatic manner (Handler and Mulkern, 1982). In other words, firms appear to contribute to the same candidates because they share interests, either initially or as a result of network ties, that are represented by those *individuals*, but these shared interests cannot be easily expressed by substituting a contribution to another candidate with a similar ideology. This interpretation holds, although to a lesser extent, for the effect of indirect interlocking. Although this effect is statistically significant in two of the three equations, it is smaller than the corresponding effects on contributions to the same candidates. The effects of direct interlocks and the asymmetry variables are also virtually zero. Only headquarters proximity has a stronger effect on similarity of ideology than on contributions to the same candidates and this difference is relatively small.

The findings in Table 6.5, in which contributions to members of the same party is the dependent variable, are similar to those in Table 6.4. The only two variables that are significant predictors of similarity of party contributions in all three equations are headquarters proximity and indirect interlocking. The probability level of production in several common industries drops below .10 in Equation 2 but rises above this level when the political-economic variables are controlled (Equation 3). As with ideological similarity, none of the political-economic variables is a significant predictor of similar party contributions.[13]

Discussion

Interestingly, although common headquarter location was not significantly associated with contributions to the same candidates in the QAP analysis, it was a significant predictor of both common ideolog-

[13] The capital intensity effect, despite its low probability, is not statistically significant because of its opposite-from-hypothesized sign in the one-tailed hypothesis. In an earlier analysis in which similarity of ideology and party contributions were dependent variables (Mizruchi, 1990a), findings based on LSDV models revealed that the concentration of the two firms' primary industries was a strong predictor of both variables. Concentration had no effect on either variable in the quadratic assignment analyses. This issue is discussed in the chapter Appendix.

Table 6.5. Determinants of similarity of party contributions

Independent variable	(1)	(2)	(3)
Constant	0.168 (.458)	0.174 (.368)	0.181 (.175)
Proximity	-0.021[a] (.075)	-0.022[a] (.061)	-0.019[a] (.075)
Same primary industry	0.000 (.448)	0.010 (.248)	0.006 (.341)
Common industries	-	-0.028[a] (.094)	-0.021 (.185)
Market constraint	-0.002 (.341)	-0.003 (.316)	-0.001 (.453)
Common stockholders	0.007 (.282)	0.007 (.273)	0.009 (.181)
Direct interlocks	-0.003 (.422)	-0.004 (.407)	-0.003 (.405)
Indirect interlocks	-0.015[b] (.017)	-0.014[b] (.017)	-0.011[a] (.069)
Asymmetry	-0.005 (.342)	-	-
Constraint*asymmetry	0.006 (.158)	-	-
Capital intensity	-	-	-0.024 (.060)
Regulated industries	-	-	-0.016 (.192)
Defense contracts	-	-	0.009 (.363)
R^2	.020	.020	.033

a. $p < .10$
b. $p < .05$

Note: OLS estimates with QAP probabilities. All probabilities are one-tailed except for those involving asymmetry, which are two-tailed. N = 1596 in all equations. Metric coefficients are reported, with quadratic assignment probabilities in parentheses. Because the dependent variable is a difference score, a negative coefficient indicates a positive association with similarity of political behavior (except for capital intensity).

ical and party contributions. There are two widely held views that could account for this effect. The first is the argument that there are geographically based coalitions within the business community. One popular version of this argument is the so-called "Yankee-Cowboy" thesis (Sale, 1976), which posits that the business community is organized into two broad factions: the moderate, old wealth–based

"Eastern Establishment," which is usually thought to consist of Northeastern and, to a lesser extent, Midwest-based firms; and the conservative, new wealth–based Sunbelt interests, which are thought to include Southern, Southwestern, Mountain, and California-based firms. In this view, Eastern and Northern firms are more likely to contribute to liberals and moderates and Sunbelt firms are more likely to contribute to conservatives.

The second possible explanation for the finding on geographic proximity is simply that firms are more likely to contribute to candidates representing their own geographic regions. Since candidates of various parties and ideological positions tend to be concentrated in particular regions, firms in close proximity are more likely to contribute to candidates of the same ideology and/or party.

In a study of determinants of contributions to incumbents, Republicans, and New Right-backed candidates, Burris (1987) found that Sunbelt based firms were more likely to contribute to candidates backed by New Right organizations. He interpreted this finding as indicative of support for the Yankee-Cowboy thesis. In a related study, however, Clawson and Neustadtl (1989) argued that since Burris failed to control for the fact that New Right–backed candidates were more likely to be from Sunbelt states, his results might have been spurious.[14]

This is a difficult issue to resolve with data on PAC contributions. The finding that firms with headquarters in the same states are more likely to contribute to candidates with similar ideologies and party affiliations is consistent with either interpretation. There are two findings that call into question the Yankee-Cowboy thesis, however. First, I created a dummy variable for headquarters region (Frostbelt or Sunbelt) based on Burris's classification scheme, with the variable coded 1 if both firms' headquarters were in the same region and 0 if they were in different regions. In a separate coding I classified dyads as 1 if both firms' headquarters locations were in Sunbelt states and 0 if not. In both cases this variable had no effect on the similarity of either ideological or party contributions, regardless of whether the variable for headquarters in the same state was included in the equation. In other words, firms with common headquarters location in Sunbelt or non-Sunbelt states were no more likely to contribute to candidates of

[14] Barton (1985) found that business elites residing in the South and Southwest were more conservative on a series of economic attitude measures, but this effect disappeared when region of birthplace was controlled, and the latter effect was mediated by attendance at elite schools and colleges, membership in national policy-making organizations, and network ties to other economic elites.

similar ideology or party than were firms headquartered in different regions.[15] Second, as we shall see later in this chapter, common headquarter location is actually associated with interfirm opposition (as indicated by contributions to opposing candidates in the same race) as well as with similarity. This finding also suggests that Sunbelt firms contribute to more conservatives because there are more conservative candidates in Sunbelt states.

In line with the findings on contributions to the same candidates, direct interlocks between two manufacturing firms were not associated with common ideological or party contributions. Firms that were directly interlocked were no more likely than non-interlocked firms to contribute to candidates of the same party or similar ideologies. However, also consistent with the findings on contributions to the same candidates, the frequency of indirect interlocks through financial institutions was positively related to the similarity of both ideology and party contributions.

Although the finding on indirect interlocks is consistent with the structural equivalence–similarity argument discussed above in relation to contributions to the same candidates, the absence of a significant industry effect on ideological and party similarity is not consistent with it. The fact that firms in the same primary industry or in several common industries are no more likely than others to support members of the same party or ideology must be regarded as surprising. This finding may also reflect the general tendency of firms to contribute based on pragmatic rather than ideological grounds. Because pragmatic contributions are focused on the candidate rather than the candidate's party or ideology, there is no inherent tendency for the contributions by firms within an industry net of their contributions to the same people to exhibit any particular ideological or party pattern.

Summary of Findings on Ideological and Party Similarity

Studies of network relations and homophily within the business community have yielded mixed results. On the one hand, several studies

[15] A dummy variable for common headquarters location in either Sunbelt or Frostbelt states was positively associated with contributions to the same candidates (when inserted into the equations in Table 6.2), even when location in the same state was controlled. However, even this finding does not demonstrate the tenability of the Yankee-Cowboy thesis since it may reflect a tendency to contribute to candidates in geographically proximate states as well as the same state.

(Useem, 1978; Barton, 1985; Whitt and Mizruchi, 1986; Burris, 1987) have failed to provide clear evidence that network centrality is positively associated with greater liberalism. On the other hand, Clawson and Neustadtl (1989) found that highly interlocked firms were more likely to contribute to Democrats and moderates and Koenig and Gogel (1981) found that highly interlocked firms were more likely to contribute to Richard Nixon's 1972 reelection campaign. The results presented here provide one possible explanation for this discrepancy. I found no relation between direct interlock ties and ideological or party similarity, but I did find a positive relation between indirect interlock ties through financial institutions and party similarity and a nearly significant effect on ideological similarity. This is consistent with the findings based on contributions to the same candidates. It suggests the possibility that similar political preferences can be forged through common social relations with financial institutions (Mintz and Schwartz, 1985). In network terms, firms in structurally equivalent positions with respect to financial institutions are more likely to contribute to members of the same party, even when geographic and industry similarity are controlled.

As noted above, the fact that the model predicts contributions to the same candidates more strongly than it predicts contributions to candidates of particular ideologies or party affiliations suggests that a candidate's ideology and party may be less important to a firm than his or her committee assignments or the region he or she represents. Thus, the findings presented here, combined with those based on contributions to the same candidates, suggest that PAC contributions cannot be relied upon as a valid indicator of the worldviews of corporate elites. Organizational and social network factors affect the extent to which firms contribute to particular candidates but they play a much smaller role in predicting general ideological similarities between firms.

It would be a mistake to view this as a negative finding, however. For those interested in the topic of corporate political power, the crucial variable is not what corporate officials believe (or say they believe) but rather what they do. This is especially important given the repeated finding of low levels of variation in attitudes among corporate elites. Although these high levels of agreement may reflect a genuine absence of interfirm (or interindustry) conflict, researchers would be hard-pressed to defend this conclusion in the absence of reliable data on corporate behavior. A focus on behavior independent of ideology may thus provide a more relevant indicator of the role of corporations in contemporary political life.

Opposition

Interestingly, although social scientists have focused considerable attention on the extent to which the business community is unified, few studies have systematically examined the determinants of corporate conflict. That is, under what conditions do corporations compete head-to-head over particular issues? Most of this work, including my own, has operated under the assumption that the absence of unity is equivalent to (or not analytically distinct from) conflict.[16]

In their analysis of unity and opposition in congressional races, Clawson, Neustadtl, and Bearden (1986) noted an interesting paradox. Political scientists specializing in business political behavior had argued that business was not unified because firms engaged in two very different strategies toward campaign contributions, termed by Handler and Mulkern (1982) "pragmatic" and "ideological." Although Clawson et al. found a considerable amount of variation in the extent to which particular firms engaged in pragmatic versus ideological strategies, they found that corporations rarely engaged in direct conflict in particular congressional races. In 73 percent of the 461 U.S. congressional races in 1980, more than ninety percent of the business contributions went to the same candidate. In only 6.9 percent of the races did fewer than two-thirds of the business contributions go to a single candidate. In other words, although corporations engaged in different strategies, they rarely engaged in opposing ones. This is consistent with Whitt's (1982) finding that corporations tend to avoid direct political conflict. Do corporations that contribute to the same candidates also avoid contributions to opposing ones? Are the variables that predict contributions to the same candidates negatively associated with contributions to opposing ones? In this section I examine these questions.

We have already paid considerable attention (in Chapter 5) to the question of the validity of campaign contributions as a measure of business unity. To what extent can these contributions be used to identify cleavages within business? As we have seen, firms may contribute to the same candidates for several reasons, only some of which

[16] Laumann and his colleagues (see, for example, Laumann and Marsden, 1979 and Laumann and Knoke, 1987, especially chapter 12) have devoted considerable attention to the sources of political conflict. Their focus, however, has been on a broad range of organizations, of which corporations are only a subset. Not surprisingly, most of the conflict they observe takes place across organizational types (for example, business versus labor) rather than within them.

are indicative of shared views or interests. In fact, two firms with *opposing* interests might both contribute to the same candidate in an attempt to gain access to him or her. It is necessary to reiterate, however, that regardless of the motives that underlie particular contributions, the objective consequences of the common contributions are the same (see Chapter 3). Therefore, the extent of common contributions is an interesting issue in its own right, even if it is not necessarily indicative of an ideological or interest-based consensus.

But what of contributions to opposing candidates? Can these be viewed as expressions of opposing interests or viewpoints? First, although many social scientists believe that corporate PACs play "both ponies" by contributing to both candidates in an election to ensure that the winner will have received money from them, we have already seen that this practice is no longer widespread (Handler and Mulkern, 1982, p. 84; Rothenberg and Roldan, 1983, p. 10; Sabato, 1984, p. 88). One reason for the rarity of split giving is undoubtedly the easy access to contribution records, which by law must be made available to the public. Whatever the reason, contributions by individual firms to two or more opposing candidates in a race are generally rare (Mizruchi and Koenig, 1986).

To the extent that multiple contributions in particular races exist, they are likely to occur when a firm contributes to a candidate who loses in the primary, as in the example of the attempt, described earlier, to unseat Texas Representative Bob Eckhardt. Firms often subsequently contribute to one of the other candidates in the general election. Multiple contributions of this type within a race are generally considered to be acceptable behavior within the PAC community (Handler and Mulkern, 1982; Sabato, 1984). For this reason, when examining conflict within particular races, it is preferable to focus only on contributions to candidates in the general election, where it is clear that they are running against one another. An examination of the 57 PACs on which this study is based revealed only 81 cases of a firm contributing to two candidates who opposed one another in the general election (about 1.5 percent of all contributions). In most cases, these contributions appeared to be cases in which a firm made an early contribution to an incumbent liberal Democratic senator (for example, Frank Church, Birch Bayh, or John Culver) who was later opposed by a well-financed conservative Republican. One plausible interpretation of this finding is that when the firms that had contributed to the incumbent saw that many other firms were contributing to the challenger and that the latter had a good chance of winning, the former firms decided to also contribute to the challenger. Because cases of split giving exaggerate the extent of opposition, all contributions to opposing candidates by the same firms (81 cases) were removed from the data set.

To return to the original question, to what extent are contributions to opposing candidates in the general election indicative of actual political conflict within the business community? My response to this question is the same as that regarding contributions to the same candidates. Regardless of the motives behind particular contributions, the objective consequences of opposing contributions operate *as if* the firms have opposing interests. The purpose of this analysis, then, is to see whether we can identify the conditions under which firms contribute to opposing candidates.

As noted in Chapter 5, the focus of this study is confined to manufacturing firms. This focus prevents us from examining relations between financial and nonfinancial firms, but it enables us to examine several other possible sources of cleavage, including those between firms with and without military contracts, between heavily regulated and less-regulated firms, and between labor and capital intensive firms.

Measurement of Opposition

In 1980 there were 420 general elections contested by candidates of major parties. As with studies based on contributions to the same candidates, firms that contribute to large numbers of candidates may, *ceteris paribus*, have a greater likelihood of contributing to opposing candidates. In order to base the analysis on a measure that is independent of the number of contributions, I employed a Pearson product-moment correlation coefficient, defined as:

$$O_{ij} = (Ng_o - g_ig_j)/[g_ig_j(N - g_i)(N - g_j)]^{\frac{1}{2}}$$

where O_{ij} equals the measure of opposition, N equals the number of candidates in the general elections (840 in this case), g_o equals the number of contributions to opposing candidates, and g_i and g_j equal the number of contributions made by firms i and j to candidates in the general election (as distinct from c_i and c_j, the number of contributions to all candidates). The expected value of this measure, based on

Table 6.6. Frequency distribution of opposing contributions by dyad (N = 1596)

Opposing contributions	AF[a]	RF	RCF
None	417	26.1	26.1
One	342	21.4	47.6
Two	227	14.2	61.8
Three	177	11.1	72.9
Four	129	8.1	81.0
Five	92	5.8	86.8
Six	52	3.3	90.1
Seven	39	2.4	92.5
Eight	38	2.4	94.9
Nine	17	1.1	96.0
Ten	18	1.1	97.1
Eleven	11	0.7	97.8
Twelve	9	0.6	98.4
Thirteen	9	0.6	99.0
Fourteen	4	0.2	99.2
Fifteen	1	0.1	99.3
Sixteen	4	0.2	99.5
Eighteen to Twenty-seven	10	0.6	100.0

a. AF = absolute frequency; RF = relative frequency; RCF = relative cumulative frequency. RCF may not always equal previous RCF plus RF due to rounding error.

a random assignment of the number of contributions made by each firm, is always zero. Thus, the measure provides a convenient indicator of the extent to which two firms oppose one another more or less than would be expected by chance, given the range of their contributions.[17]

Results

As mentioned above, one of Clawson et al.'s (1986) most important findings was the relative absence of races in which corporate PACs engaged in head-to-head competition. Table 6.6 presents a frequency distribution of the level of interfirm opposition. The results are striking. Although the mean number of common contributions among the 1,596 dyads is 24.1 and the mean Pearson correlation is

[17] This measure of association differs slightly from that employed in the analysis of contributions to the same candidates (see Chapter 5). In the study of contributions to the same candidates, the pool of candidates from which firms may pick is theoretically indeterminate, since there is no limit on the number of candidates who can receive contributions. Because the present analysis of opposing contributions deals only with major party candidates in general elections, the size of the candidate pool is fixed. In this case a Pearson correlation is more appropriate.

.205, the mean number of opposing contributions is only 2.65. The highest opposition correlation is .079 (Champion International and Uniroyal) while the mean is − .072. More than one fourth of the dyads had no opposing contributions, and over 60 percent had two or fewer. Only 92 dyads (5.8 percent) had correlations above zero. Only 12 had scores more than one standard deviation above zero, while 955 had scores more than one standard deviation below zero. Other dyads with relatively high levels of opposition include E G & G and Potlatch (.071), Chrysler and National Gypsum (.062), and Blue Bell and Philip Morris (.058). Dyads with relatively low levels of opposition include General Electric and General Motors (the lowest, at − .312), General Electric and Pepsico (− .284), and LTV and United Technologies (− .283). The dyad with the highest number of opposing contributions (27) was Dow Chemical and LTV. Because of their large number of total contributions (191 and 221 respectively), however, their opposition score of − .150 was actually below the mean.

Despite the highly skewed distribution of the absolute number of opposing contributions, the Pearson correlations closely approximate a normal distribution.[18]

Correlations between opposition and each of the exogenous variables are included in Table 6.1. Table 6.7 presents the results of three multiple regression equations with associated quadratic assignment probabilities. These models contain the same independent variables as those in the previous analyses in this chapter. As with the earlier analyses, the effects of the asymmetry variables were negligible. As a result, they were deleted from the model. In Equation 2, the variable for common multiple industries is inserted. Finally, Equation 3 includes the political conflict variables hypothesized in Chapter 4 to affect the similarity of political behavior. The hypotheses here are that firms that share characteristics on these variables (similar levels of capital intensity, common sources of regulation, and common interests in defense spending) will be less likely to engage in political opposition.

Most of the effects in Equation 1 are in accordance with expectations.[19] Although headquarter proximity is positively associated with

---

[18] Due to the nonparametric nature of the quadratic assignment procedure, a normal distribution of the dependent variable need not be assumed.

[19] Values on the opposition score range from − .312 to .079. Our illustration dyad, Bethlehem Steel and Monsanto, has a score of − .073, which puts them at about the mean. Bethlehem contributed to 92 general election candidates while Monsanto contributed to 78. Three of their contributions were to opposing candidates. Using the model in Equation 1, an increase of one indirect interlock would lower the opposition

contributions to the same candidates, it was noted above that it might also be correlated with contributions to opposing candidates since firms tend to contribute to candidates proximate to their headquarters regardless of party or ideology. This in fact is what the findings reveal. Firms with headquarters in the same state are more likely than other firms to contribute to opposing candidates. Three other variables produce significant effects in the expected direction. The extent to which firms' stock is owned by the same financial institutions is negatively related to opposition, as is the number of indirect interlocks through financials. Direct interlocking is not associated with absence of opposition, but this finding is not surprising given the findings on contributions to the same candidates and those on ideological and party similarity. Market constraint is also negatively associated with opposition, although the probability of the coefficient in Equation 1 slightly exceeds .05. Finally, as hypothesized, neither the asymmetry of constraint nor the constraint*asymmetry interaction term is significantly associated with opposition.

The main surprise in Equation 1 is the fact that membership in the same primary industry is *not* a deterrent to opposition. Moreover, when the standardized number of common industries is inserted into the model (Equation 2), neither variable is a significant predictor of opposition, although both coefficients are in the expected direction. In Equation 3, when common receipt of defense contracts is controlled, the coefficient for same primary industry actually reverses to the opposite-from-expected direction, although not significantly so.

One possible reason for the null effect of the same industry variable might be that members of certain industries are especially politically active. This would suggest that firms that contribute to the same candidates are also more likely to contribute to opposing ones. But a spurious effect of common activism cannot be the reason for this finding, since (1) the dependent variable in the present analysis is

---

index by .0196, to just over −.093. Given the two firms' number of contributions, a decrease of one opposing contribution would lower their opposition score by about .013. This means that the addition of one indirect interlock would be expected to remove between one and two of the three opposing contributions between the two firms. A one-unit change in each of the significant variables in the equation would be expected to drop the Bethlehem-Monsanto opposition score from −.073 to −.128. This would be equivalent to removing all three opposing contributions and adding about ten non-opposing contributions for each firm. Using Equation 3, a one-unit change in each significant variable would be expected to lower the opposition index to −.188 (−.207 with the non-significant variables included). This is equivalent to removing the three opposing contributions and adding about 60 contributions each with no opposition.

Table 6.7. Determinants of corporate political opposition

Independent variables	(1)	(2)	(3)
Constant	-4.678[c] (.004)	-4.563[c] (.005)	-4.158[c] (.008)
Proximity	1.448[b] (.031)	1.403[b] (.026)	1.521[b] (.022)
Same primary industry	-0.534 (.177)	-0.459 (.259)	0.371 (.317)
Common industries	–	-0.138 (.457)	0.198 (.432)
Market constraint	-0.526[a] (.060)	-0.602[b] (.049)	-0.500[a] (.088)
Common stockholders	-1.644[b] (.013)	-1.648[b] (.016)	-1.473[b] (.045)
Direct interlocks	-0.469 (.269)	-0.487 (.237)	-0.691 (.161)
Indirect interlocks	-1.960[d] (.001)	-1.964[d] (.001)	-1.947[d] (.000)
Asymmetry	-0.238 (.578)	–	–
Constraint*asymmetry	0.223 (.433)	–	–
Capital intensity	–	–	-0.644 (.245)
Regulated industries	–	–	-0.063 (.468)
Defense contracts	–	–	-6.073[c] (.002)
R^2	.147	.145	.206

a. $p < .10$
b. $p < .05$
c. $p < .01$
d. $p < .001$

Note: OLS estimates with QAP probabilities. All probabilities are one-tailed except for those involving asymmetry, which are two-tailed. N = 1596 in all equations. Metric coefficients are reported, with quadratic assignment probabilities in parentheses. Coefficients are multiplied by 100.

independent of activism and (2) membership in the same industry is not positively related to opposition; it simply is not strongly negatively related. A more plausible reason is that since members of particular industries compete economically, they at least occasionally oppose one another politically as well. Although such opposition is infrequent, it may occur often enough to dampen the otherwise negative association between common industry membership and contributions to opposing candidates.[20]

The fact that market constraint is negatively associated with opposition is consistent with the findings of Whitt (1982) and others (see, for example, Lieberson, 1971) that firms prefer to avoid conflicts with companies on which they are dependent for purchases or sales. Constraint was also found to be positively associated with contributions to the same candidates. The effect of constraint as a deterrent to conflict actually increases slightly when the number of common industries is controlled (Equation 2). As Whitt's findings suggest, the similar behavior that is generated by constraint may mask an underlying source of tension between members of heavily interdependent industries. In the example from Whitt's study (discussed above), the banks viewed their political interests as conflicting with those of their major customers (the oil companies) but they felt it necessary to go along with the oil companies so as to not upset the delicate balance of dependence. In that example, the banks simply refused to oppose the oil companies, although they did not support them either. In the case of BART, the oil companies actually supported the financial community. Thus, there are three possible responses to situations in which political conflicts of interest exist between firms with market constraint relations. The first is for the firms to actively support the same position. The second is for one firm to support a position and the other to "sit it out," that is, not directly oppose the other. And the third is for direct conflict to ensue. Since it is less risky for a firm to "go along" (options 1 and 2) than to directly oppose a firm on which it is heavily dependent (option 3), it is not surprising that constraint is associated with an absence of opposition.

In the analysis of common contributions presented earlier, I found that direct interlocking was only a marginally significant predictor of similarity but that indirect interlocking through financial institutions was a strong predictor. The same finding appears to hold with regard to opposition. Direct interlocks are not associated with the level of opposition. However, indirect ties through financial institutions are strongly (negatively) associated with opposition. Once again, the Mintz and Schwartz "finance hegemony" argument and the Burt structural equivalence argument receive support.

---

[20] In corporate testimony before Congress, for example, I found thirty-six instances over a twelve-year period in which firms in the same primary industry publicly opposed one another on an issue. See Chapter 7.

Interestingly, although most of the network variables hypothesized to affect political opposition had their expected effects, only one of the political-economic variables behaved in its predicted fashion (see Equation 3 of Table 6.7). The dummy variable for dyads in which both firms received military contracts was negatively associated with opposition.

It should be noted that an earlier analysis (Mizruchi, 1990b), based on an alternative coding of the military contracts variable, revealed a tendency toward opposition in dyads in which both firms have military contracts or both firms do not. In other words, dyads in which one firm has military contracts and the other does not had *lower* levels of opposition, exactly the opposite of what Ferguson and Rogers (1986) and others would expect. Several researchers have found that military contractors are among the most likely firms to contribute to incumbents, who are more likely to be Democrats (Handler and Mulkern, 1982; Herndon, 1982; Eismeier and Pollack, 1984; Maitland and Park, 1985). Whether this represents a clear conflict of interest between military and non-military firms (Lieberson, 1971) or simply a difference in strategy[21] is unclear, but one would expect firms with common interests in defense contracts to oppose one another less frequently than firms without such interests. Why was this not the case in the earlier study? One possibility is that the way in which the variable was coded in that study biased the results against the theoretically expected finding. The dummy variable for defense contracts was coded "0," or "no," if one firm had military contracts and the other did not. Thus, the variable was coded "1," or "yes," if both firms had military contracts or if neither firm had military contracts. As a result, 1,056, or 66 percent, of the dyads were coded as having similar interests in defense spending. On the other hand, only 13 of the 57 firms, accounting for 78 dyads (4.9 percent), received defense contracts in 1980. See Mizruchi (1990b) for the results of this analysis.[22]

The two other political conflict variables, capital versus labor intensity and regulated versus non-regulated industries, were not significantly associated with the level of political opposition. Recoding of the dummy variable for regulated–non-regulated industries similar to that described above for defense contracts did not alter the findings.

[21] Different strategies, of course, could be a result of conflicts of interest.
[22] In that analysis, membership in the same primary industry was a marginally significant predictor of absence of opposition. This variable drops from significance in the present analysis because the coding of defense contracts here subsumes a portion of the variable for membership in the same industry.

And inclusion of a variable for common Sunbelt location also had no effect.

Discussion

Despite the low level of opposition among the 57 firms in the study, the findings on the network variables are strikingly similar to those in the analysis of contributions to the same candidates. The findings suggest that market constraint, common stockholdings by financial institutions, and, especially, indirect interlocks through financials, are associated with low levels of opposition as well as with high levels of similarity. Similar to the findings on contributions to the same candidates, indirect board interlocks through financial institutions were more likely to prevent opposition than were direct interlocks. Unlike the findings on contributions to the same candidates, however, membership in the same primary industry is not significant in lowering opposition; and the number of common industries is unrelated to the level of opposition. Moreover, having headquarters locations in the same state actually increases the level of opposition. This finding is undoubtedly due to the fact that firms tend to contribute to candidates from their geographic region regardless of ideology or party. The findings on same primary industry and common industries are the only ones that were unexpected based on the model presented earlier. As noted above, a possible explanation for the null effect of same industry is the fact that members of particular industries occasionally oppose one another politically as a result of their competition in the market.

Unlike the findings on the network variables, only one of the three political-economic variables behaved as expected. There was no increased likelihood of opposition between regulated and non-regulated firms or between labor and capital intensive firms, even though several theorists have posited such variables as the basis for divisions within the business community. It should be emphasized, however, that the effect of common receipt of military contracts was a strong predictor of the absence of opposition. Moreover, this effect is in some respects similar to a "same industry" effect, since both firms in these dyads are involved in production of equipment used by the military.

Because of the low level of overall opposition that exists, it would be premature to conclude that there is nothing to the cleavage models presented by Ferguson and Rogers (1986) and others (discussed earlier). Consistent with the findings of Whitt (1982) and Clawson et al. (1986), however, even when opposing interests exist, firms appear to avoid direct political conflict. As we saw in Table 6.6, no opposing contributions occurred in more than 26 percent of our dyads and two or fewer occurred in more than 60 percent. Within this context, it is encouraging that we were able to detect the effects of the network variables on the opposition that does exist.

In fact, the absence of situations in which corporations engage in direct political opposition is the most striking finding in this analysis. Even such a seemingly minor act as a contribution to a congressional candidate reveals a relative absence of firms in head-to-head conflict. This conclusion is consistent with the findings of Whitt (1982) and Clawson, Neustadtl, and Bearden (1986) that business tends to avoid overt political conflict.

One possible explanation for this state of affairs is presented by Lieberson (1971). According to Lieberson, the fact that some industries stand to gain, for example, from a decline in military spending, does not mean that it is in their short-term interests to work for such a decline. Instead, it may be more feasible for firms pursue their own direct interests, which often differ but rarely come into conflict. Meanwhile, as Whitt suggests, when conflicts do occur, firms may try to resolve them prior to reaching the political arena because the costs of open political conflict may exceed whatever short-term gains particular firms might achieve. Moreover, because of the high level of interaction at the top levels of the corporate world, the provocation of conflict on one issue may jeopardize future relations. This is consistent with the finding that to the extent that opposition does occur, firms with broadly based social network ties (indirect interlocks) are the least likely to engage in it.

The overall level of conflict is far below the level of similarity and is far below what would be expected by chance. In fact, the frequency of contributions to the same candidates exceeds that of contributions to opposing candidates by a factor of nearly ten. Giddens (1973, p. 171) has argued that "in the United States there is a considerably greater degree of fragmentation, if not necessarily overt conflict, between elite sectors than in most other societies." But this conflict is rare in the electoral arena. If it is as common as some suggest, we shall have to look elsewhere to find it.

This chapter has presented a test of the structural model of corporate political behavior outlined in Chapter 4 using four relational measures of political behavior: contributions to the same candidates, contributions to candidates with similar ideologies, contributions to candidates of the same party, and contributions to opposing candidates. Most of the variables specified in the model were successful in predicting contributions to the same candidates and (negatively) contributions to opposing candidates. These variables include membership in the same primary industry, market constraint relations, common stockholdings, and indirect interlock ties through financial institutions. The effects of these variables remained generally stable even when three important political-economic variables (common object of regulation, common interest in defense contracts, and common levels of capital intensity) were controlled. Except for indirect board interlocks through financial institutions, however, the variables were not successful in predicting contributions to candidates with similar ideologies or members of the same party.

What do these findings contribute to the debate over business unity with which I opened the book? The key point to remember is that whether, or even the extent to which, business is unified is not my question. Clearly, both unity and opposition exist as do differences in focus. My findings indicate that unity is far more prevalent than is opposition. But many firms focus on different areas and therefore have low levels of both unity and opposition.

The existence of variation in the degree of unity as well as the differences in focus among firms could be used as support for a pluralist argument. On the other hand, the high level of unity in relation to opposition and the significant effects of the network variables in contributing to this unity could be taken as support for a class perspective. Pluralists could argue in response that the network variables do not appear to explain a majority of the variation in similarity of behavior among firms. Class theorists could, with equal justification, argue that the observed effects are substantively powerful.

The ability of both perspectives to account for my findings illustrates the problem with the pluralist-unity dichotomy. The advantage of the conditional model that I have proposed is that the focus shifts from global statements about business unity toward identifying variables whose presence affects the level of unity. The findings in this chapter demonstrate the importance of network factors in influencing the extent to which firms contribute to particular candidates. In particular, they are consistent with two key tenets of the model developed in Chapter 4: first, that mediating mechanisms exist that contribute to similar political behavior among firms; second, that firms that share positions in the network (and therefore have similar relations to other firms) are more likely to behave similarly than are firms located in different positions in the network.

The relatively weak findings with regard to ideology and party contributions, however, suggest that these network factors have their primary effect on influencing contributions to specific individuals rather than to certain types of individuals. This finding highlights the importance of pragmatism in the contribution decisions of major corporate PACs, even in the ideologically charged election of 1980. At the same time, the data indicate overwhelmingly that within this pragmatic framework, firms' contribution decisions were influenced by the interfirm networks within which they were embedded.

APPENDIX: LSDV vs. QAP

This appendix deals with the three cases in which the effects of a variable in the quadratic assignment (QAP) analyses presented in this chapter diverge from the effects of the same variable based on least squares with dummy variables (LSDV) models reported in previously published work. The first two include the null effects of geographic proximity and the standardized number of common industries on contributions to the same candidates. The third case deals with the strong LSDV effect of the concentration of the firms' primary industries on similarity of ideological and party contributions. In all three cases, statistically significant findings observed using LSDV models were not reproduced in the QAP models.

Proximity and Common Industries

In a previously reported analysis (Mizruchi, 1989), I found that whether firms' headquarters were located in the same state was strongly and positively associated with their contributions to the same political candidates. This finding was in accord with theoretical expectations. Firms are, *ceteris paribus,* more likely to contribute to local legislators, who may have strong incentives to assist the firms. Furthermore, the CEOs and board members of *Fortune* 500 firms headquartered in the same geographic locale are likely to know one another and to interact socially (Palmer et al., 1986).

The simple effect of common headquarters location on common contribution patterns is strongly significant. The effect becomes nonsignificant when common stockholders and indirect interlocks are inserted into the equation. In Table 6.3, however, geographic proximity is the strongest predictor of both common stockholdings and direct interlocks and it is the second strongest predictor of indirect interlocks (only direct interlocking is stronger). In other words, geographic proximity affects common stockholdings and interlocks, which themselves are predictors of common campaign contributions. This can be demonstrated by a decomposition of the effect of geographic proximity. Of the total correlation between proximity and similarity of contributions (.119), only .049 is contained in the direct path between the two variables. The remainder of the effect is indirect, primarily through common stockholdings and indirect interlocks. In the LSDV model, the effects of common stockholdings and indirect interlocks, although statistically significant, are not as strong as in the QAP model because firms that are heavily involved in common stockholding and interlock relations are themselves more likely to contribute to the same candidates, a factor that is controlled in the LSDV model. Because firms that tend to be geographically proximate to other firms are no more likely to be involved in common contributions than are other firms and because some of the variation accounted for by the network variables in the OLS model is controlled in the LSDV model, the proximity effect actually increases in the LSDV model.

Although membership in the same primary industry is associated with contributions to the same candidates in the QAP models presented here, the standardized number of industries in which both firms operate does not even approach statistical significance. In the LSDV model, both variables were simultaneously significant, despite the fact that the latter is partly defined in terms of the former.[23] In the LSDV model, the insertion of common industries into the equation nullifies the effect of market constraint. In the QAP model, the insertion of common industries has no effect on the constraint coefficient. Which is the more appropriate finding?

In Chapter 5 I noted that the key assumption behind the LSDV model was that an actor's tendency to be involved in particular types of relations must be treated as independent of the actor's network position. In other words, all variation in network variables that is specific to a particular actor must be stripped of substantive content and treated as a control. The use of this procedure (in the LSDV model)

---

[23] Firms in the same primary industry will automatically have a non-zero value on this measure and both will tend to operate in similar secondary industries.

lowered the effects of three of the network variables (market constraint, common stockholdings, and indirect interlocks) from their corresponding OLS coefficients. The use of QAP, however, led to effects for these variables that were similar to their LSDV effects (although the QAP effects accounted for a greater portion of the variation). As with the effect of headquarters location in the same state, the effect of the standardized number of common industries increased considerably in the LSDV analysis. The reason for this increase appears to be that firms that tended to be involved in dyads with high levels of common industries tended to have low correlations between common industries and contributions to the same candidates. Once this firm-specific effect was controlled, a large portion of the high common industries–low contributions to the same candidates covariance was moved into the dummy variable effects. The remaining association between common industries and contributions to the same candidates therefore increased.

Concentration

The concentration of the firms' primary industries has already been included in the analysis (as a partial component of the concept of market constraint). As noted above, its partial effect on contributions to the same candidates is only marginally significant when the variable is added to an equation containing firm size and common Business Roundtable membership. In a previously published analysis of similarity of ideological and party contributions using LSDV (Mizruchi, 1990a), I found a strong association between both variables (similarity of ideology and party) and the concentration of the primary industries in which the firms operated. In the QAP analysis, concentration has no association with either ideological or party similarity. In the LSDV model, the effect of concentration indicates that for particular firms, the more concentrated the industry of the partner in a dyad, the more similar are the ideological and party contribution patterns between the firms. But this finding ignores the extent to which the similarity of behavior between firms is a function of the simultaneous concentration of both. Although industry concentration does not appear to play a role in producing similar political behavior across industries, it might play a role in producing similar political behavior within industries. This issue is examined in Chapter 8.

7 · Business Testimony before Congress: Unity and Conflict

Political campaign contributions have been widely used as a data source on corporate political behavior. But PAC contributions constitute only one aspect of corporate political activity. That this may be a problem is recognized by virtually all of the authors of studies based on PACs.

There are two primary reasons that PAC contributions are, by themselves, insufficient to resolve questions about corporate political unity. First, PAC contributions cover only one arena of politics: support of candidates for public office. But a great deal of corporate political behavior occurs independent of electoral politics.

Second, one of the dangers of focusing exclusively on PAC contributions is that these contributions are gifts presented to particular *individuals*. Therefore, they are not necessarily indicative of support for a particular policy or political position. In fact, as we have seen, many investigations of the behavior of corporate PACs suggest that contributions tend to be primarily pragmatic in origin (Handler and Mulkern, 1982; Clawson et al., 1986). In other words, firms may support particular candidates not out of shared ideology or even a desire to see the candidate elected, but rather because the candidate is likely to win reelection and the firm wants to ensure access to him or her.

Thus, our knowledge of corporate political behavior would be strengthened by an analysis of data based on support of actual political policies. Contributions to legislative propositions that are decided by popular ballot, such as those studied by Whitt (1982), is one source of data. But these data are not widely available and those that are exist primarily at the local level. Another potential source of data is corporate lobbying activities. Many of the largest U.S. corporations have Washington offices that are used for various types of lobbying (Sabato,

1984), and even those that do not have such offices find themselves lobbying for a particular policy at one time or another. Many studies of lobbying have been conducted (for example, Bauer, Pool, and Dexter, [1963] 1972; Esty and Caves, 1983; Laumann and Knoke, 1987; Wright, 1989). Because of these studies' differences in focus, however, it is difficult to identify firms' positions on a set of specific issues. One unique source of publicly available data on corporate political behavior is the testimony of firm representatives before congressional committees. Although considerable effort must be expended to assemble these data in systematic form, they provide an excellent opportunity to decipher the political positions of business.

In this chapter I apply my model to the study of agreement and opposition in firms' testimony before Congress. I examine the effects of organizational and social network factors on the extent to which firms express similar or opposing positions on issues of concern to federal legislators.

Before proceeding, it is important to note that, as with the study of campaign contributions, the analysis of testimony usually requires a focus on the legislative rather than the executive branch of government. This raises the question, presented initially by Mills (1956) and later by O'Connor (1973), of whether such analysis is simply tapping the "middle levels of power." It is certainly true that corporations can disagree on relatively narrow issues discussed in congressional committees while remaining unified on more general issues of concern to the broader business community. A focus on firms' positions on legislative matters should not be taken to imply that every disagreement that appears indicates a serious cleavage within the capitalist class. We saw in Chapter 2, however, that many theorists, both pluralist and Marxist, have argued that the business community is characterized by systematic tendencies toward political conflict. Proponents of these two perspectives have different theoretical purposes for identifying unity and conflict among corporations. But few theorists deny that the phenomena themselves are important. Agreement and disagreement over proposed legislation is one arena in which corporate unity and conflict are likely to manifest themselves.

Corporate Testimony before Congress

Congress regularly holds hearings to gather information from various sectors of the public as it prepares new legislation. Whether a hearing will occur is usually determined by the chair of a House or Senate committee in consultation with a relevant federal agency. Some hearings (such as those on the Iran-Contra affair) are investigatory proceedings in which the committee has subpoena power and organizational representatives testify under oath. In most cases hearings are primarily informational. Typically, congressional committees invite various organizations to send representatives to testify by expressing their opinions or lending technical support. On other occasions, corporations and other groups actively seek representation at the hearing.

All testimony from the hearings is recorded in publicly available documents. In addition, a brief synopsis of each hearing, including a listing of all organizations and individuals who offered testimony, is recorded in the *Congressional Information Services Index*. The analysis in this chapter draws on testimony from all appearances of representatives of the 57 firms from 1980 through 1987. The *Index* was searched to identify hearings in which representatives of the firms appeared. In some cases a representative of a firm testified on behalf of an industry trade association. In order to ensure our ability to distinguish the positions of individual firms, I examined only those cases in which a firm representative testified on behalf of his or her own firm. During the 1980–1987 period, 728 such hearings were identified. All but five of the 57 firms testified in at least one hearing. General Electric and General Motors representatives each appeared at 84 hearings during this period. The average firm appeared 17.5 times. Representatives of two or more of the 57 firms appeared at 150 of these hearings. (Table A.1 contains a listing of the number of appearances made by each of the 57 firms.)

Because my interest throughout this study has been the relations between firms, I followed up in detail only those 150 cases in which two or more of the 57 firms appeared jointly. A team of research assistants and I read the complete testimony of each firm's representative at each hearing. The typical pattern of corporate presence at these hearings involved a representative of the firm, usually a vice-president in charge of a specific operation that was affected by the proposed bill, submitting a written statement for the record. The firm representative then generally summarized the statement and answered questions from members of the committee (representatives or senators).

The issues discussed at hearings reflect the interests of congressional committees at particular points in time. These interests themselves, of course, are likely to reflect areas of concern to the constituents of various committee members. The 150 hearings in which two or more of the 57 firms appeared between 1980 and 1987 spanned 12 Senate committees, 20 House committees, and one joint committee. Virtually all of the hearings could be classified into one or more of eight major issue areas. These were energy (43 hearings), automobile and transportation (35), government regulation and taxes (31), environmental protection (30), industrial health and structure (22), public works and government budget (22), science, technology, and education (22), and foreign trade (18). Other issues included national defense (3), foreign policy (1), and health care (1).

The content of joint appearances was coded based on an intensive examination of the testimony offered by each firm. Corporate positions in joint appearances were divided into three broad categories, labeled *agreement, unrelated,* and *opposition*. The first two categories were originally divided into subcategories, although for the purposes of analysis only general agreement and opposition were employed.[1]

Agreement

Agreement took three forms. The first I called "explicit coordination." These were cases in which the two firms expressed the same view-

---

[1] The issues discussed at hearings vary in their relevance to particular firms, and not all firms for whom an issue is relevant will be invited to testify. Whether a firm is invited to testify may depend on its previously established relations with members of a congressional committee; the frequency with which two firms appear will, other things being equal, affect the frequency with which they support and oppose one another. Because my chief concern is with the positions on public issues taken by firms that appear simultaneously at congressional hearings, the act of public agreement itself is the phenomenon on which I focus. No assumptions are made about the positions of firms that do not appear at particular hearings. Some evidence indicates that the firms that do appear are likely to be those viewed as influential on the issues under discussion (Laumann and Knoke, 1987). In addition, interviews with congressional staff members suggest that organizations' requests to testify are rarely refused. Firms that rarely or never appear at the same hearing may have interests in such different areas that they have little involvement as either allies or opponents. The hearings at which firms testify do not necessarily represent an exhaustive cross-section of issues that unite or divide the business community. It is plausible to assume, however, that firms that consistently agree on issues in their testimony are more likely to be allies in business political conflicts than are firms that consistently oppose one another in their testimony. One finding that strongly supports this notion is the fact that when testimony data from 1975 through 1979 are used to code the dependent variable, the findings are substantively identical to those based on the 1980 through 1987 data, even though hearings from the earlier years touched on different sets of issues. In the section entitled "Frequency of Joint Corporate Testimony," I discuss the ways in which these issues were taken into account in the operationalization of the dependent variable.

point in virtually identical language, strongly suggesting that prior coordination occurred. An example of this involved a case in which representatives of Armco Steel, Bethlehem Steel, and U.S. Steel made a joint statement on their violations of the Clean Air Act which they claimed were brought on by excessive controls by the Occupational Safety and Health Administration. In other cases explicit coordination cannot be demonstrated but the statements were similar enough to raise the possibility that communication between the firms took place.[2] An example of this involved a case in which representatives of Exxon and Mobil argued almost identical positions before the Senate Subcommittee on Energy Regulation and Conservation. The issue addressed at this hearing involved an 1895 Federal Regulatory Commission order to revise regulations on the transportation of natural gas by pipelines. C. M. Harrison, senior vice president of Exxon, and Henry K. Holland, Jr., vice president of production for Mobil, both supported most aspects of the order. Both representatives, in their separate testimonies, strongly objected to a block billing mechanism under study by the Commission. Both argued that this mechanism would reduce badly needed gas reserves, lead to reduced gas exploration and drilling activity, and lock in place outmoded gas prices at below market value. The almost identical nature of these arguments suggests the possibility that prior discussion occurred between the firms.

"Complete agreement" involved cases in which one company representative explicitly pointed out that he or she agreed with testimony given previously by a representative from another company. Such cases may or may not have involved explicit coordination. An example occurred at a 1982 hearing of the House Subcommittee on Oversight and Investigations called to consider the competitive problems of the U.S. steel industry, especially in the area of capital formation and reinvestment. Peter B. Mulloney, a vice president of U.S. Steel, and William L. Hoppe, manager of economic studies in the planning department of Bethlehem Steel, both defended the steel industry's revitalization efforts. Both speakers criticized the government's trade policies and expressed concerns about the impact of European government subsidies, arguing that both policies represented a threat to the U.S. steel industry. At one point in his testimony, Hoppe, in de-

---

[2] Because what I label explicit coordination is not distinguished from other types of agreement in the analysis, it is not necessary to demonstrate the existence of prior communication between firm representatives.

fending the industry's reinvestment policies, referred to Mulloney's testimony, noting that "as Mr. Mulloney has already pointed out, the industry as a whole was already spending more than its generated cash flow to reinvest in the business." At that point Mulloney interrupted Hoppe's testimony and reaffirmed Hoppe's point. Hoppe then noted the appropriateness of Mulloney's remarks when he resumed his testimony.

Another example occurred in 1983 when a Westinghouse representative testified in support of continued funding for the Clinch River Breeder Reactor, arguing that the project, even if not economically competitive, demonstrated the viability of new energy technology. A representative from General Electric, whose testimony followed, stated that the Westinghouse representative had "stolen my lines" and went on to reiterate the need for funding the reactor for essentially the same reason.

The third category I termed "general agreement." These were cases in which two firms expressed the same general position but used different language, or cases in which two firms took the same positions but for different reasons. An example of general agreement occurred at a June, 1980 hearing of the Subcommittee on Oversight and Review of the House Public Works Committee on implementation of the Federal Water Pollution Control Act of 1977. Representatives from Monsanto and Weyerhaeuser both argued that no significant revisions should be made to the 1977 Act. Michael A. Pierle, regulatory management director of water at Monsanto, argued that no amendments were needed because existing technologies had been effective in reducing the disposal of toxic pollutants. He went on to describe the steps that Monsanto had taken to comply with the clean water legislation. Pierle argued against a proposal for frequent compliance monitoring, indicating that it would result in extensive and unnecessary costs to his firm. John S. Larsen, vice president of regulatory affairs at Weyerhaeuser, described the steps that Weyerhaeuser had taken to control waste waters at its ten pulp and paper mills. Larsen concurred with Pierle that the Act should remain essentially as it was. Larsen's emphasis, however, was on the need to evaluate facilities on a case-by-case basis so that unreasonable standards would not be applied to firms already in compliance with the law.

Another example of general agreement occurred at a 1982 House Banking and Finance Committee hearing. Exxon and Texaco representatives both spoke in opposition to a bill designed to provide a series of protections for independent gas station owners against the major oil companies. The Exxon representative spoke in general terms about market freedom and protecting consumers' rights, whereas the Texaco representative spoke more about his firm's behavior, denying that the company had engaged in any anticompetitive activities.

Unrelated

The second category of joint appearance was termed *unrelated*. This took two forms. The first I termed "indifferent." These were cases in which what one firm representative said was of little concern, either positive or negative, to the other. Testimony which for at least one firm was primarily technical in nature was likely to fall into this category. An example occurred at a Senate Finance Subcommittee hearing in April, 1986 on proposals relating to excise taxes. J. Tylee Wilson, chairman and CEO of R. J. Reynolds, argued against a proposal to prohibit deductibility and indexing of excise taxes, claiming that it would have a devastating impact on consumers, suppliers, employees, and the American farmer. In separate testimony, John K. Meagher, vice president of government relations for LTV, spoke in favor of a tax program that taxes imports and subsidizes exports, encourages savings and penalizes consumption, provides relief in the pension area, and subsidizes domestic credit for business expansion as well as foreign industrial expansion. In this and other hearings on tariff legislation, a parade of firm representatives appeared and spoke about the need for tariffs specific to their interests. In most cases these interests did not conflict directly with those of other firms testifying at the hearing.

Other joint appearances that fell under the unrelated category contained the potential for opposition although none was observed. In these cases, firm representatives spoke to different issues that could potentially have led to conflict had Congress chosen to favor one side over the other but for which no evidence of conflict existed. These cases occurred frequently in hearings dealing with appropriations. An example occurred at a March 1983 hearing of the House Subcommittee on Energy and Water Development Appropriations. Robert W. Clark, president of Goodyear Aerospace Corporation, a subsidiary of Goodyear Tire and Rubber, requested support for the continuing construction of the Portsmouth, Ohio, Gas Centrifuge Enrichment Plant facilities and related equipment. Clark argued that the development of technologies for effective uranium enriching services would, by improving the efficiency of uranium usage, reduce U.S. dependence on foreign energy sources, save thousands of jobs, and render further federal subsidies unnecessary. David Kummer, director of fusion energy for McDonnell Douglas, argued that Congress should facilitate the "aggressive development" of fusion technology, suggesting that fusion provided an inexhaustive supply of energy with few environmental repercussions. He also warned of the potential damage to the American position in the domestic and world economy if a foreign nation were to become the first to commercialize fusion.

Another example, at a 1982 Department of Energy authorization hearing, involved a General Electric representative who spoke in support of funding for high temperature gas-cooled nuclear reactors (which they were developing) and a McDonnell-Douglas representative who spoke in support of funding for research on the design and fabrication of hardware for fusion power plants (which they were developing).

In both of these cases, no evidence of actual opposition between the firms was uncovered. To the extent that the available research funds were fixed, however, the potential existed for conflict between the parties, since each firm had a stake in a particular component of funds.

Opposition

The third category of joint appearance was *opposition*. These were cases in which two firms adopted clearly contrary positions. Two examples should illustrate this classification. At a Senate Committee on the Environment and Public Works hearing in June 1981, representatives from the three major auto companies (General Motors, Ford, and Chrysler) spoke in opposition to the implementation of the Clean Air Act, focusing on factors involving motor vehicle emission standards. David S. Potter, vice president of the public affairs group at General Motors, Herbert L. Misch, vice president of environmental and safety engineering at Ford, and John D. Withrow, Jr., vice president of engineering at Chrysler, issued a series of arguments. They spoke in favor of retaining the 1980 carbon monoxide and nitrogen oxide standards, argued against the proposed rule that would have required all automobiles to comply with high altitude emission standards, and argued in favor of providing the EPA with the authority to set heavy-duty engine standards at a more cost-effective level, thus negating the need for catalytic converters in heavy-duty trucks (which they argued would not significantly improve air quality). The auto companies exhibited complete agreement (and possibly explicit coordination) at this hearing. They were opposed by Roger Ackerman, senior vice president of Corning Glass Works, who argued in favor of more stringent clean air standards. (Corning Glass produced the ceramics that were used in the catalytic converter.) Ackerman argued that a rollback of the Clean Air Act would constitute a waste of all the money that had been spent in the development of sophisticated pollution control equipment. Turning back the clock on auto emission controls, he argued, would threaten the environment and, in the long run, the health of the auto industry as well.

In another example, representatives from LTV and American Can spoke in support of federal loan guarantees for the development of synthetic fuels. An Exxon representative spoke against this plan, arguing instead that the government should remove what the firm felt were the already existing disincentives to synthetic fuel development.

In the analyses that follow, the dependent variable was operationalized in terms of the general categories of agreement and opposition.[3]

Frequency of Joint Corporate Testimony

The 1,596 observations in the data set included 97 dyads with one or more cases of agreement on a bill and 31 with one or more cases of opposition. Twenty-two dyads had two or more cases of agreement but only three had two or more cases of opposition. Chrysler, Ford, and General Motors had a total of 68 cases of agreement among them, nearly half as many as the remaining 1,593 dyads combined. Table 7.1 presents a list of the 22 dyads with at least two cases of agreement.

As we saw in the previous chapter, corporations rarely engage in direct political conflict. The results from the analysis of congressional testimony lend further support to this finding. Between 1980 and 1987 the incidence of agreement was nearly four times that of opposition (207 cases versus 56). Interestingly, although they had the highest levels of agreement, the three auto companies were also the firms with the highest amount of opposition, accounting for 28 of the 56 cases of opposition. No other dyad had as many as two cases of opposition. In fact, eight of the 31 dyads in which opposition occurred also contained cases of agreement.

---

[3] The majority of coding decisions were made by graduate research assistants. As a reliability test, we randomly selected 20 hearings, accounting for 39 dyads. The pairs of coders agreed on the general category (agreement, unrelated, opposition) in 37 of 39 sampled dyads. For two dyads, the coders disagreed about whether the case should be coded "unrelated" or "agreement." I classified all ambiguous cases myself.

Table 7.1. Dyads with two or more cases of agreement

Firms	Agreements
Ford- General Motors[a]	31
Chrysler- Ford[a]	23
General Electric- Westinghouse[a]	16
Chrysler- General Motors[a]	14
Rockwell Intl.- Westinghouse	6
Rockwell Intl.- General Electric	5
Exxon- Texaco[a]	4
Bethlehem Steel- U.S. Steel[a]	4
General Electric-United Technologies	3
Burlington Inds.- Champion Intl.	2
Burlington Inds.- Intl. Paper	2
Champion Intl.- Louisiana-Pacific	2
Exxon- Mobil[a]	2
General Electric- General Motors	2
General Electric- McDonnell-Douglas	2
General Motors- U.S. Steel	2
General Motors- Westinghouse	2
Goodyear- Union Carbide	2
Goodyear- U.S. Steel	2
Intl. Paper- Louisiana-Pacific	2
Louisiana-Pacific- Potlatch	2
Monsanto- Union Carbide[a]	2

a. members of same primary industry

Table 7.2 presents a list of the 31 dyads in which opposition occurred. Seven of the 31 dyads contain members of the same primary
industry. Among the eight dyads with cases of agreement as well as
opposition, five were members of the same primary industry, while
among the 23 dyads with no cases of agreement, only two included
members of the same primary industry (Fisher's exact test $p = .006$).

The presence of the three auto company dyads among those with the
highest levels of both opposition and agreement raises the question of
whether agreement and opposition in congressional testimony are
both functions of frequent appearances. In the analyses of PAC contributions I controlled for firms' levels of activism on the ground that
firms that made large numbers of contributions would, by random
chance, tend to contribute to more of the same candidates than would
firms that made few contributions. The unequal distribution of appearances at congressional hearings warrants a similar control. It is difficult to employ correlation coefficients between firm testimony
profiles (as I did with their campaign contributions), however, since
the vast majority of dyads have no instances of agreement or opposition. In fact, the key distinguishing feature of a given dyad is whether
it had any cases of agreement or opposition. Thus, the measures of
agreement and opposition are best treated as dichotomous variables.

If agreement in testimony between firms is simply a consequence of

Table 7.2. Dyads with one or more cases of opposition.

Firms	Opposition
Chrysler- General Motors[a]	14
Ford- General Motors[a]	8
Chrysler- Ford*	6
Bethlehem Steel- U.S. Steel[a]	1
Burlington Inds.- Georgia Pacific	1
Burlington Inds.- National Gypsum	1
Burlington Inds.- Weyerhauser	1
Chrysler- Corning Glass	1
Chrysler- LTV	1
Corning Glass- Ford	1
Corning Glass- General Motors	1
Dart & Kraft- Exxon	1
Dart & Kraft- Mobil	1
Deere- General Electric	1
Dow Chemical- Union Carbide[a]	1
Exxon- General Motors	1
Exxon- Goodyear	1
Exxon- Minnesota Mining & Mfg.	1
Exxon- Sperry	1
Exxon- U.S. Steel	1
General Motors- Mobil	1
Goodyear- Minnesota Mining & Mfg.	1
Goodyear- Mobil	1
International Paper- Weyerhauser[a]	1
LTV- Louisiana-Pacific	1
Minnesota Mining & Mfg.- Mobil	1
Mobil- Georgia Pacific	1
Mobil- National Gypsum	1
Mobil- Sperry	1
Mobil- Texaco[a]	1
Mobil- U.S. Steel	1

a. members of same primary industry

frequent appearances, then the firms with cases of agreement should also display instances of opposition. The correlation between dichotomous variables for agreement and opposition was positive (.116), but it was low enough to suggest that frequent appearances was only a minor component of agreement. One way to handle this problem is to combine agreement and opposition into a single measure. This was done by subtracting the number of cases of opposition between firms from the number of cases of agreement. Dyads with more cases of agreement than opposition were coded 1, those with equal frequencies of agreement and opposition (or with neither of each) were coded 0, and those with more cases of opposition were coded -1. This resulted in a distribution of 92 "agree" dyads and 23 "oppose" dyads, with the remainder coded 0.[4]

---

[4] One alternative is to code the variable 0 if there are any cases of both agreement and opposition. This coding alters the value of only three dyads, however, and yields vir-

Table 7.3. Determinants of agreement in corporate testimony

Independent variable	(1)	(2)	(3)
Constant	-0.733[c] (.003)	-1.229[c] (.002)	1.408[a] (.096)
Proximity	-2.175 (.196)	-2.132 (.205)	-1.784 (.248)
Same primary industry	18.635[d] (.001)	17.367[d] (.001)	16.291[d] (.001)
Common industries	–	3.898 (.152)	1.564 (.331)
Market constraint	2.971[c] (.002)	2.674[c] (.003)	2.234[c] (.010)
Common stockholders	1.996[a] (.093)	1.981[a] (.096)	1.959[a] (.098)
Direct interlocks	7.566[c] (.009)	7.665[c] (.008)	7.826[c] (.006)
Indirect interlocks	3.829[d] (.001)	3.764[c] (.002)	3.384[c] (.005)
Asymmetry	-1.777[a] (.074)	-1.514[a] (.080)	-1.152 (.204)
Constraint*asymmetry	0.220 (.698)	–	–
Capital intensity	–	–	-3.749[b] (.020)
Regulated industries	–	–	0.318 (.401)
Defense contracts	–	–	6.458[a] (.065)
R^2	.062	.063	.069

a. $p < .10$
b. $p < .05$
c. $p < .01$
d. $p < .001$

Note: OLS estimates with QAP probabilities. All probabilities are one-tailed except for those involving asymmetry, which are two-tailed. N=1596 in all equations. Metric coefficients are reported, with quadratic assignment probabilities in parentheses. Coefficients are multipled by 100.

---

tually identical results. Another alternative is to treat agreement as the dependent variable and opposition as a control variable. This also does not affect the findings. Controls for the number of appearances by each firm in the dyad were not significant predictors of the combined measure of agreement, nor did inserting them into the regression equations affect the strength of the other coefficients.

Test of the Model

As a brief recapitulation, recall that the model outlined in Chapter 4 and tested on campaign contribution data in Chapter 6 provides the basis for several hypotheses about the sources of similar political behavior between firms. These include the expectations that the level of economic interdependence (market constraint) between firms and the extent to which the firms share directors will be positively associated with their level of political agreement. In addition, geographic proximity, membership in the same primary and secondary industries, and common ownership of the firms' stock were specified as factors that could provide sources of corporate political agreement. Finally, based on the arguments of several political theorists, common interests in regulation, labor policy, and military spending were also examined as sources of political unity and cleavage.

Means, standard deviations, and correlations among the variables in the analysis are presented in Table 6.1 in the previous chapter. Table 7.3 presents the results of three multiple regression equations (with quadratic assignment probabilities) with the existence of agreement as the dependent variable. Although the dependent variable in this analysis is categorical, quadratic assignment, as a nonparametric test, is an appropriate technique (see Chapter 5). As in the previous chapter, Equation 1 presents a reduced-form model containing the effects of the network variables, headquarters proximity, and membership in the same primary industry but excluding the effect of the standardized number of common industries. Equation 2 is identical to Equation 1 except for the insertion of the standardized number of common industries and the omission of the constraint*asymmetry interaction term, which was not significant in Equation 1. I retained the asymmetry of constraint term here (unlike in Chapter 6) because its effect was significant in Equation 1. Equation 3 presents the full model including the three political-economic variables.

The findings in Equation 1 are consistent with all but two of the hypotheses.[5] Production in the same industry, market constraint re-

---

[5] The coefficients in Table 7.3 describe the proportion of a unit's change in agreement corresponding to a one-unit change in the independent variable. For example, an increase in one direct interlock would increase the probability of agreement over neutrality (a score of zero) by about 7.6 percent. A one-unit change in all of the statistically significant variables in Equation 1 would increase the probability of agreement relative to neutrality by 36.8 percent (39 percent if all variables are included). The figure is 41.9 percent for Equation 3 (46.7 percent if all variables are included). The change in the probability of moving from an oppose to an agree position (−1 to 1 in terms of the

lations, common stock ownership, and both direct and indirect interlocks are significantly and positively associated with agreement,
while the asymmetry of market constraint between firms does not
alter the effect of market constraint on agreement (as indicated by the
null effect of the constraint*asymmetry interaction term). The principal null finding in Equation 1 was the absence of an effect of geographic proximity. But this finding is not surprising since few of the
hearings in which two or more of the 57 firms appeared concerned
issues specific to geographic areas. Contrary to the hypothesis of no
association, the level of asymmetry is negatively related to agreement.
That is, the more equal the constraint relations between two firms,
the higher their level of agreement. Although the substantive basis for
this finding is unclear, it is possibile that coordination of testimony
between firms is facilitated by equal exchange relations. Constraint
and asymmetry are strongly correlated (.370) and, although the simple
correlation between asymmetry and agreement does not differ significantly from zero (− .019), the effect increases sharply when constraint
is controlled and it declines sharply when constraint is removed from
the equation. The effect remains significant when the interaction term
is removed (Equation 2) but it becomes insignificant in the full model
in Equation 3.

The strongest predictor of agreement is membership in the same
primary industry. This corresponds to the expectation, shared by both
pluralists and class theorists, that the largest members of a particular
industry will act collectively to support their common interests. Of
the 97 cases of agreement, 23 involved members of the same primary
industry. Nearly 29 percent of the dyads with the same primary industry had cases of agreement, compared with only 4.9 percent of the
dyads with different primary industries (Yates's chi-square = 71.72, p
< .0001).[6] Even with controls, being in the same primary industry
increased the likelihood of agreement over neutrality by more than 18
percent.

Market constraint is also a positive predictor of agreement. The
greater the level of dependence between the industries in which the

---

agreement index) is one-half of these values (for example, over 20 percent based on
Equation 3).

[6] If we include only the 92 dyads that had more agreement than they had opposition,
the results are the same. Twenty-one of these 92 dyads were members of the same
primary industry, compared with only two of the 23 dyads in which opposition exceeded
agreement. More than 26 percent of the dyads with the same primary industry had
scores of one on agreement, compared with only 4.7 percent of the dyads with different
primary industries (chi-square = 66.183 with 2 d.f., p < .0001).

firms are involved, the more likely the firms are to agree politically. One possible explanation for this finding is that firms tend to vertically integrate into industries by which they are constrained (Chandler, 1962; Williamson, 1975; Burt, 1983a) In other words, firms' behavior should parallel members of constraining industries because both firms are likely to operate establishments in the same secondary industries. As Equation 2 demonstrates, however, the insertion of a control for the number of common industries has virtually no effect on the magnitude of the constraint coefficient. The finding that interfirm market constraint is positively associated with political agreement, then, is consistent with the argument that economic leverage between firms can serve as a source of political unity. The extent to which this finding is a result of similar interests between members of constraining industries or direct influence between them cannot be determined from these data. But if the effect were due simply to similar interests, the insertion of common industries into Equation 2 and the other common interests variables into Equation 3 would be expected to remove the effect of constraint. In both cases, the constraint coefficient remains strongly positive.

One of the most interesting findings in Equations 1 and 2 is the effect of direct interlocks. In the analyses of campaign contributions, direct interlocking was either marginally significant or not significant while indirect interlocking was a significant predictor in virtually all cases. Indirect interlocking remains a strong positive predictor of agreement in this analysis. Interestingly, however, direct interlocking has an equally strong effect. Its coefficient is actually higher than that of indirect interlocks, although its probability level is slightly less strong. In Chapter 6 I interpreted the stronger finding on indirect ties in the context of two theoretical issues. The first was based on the purportedly unique role of financial institutions as an integrating mechanism within the business community (Mintz and Schwartz, 1985). According to Mintz and Schwartz, financial institutions possess disproportionate power within the business world due to their control over capital. This enables members of the financial community to resolve economic conflicts between sectors of business based on what the former believe are the best interests of business as a whole. In this argument, the boards of financial institutions become arenas in which the general interests of business are discussed and conflicts are resolved. It would follow that firms that share director ties with the same financial institutions would take similar positions on political issues. This argument is also buttressed by the positive effect of common stockholdings by financial institutions, although the effect of this variable is not as strong with regard to congressional testimony as it is for PAC contributions.

The second issue involved the debate among network analysts over the relative importance of structural equivalence versus cohesion as a source of social homogeneity (Friedkin, 1984; Burt, 1987b). Cohesion refers to the existence of strong, intense ties between actors. Structural equivalence refers the existence of actors with identical relations to other members of a social network, regardless of whether they have relations with one another (Lorrain and White, 1971). In a series of articles, Burt (for example, 1987b) has presented evidence to suggest that structural equivalence is a stronger predictor of homogeneity of attitudes and behavior than is cohesion. Friedkin (1984), however, has presented evidence to suggest that cohesion is a stronger predictor. Some of the dispute on this issue is based on interpretation of data rather than on actual empirical discrepancies. Friedkin and others (Kadushin, 1968; Alba and Moore, 1983) have argued that cohesive relations include indirect as well as direct ties. On the other hand, structural equivalence is by definition based on indirect ties since a common tie to the same third party is an indirect tie.

In the previous chapter I suggested that direct interlock ties are representative of cohesive relations and indirect ties are indicative of structural equivalence. We have already reviewed the debate involving Friedkin, Burt, and others about whether two-step ties should be viewed as components of cohesion or structural equivalence. In the findings on campaign contributions, this debate had real consequences for the substantive interpretation of the data. Unlike the findings on campaign contributions, however, the findings on corporate testimony suggest that direct interlocking does correspond with similar political behavior. Thus, even if one views indirect ties as indicative of structural equivalence, the effect of direct ties suggests that cohesion plays a role in common testimony at congressional hearings. The question is why direct ties have a stronger effect on agreement at congressional hearings than they do on common campaign contributions. One possible explanation is that the decision to contribute to a candidate can easily be made without direct consultation with one's peers. The decisions of one's peers can play an important role in one's own decisions (Whitt, 1982; Useem, 1984; Galaskiewicz, 1985) even without the existence of direct communication, although the latter does play a role. In testimony before congressional committees, on the other hand, direct communication is a

174 · The Structure of Corporate Political Action

frequent occurrence. The testimony of representatives from two or more firms often consists of joint statements or is nearly verbatim. In other cases there is virtually no overlap, which raises the possibility that an explicit division of labor was engineered. Firms with direct interlock ties are in a better position to communicate than are firms with indirect ties.

To summarize, the significant positive effects of common stock-holdings by financial institutions and indirect interlocks through banks and insurance companies provide additional support for the Mintz and Schwartz argument, and the finding on indirect interlocks provides support for the argument that structurally equivalent actors are likely to behave similarly. Unlike previous findings based on campaign contributions, however, the effect of direct interlocks is also strongly significant. Thus, although the effect of structural equivalence observed in previous studies continues to hold here, there is little indication that structural equivalence has a greater effect on similarity of behavior than does cohesion.

Equation 2 of Table 7.3 contains all of the predictors from Equation 1 except for the constraint*asymmetry interaction term. In addition, as noted above, the standardized number of common industries is included. The effect of membership in several industries is not statistically significant, although the coefficient is in the expected direction. Moreover, the insertion of this variable has virtually no effect on the strength of the other coefficients. A primary reason for the non-significant effect of common industries is that the variable is partly subsumed by same primary industry (the two have a simple correlation of .358). When same primary industry is removed from the equation (not shown here), the effect of common industries becomes statistically significant.

Equation 3 includes all of the variables from Equation 2 plus the three political-economic variables discussed above. The effects of the variables in Equation 2 remain basically the same except for that of asymmetry of constraint, which drops below statistical significance even at the .10 level. Two of the three political-economic variables, similar levels of capital intensity and common interests in defense contracts, are positively associated with agreement.[7] Both of these findings support Ferguson and Rogers's (1986) argument that firms

---

[7] The negative coefficient of capital intensity supports the hypothesis because the variable is a difference score; that is, firms with similar levels of capital intensity tend to express political agreement.

with similar interests in labor policy and similar levels of dependence on military spending will tend to form political coalitions. The effect of common interests in defense spending would not be surprising since defense contractors tend to be members of the same industry (the simple correlation is .201). But the effect holds even when same industry is controlled and the insertion of defense into the equation has virtually no downward impact on the effect of same primary industry. It should be noted, however, that the effect of defense contracts is only marginally significant, and neither defense contracts nor similar levels of capital intensity are as strong as the effects of market constraint and interlocking.

Common interests in government regulation were not significantly associated with agreement. It is possible that a sizable portion of the variation accounted for by this variable is also subsumed in the variables for same primary industries and common industries. To examine this, I recomputed Equation 3 with same primary industry and common industries omitted (not shown here). Because the industry variables are important controls, the effects of the other variables increased. But the effect of common interests in regulation did not approach statistical significance.[8]

The findings in Equation 3 suggest that even when we control for the three political-economic variables, two of which are significant predictors of agreement, the strength of the network variables in predicting interfirm political agreement continues to hold. Using Equation 3, a one-unit increase in the four key network variables (market constraint, common stockholdings, and direct and indirect interlocks) raises the probability of agreement versus neutrality by 15.5 percent.[9]

In this chapter we have extended the analysis of the sources of political agreement and disagreement among large corporations from an

[8] As in the analyses in Chapter 6, I examined the effect of common plant locations and common foreign subsidiaries. As in those analyses, I found no significant association between these variables and testimony agreement.

[9] I suggested in the previous chapter that firm size might be of considerable importance in predicting similar political behavior. As I noted, dyads containing the largest firms tend to have high levels of similarity of campaign contributions. As in Chapter 6, I computed the dyadic firm size by taking the product of the *Fortune* 500 size ranks of each firm (transformed by taking the reciprocal of the square root of this figure). Interestingly, the effect of size was not statistically significant in any of the three equations. Evidently, because both agreement and opposition were positively correlated with size (.179 and .283 respectively), the combined agreement minus opposition measure essentially nullified the impact of size (the simple correlation between size and the combined measure of agreement was a non-significant .028).

analysis of corporate campaign contributions to one based on corporate testimony before congressional committees. The hypotheses developed in Chapter 4, in which firms are expected to behave similarly as a consequence of membership in the same primary industry, market constraint relations, common stock ownership by financial institutions, and direct and indirect interlock ties, were once again confirmed. Hypotheses regarding the role of common interests in regulatory, defense, and labor policy received mixed support. Overall, the key economic and social network variables (market constraint relations between firms, common stock ownership by financial institutions, direct interlock ties between the manufacturing firms, and indirect interlocks through banks and insurance companies) were all significantly associated with agreement in political testimony. In every case, the variables that were associated with contributions to the same congressional candidates in electoral campaigns were also associated with agreement in congressional testimony. The effects of two political-economic variables, similar levels of capital intensity and common interests in defense contracts, were also significant predictors of agreement. But the inclusion of these variables into a multiple regression equation did not alter the effects of the network variables.

Membership in the same primary industry was by far the strongest predictor of joint appearances in support of a particular bill. Although members of the same primary industries also opposed one another on occasion (a total of 36 times between 1975 and 1987), the number of cases of agreement exceeded cases of opposition by a margin of nearly four to one. Except for a large number of instances involving the three large auto companies, cases of direct disagreement at a particular hearing were relatively rare. Not including the auto companies, the ratio of agreement to disagreement was about five to one.

Despite the accordance of the findings with the theoretical model of corporate political behavior presented earlier, an examination of the content of the statements by firm representatives indicates that testimony at congressional hearings is generally focused on specific, often narrow, corporate interests rather than on the broad class interests that constitute the topic of many discussions of business political behavior. This behavior is consistent with what Useem (1984) termed "company rationality," a concern with the specific interests of the firm without regard for the consequences for business as a whole. Issues of a more general nature may be the province of broad, policy-making organizations such as the Business Roundtable and the Committee for Economic Development. The firms whose representatives testified before congressional committees may have invoked the general welfare of the business community or the society as a whole when lobbying for a proposed bill. But such pronouncements were made to bolster claims for a clearly defined set of very specific interests. This raises an important question for researchers of corporate political behavior. Do the findings presented here demonstrate that a company-rational, pragmatic view of the world informs corporate political behavior (a view that might be used as evidence for a pluralist model of political power)? Or is this finding specific to the source of the data? That is, do these corporations appear to be pragmatic because of the nature of the topics addressed at congressional hearings?

These questions may never be definitively answered. It is important to note, however, that the existence of pragmatic, company-rational firms does not necessarily lend exclusive support to a pluralist model of intercorporate relations. The pragmatic interests of firms frequently coincide, and not only among members of the same industries. Moreover, corporations support one another far more often than they oppose one another. In fact, considering that members of the same and related industries compete economically, the extent of their political unity is striking. If large American corporations are not a highly disciplined collectivity that acts as a monolithic bloc, neither are they the amorphous mass of "partly agreed, partly competing, partly simply different groups" of which Dahrendorf (1959, p. 47) wrote. The fact that common stockholdings, market constraint, and interlocking directorates are positively associated with political agreement and negatively associated with opposition suggests once again that in analyzing corporate political behavior, the integrating mechanisms of the business community cannot be ignored.

8 · Differentiation across Industries: Within-Industry Integration and Political Success

The model described in Chapter 4 and tested in the last two chapters has enabled us to predict the extent to which pairs of corporations engaged in similar political behavior. In this chapter the focus shifts. First, I examine the sources of differentiation in the similarity of behavior across industries. Second, using the leading members of the industries as units of analysis, I examine the extent to which similarity of political behavior affects an industry's political success. The focus of the first topic is the issue of industry concentration and political organization. The focus of the second topic is the issue, raised in Chapter 3, of the link between similarity of behavior and power. I begin with a discussion of the role of economic concentration.

Background

In the widely quoted conclusion to his *Politics and Markets*, Charles Lindblom wrote that "[t]he large private corporation fits oddly into democratic theory and vision. Indeed, it does not fit" (1977, p. 356). The concern expressed by Lindblom has a long history in American social and political criticism. Public fear of the large corporation goes back more than a century. During the early 1900s, critics of corporate power warned of the "community of interest" allegedly created by J. P. Morgan and other major financiers (Cochran and Miller, 1961, pp. 196–197). Three decades later, Berle and Means ([1932] 1968) alluded to the unchecked corporate power that they feared might result from the increased concentration of economic assets. More recently, Baran and Sweezy (1966), Herman (1981), Useem (1984), and Jacobs (1988), among others, have argued that concentration leads to increased interfirm cohesion and ultimately to greater corporate power.

Interestingly, the theoretical basis for this argument lies in the two factors identified by Dahl (1958), and discussed in Chapter 3, as necessary for a group to be powerful: a high level of resources and a high level of unity. The largest firms in the most concentrated industries represent a group with considerable resources that is well situated to form organizations to pursue collective goals. To the extent that an industry is concentrated, there will be relatively few actors with these resources. Olson (1965) has suggested that the organization of collective interests will, *ceteris paribus,* pose fewer difficulties for smaller numbers of actors. Similarly, Blau (1977) has argued that cohesion is more easily achieved in smaller groups. The problems of effective collective action among firms due to free rider problems have been well documented. Chandler (1977) and Bowman (1989) provide historical examples of the problems faced by firms both in attempting to organize and in maintaining discipline once the organization was established.[1]

If the arguments by Olson and Blau are correct, then the largest members of concentrated industries should possess a high potential for unity as well as high levels of resources. In the analysis that follows I examine whether firms in highly concentrated industries are more likely to exhibit similar political behavior than are firms in less concentrated industries.

Recent Research on Concentration and Unity

Despite considerable theorizing on the issue of concentration, unity, and power, there has been little systematic empirical analysis. An important recent contribution is by Jacobs (1987; 1988). Using corporate tax rates as an indicator of business power (based on the assumption that the lower one's taxes, the more powerful one is), Jacobs found that corporate tax rates declined as the concentration of corporate assets increased. Because he did not have data on corporate political unity, however, Jacobs was forced to assume that concentration increased the ability of business to operate in a unified fashion.

In an earlier study (Mizruchi and Koenig, 1988), Thomas Koenig and I examined the effects of concentration on corporate political unity.

---

[1] Oliver and Marwell (1988) have argued, contrary to Olson, that collective action is easier to sustain in large groups because large groups tend to have more resources. For groups with equal levels of resources, however, small size should facilitate organization. Note that my argument employs a group's level of resources as well as its potential for unity.

Using similarity of political contributions as our dependent variable, we found that members of more concentrated industries were more likely than other firms to contribute to the same congressional candidates, but that this association disappeared once factors such as the firms' director interlocks and stock ownership patterns were controlled.

That study, however, raised three questions. First, it was based on a sample of only 25 observations. Since many of our variables were strongly correlated, we do not know the extent to which multicollinearity affected our results. Second, one of our findings, that geographic proximity was negatively related to similarity of contribution patterns, was contrary to our expectations and was difficult to explain. Third, we included the four largest firms operating in each industry regardless of the extent of the firm's involvement in that industry. In the present analysis, I draw on the more extensive data set used in Chapters 6 and 7. I also employ a more fully specified model and I focus on the firms' primary as well as secondary industries.

Variables and Hypotheses

Many of the arguments about the effect of concentration on unity are historical in nature. Because the unit of analysis is typically business as a whole, the only source of variation (other than cross-national comparisons, which involve enormous data compatibility problems) is temporal. The argument should hold, however, for specific industries and sectors within the business community as well as for business as a whole. It should also hold for pairs of firms within particular industries. According to the concentration-unity hypothesis, members of highly concentrated industries should behave more similarly than members of more competitive industries.

Among the 1,596 dyads in the data set analyzed in Chapters 6 and 7 were 80 pairs of firms in which both firms operated in the same primary industry in 1980.[2] These 80 dyads were the units of analysis for the examination of cross-industry variation. In this analysis I examine two dependent variables, common campaign contributions and agreement in congressional testimony. Common contributions sim-

---

[2] Three firms in each of 19 industries would produce 57 within-industry dyads. Because I employed more than three firms in a few industries, the number of within-industry dyads exceeds 57. See Chapter 5 for discussion of the sampling procedure and Table A.1 for a list of each firm's primary industry.

ilarity is operationalized using the same measure as that reported in Chapter 6: Specifically, similarity is defined as:

$$S_{ij} = n_{ij}/(n_i n_j)^{\frac{1}{2}}$$

where S_{ij} equals similarity, n_{ij} equals the number of contributions in common, and n_i and n_j equal the number of contributions made by firms i and j respectively. As noted in Chapter 5, this measure provides an indicator of behavioral similarity that is independent of the number of contributions by each firm. Agreement in testimony is operationalized, as in Chapter 7, as an ordinal variable, coded 1 if the firms in the dyad had more instances of agreement than opposition, -1 if the reverse was true, and 0 if the number of instances of agreement and opposition were equal (including no cases of either).

Based on the above discussion, the key independent variable is the concentration of the industry in which the firms' primary production takes place. I employed the four-firm concentration ratio in 1977 for the two-digit (major) industry in which the firms' primary production took place, according to *Fortune*. The primary hypothesis of this chapter is that *the higher the concentration of the firms' primary industries, the higher their similarity of political behavior.*

Most of the remaining variables in the analysis are those, discussed in Chapter 4, that will potentially affect similar political behavior. Given the different substantive focus of this chapter, they are included here primarily as control variables. The control variables include geographic proximity, common secondary industries, the level of market constraint between the firms' secondary industries, indirect interlocks (direct ties between members of the same industry are illegal), common stock ownership by financial institutions, and combined firm size (operationalized as the negative of the geometric mean of the firms' *Fortune* 500 rank).

Theoretically, the role of size is similar to that of concentration, although size is a clearer indicator of a firm's resources. Nevertheless, the inclusion of size here may be substantively redundant. Because of this, I shall present the equations both with and without size. This analysis also provides an opportunity to follow up on the finding (described in Chapter 6) that common membership in the Business Roundtable is associated with similarity of political behavior.

Statistical Model

In Chapter 5 I discussed several statistical approaches for the handling of dyadic data. Quadratic assignment was the preferred method. That technique, however, is best suited for situations in which an entire square matrix is examined. In the analysis here, I focus on only the 80 cells of the upper triangle of the matrix that contain members of the same primary industry. Because the number of observations is small, however, it is possible to employ the iterative residual regression (IRR) approach, in which the network autocorrelation is estimated directly, for the analyses in which similarity of contribution patterns is the dependent variable.

Readers who are interested in the details of the IRR approach are referred to Chapter 5. To recap briefly, IRR involves solving the matrix equation $Y - \rho WY = (X - \rho WX)B + v$, where ρ is an autocorrelation parameter, W is an $N \times N$ matrix of overlaps among the observations, v is an $N \times 1$ vector of randomly distributed error terms, and Y and X are standard OLS terms. The W matrix employed here was created by constructing an 80×80 matrix and coding, for each pair of dyads, the number of firms in common. This produced a binary matrix in which all dyad pairs that overlap particular firms contain a one and all independent dyad pairs contain zeros. See Chapter 5 for further explanation.

Dow et al.'s simulation results suggest that at levels of ρ below the .4 to .5 range, OLS estimates are no more biased and inefficient than IRR estimates. At levels in the .2 to .3 range, OLS estimates appear to be generally sound. In the data analyzed here, the estimates of ρ were in the .25 to .3 range with common contributions as the dependent variable. Thus, the equations in which similarity of contribution patterns is the dependent variable are based on OLS estimates. Because the categorical nature of the variable for agreement in testimony violates the assumptions of OLS regression, logistic regression analyses were performed in equations involving testimony agreement as the dependent variable. To examine the network autocorrelation in equations with testimony agreement as the dependent variable, IRR analyses were employed to estimate ρ. The estimate of ρ in these equations was virtually zero (.04), indicating that autocorrelation was not a problem.

Results: Campaign Contributions

Table 8.1 presents means, standard deviations, and correlations among the variables. All of the exogenous variables are positively associated with similarity of campaign contributions, and all except stockholding are statistically significant.

Table 8.1. Means, standard deviations, and correlations among variables
(N = 80)

Variable	Mean	SD	2	3	4	5	6	7	8	9	10
1. Similarity of behavior	.273	.140	420	432	367	112	378	423	259	648	251
2. Proximity	.175	.382		284	385	071	177	372	-081	270	115
3. Common industries	.519	.161			299	149	146	309	-085	292	015
4. Market constraint[a]	.477	1.684				154	004	235	-101	279	246
5. Common stockholders[b]	1.288	.636					108	230	034	238	040
6. Indirect interlocks	.413	.791						340	090	304	270
7. Business Roundtable	.525	.503							099	536	158
8. Concentration	.449	.173								414	213
9. Size	-115.4	105.9									213
10. Testimony agreement	.238	.484									

a. Factor scores drawn from larger data set
b. In logarithms (base e)

Table 8.2 presents the results of two regression equations. Equation 1 contains the fully specified model with the exception of firm size. Equation 2 is identical to Equation 1 except that size is included. Interpretation of the coefficients is the same as in the analysis of similarity of contributions in Chapter 6. A one-unit increase in concentration increases the number of common contributions by about 23 candidates for a dyad with average numbers of total contributions (about 100 each). Since the range of concentration is less than one (from .198 in the printing and publishing industry to .898 in tobacco), the predicted difference in common contributions between dyads in these two industries is 16.2 in Equation 1 and 6.8 in Equation 2.[3] An increase of one indirect interlock produces an increase of 4.3 common contributions for an average dyad. In Equation 1, all but one of the variables that had statistically significant simple correlations with similarity of campaign contributions had significant partial effects as well, although the relative strength of the predictors differed in the multiple regression. Common stockholding relations was the only non-significant variable, a finding counter to those in Chapters 6 and 7. Common Business Roundtable membership also failed to reach

---

[3] Similarly, the common industries variable ranges from .224 to 1. The predicted difference in common contributions between these two dyads is 18.1 in Equation 1 and 14.6 in Equation 2.

Table 8.2. Similarity of political behavior within industries: Campaign contributions (Full models-OLS estimates)

Independent variables	(1)	(2)
Constant	0.306 (0.055)	19.019[b] (2.705)
Proximity	7.382[b] (2.070)	6.661[b] (2.037)
Common industries	23.373[c] (2.917)	18.762[c] (2.524)
Market constraint	1.790[b] (2.273)	1.199[a] (1.627)
Common stockholders	-0.812 (-0.423)	-1.597 (-0.903)
Indirect interlocks	4.279[c] (2.674)	3.417[b] (2.306)
Business Roundtable	3.091 (1.113)	-0.890 (-0.324)
Concentration	23.204[d] (3.344)	9.712[a] (1.339)
Size	–	0.055[d] (3.859)
rho	.26	.22
R^2	.490	.578

a. $p < .10$
b. $p < .05$
c. $p < .01$
d. $p < .001$

Note: All probabilities are one-tailed. N = 80 in all equations. Metric coefficients are reported, with T statistics in parentheses. Coefficients are multiplied by 100.

statistical significance in Equation 1, despite its strong bivariate association with similarity. Still, the effect remained in a positive direction (the effect of this variable will be discussed in detail below). Geographic proximity, which was positively but not significantly associated with similarity of campaign contributions in Chapter 6, was a significant predictor of similarity of contributions in this analysis.

Two main findings emerge from Equation 1. First, in accordance with the primary hypothesis, concentration is strongly associated with similarity of political behavior. In fact, it is the strongest predictor in the equation. Second, with the exception of common stockholdings, all of the variables that were significant predictors of similar behavior in the entire sample are also significant predictors among members of the same industry. Even among members of the same primary industries, firms that have indirect interlock ties are more likely to contribute to the same candidates. In addition, members of the same primary industries whose headquarters are within the same state, those that operate in similar secondary industries, and those that operate in secondary industries among which market constraint relations exist, are also likely to contribute to the same candidates.

As I have already noted, substantively, firm size is expected to play a role similar to that of industry concentration in that the heads of the largest firms are likely to be members of what Useem calls the "inner circle." Industry concentration and mean firm size have a simple correlation of .414. Mean firm size is entered into the model in Equation 2. This has three main consequences. First, size becomes the strongest predictor in the model (its insertion adds nearly nine percent to the explained variance). Second, the effects of both market constraint and (especially) concentration decline considerably. Both variables remain statistically significant only if a .10 probability level is employed. The coefficient for concentration declines from .232 in Equation 1 to .097 in Equation 2.[4] Third, the effects of common stock ownership and Business Roundtable membership, although not significant in Equation 1, move even farther from their predicted state. The effects of the other variables remain basically the same, although common industries and indirect interlocking do decline somewhat.

To what extent do the effects of concentration and size indicate the presence of an "inner circle" effect? This question is especially relevant considering the null finding on Business Roundtable membership, perhaps the most obvious indicator of common inner circle status. Interestingly, the process by which Business Roundtable membership moves from its strong bivariate effect to its near-zero partial effect appears to be quite consistent with the inner circle thesis, especially if one recognizes that our indicators are appropriately viewed as proxies for this concept. This can be illustrated by the equations in Table 8.3. Equation 1 includes the full model with three variables

---

[4] In the analysis in Chapter 6, size was measured by the negative of the reciprocal of the product of the two firms' *Fortune* 500 ranks, while in this analysis size was measured as the negative of the geometric mean of the firms' ranks. The latter was employed here because the former measure was potentially collinear with market constraint (the two were correlated more than .8 among the 80 same primary industry dyads). It also produced more conservative results. When the reciprocal measure of size is employed, the effect of concentration is far stronger than that of size. The T statistic for concentration is 2.650 ($p = .005$), while that for size is only 1.587 ($p = .058$).

Table 8.3. Effects of Business Roundtable membership on similarity of campaign contributions with various controls (OLS estimates)

Independent variable	(1)	(2)	(3)
Constant	10.986[b] (2.198)	-0.487 (-0.084)	11.248[b] (2.344)
Proximity	7.263[b] (1.844)	8.243[b] (2.229)	6.384[b] (1.683)
Common industries	22.248[c] (2.510)	24.671[c] (2.962)	20.973[c] (2.462)
Market constraint	1.332[a] (1.536)	1.544[b] (1.896)	1.609[b] (1.919)
Common stockholders	-0.425 (-0.199)	-0.602 (-0.301)	-0.661 (-0.323)
Indirect interlocks	–	–	4.616[c] (2.708)
Business Roundtable	6.568[b] (2.236)	5.100[b] (1.831)	4.325[a] (1.472)
Concentration	–	24.374[d] (3.380)	–
rho	.29	.24	.31
R^2	.352	.439	.411

a. $p < .10$
b. $p < .05$
c. $p < .01$
d. $p < .001$

Note: All probabilities are one-tailed. N=80 in all equations. Metric coefficients are reported, with T statistics in parentheses. Coefficients are multiplied by 100.

omitted: indirect interlocking, concentration, and mean size. Each of these three variables could be viewed as an indicator of inner circle status. With none of these variables in the equation, common Roundtable membership is a strongly significant predictor of similarity of political behavior, providing an increase of 6.6 common contributions for an average dyad.

Concentration is inserted into Equation 2. The effect of Roundtable membership declines but it is still statistically significant at the .05 probability level. In Equation 3 indirect interlocking is substituted for concentration. Based on Useem's operationalization (in terms of multiple board seats), the interlocking variable may be a more explicit indicator of inner circle status than is industry concentration. As is evident from a comparison of the effect of Business Roundtable membership in all three equations, the insertion of interlocking plays a major role in nullifying the effect of common Roundtable membership. The effect remains statistically significant only if a .10 probability level is employed. Equation 1 of Table 8.2 includes both concentration and indirect interlocks, and the Roundtable effect drops below statistical significance, although it remains positive. When size is inserted (Equation 2 of Table 8.2), the Roundtable effect drops to virtually zero.

These findings suggest that concentration, indirect interlocking, and size (especially the latter two) may be capturing processes similar to those tapped by common membership on the Business Roundtable. It is important to note that concentration is less closely associated with Roundtable membership than are size and interlocking. This suggests that concentration, more than the other variables, is measuring aspects of the interfirm environment that are independent of previously existing interfirm social and/or political ties. It is also consistent with my earlier argument that a small number of major firms in an industry might facilitate intraindustry political organization. The finding on the importance of concentration in predicting the similarity of political behavior lends support to this claim.

On the other hand, a portion of the interfirm organization effect captured by concentration may also be accounted for by firm size. As shown in Equation 2 of Table 8.2, the effect of concentration declines markedly when size is controlled. In either case, the findings suggest that the largest firms in highly concentrated industries are those most likely to contribute to the same political candidates.

Results: Congressional Testimony

Among the 80 dyads involving members of the same primary industry, only two included situations in which cases of opposition in testimony exceeded agreement. The dyads include 21 cases in which agreement exceeds opposition and 57 cases of equal levels of the two, including zero of both. As a result, the distribution of the agreement variable does not approximate normality. As noted earlier, this indicates that logistic regression is likely to be more reliable than OLS as an estimation technique. In order to compute logistic equations, however, it is necessary to either omit the two "oppose" observations (coded as -1) or to code them as zero. I have coded them as zero here, which leaves us with 21 dyads coded as "1" (agree) and 59 coded as "0" (neutral or disagree). Table 8.4 presents logistic regression models

188 · *The Structure of Corporate Political Action*

Table 8.4. Similarity of political behavior within industries: Corporate testimony (Logistic regression estimates)

Independent variable	(1)	(2)
Constant	-3.241[b] (-2.315)	-2.678[a] (-1.314)
Proximity	0.049 (0.060) (.010)	0.030 (0.036) (.006)
Common industries	0.147 (0.077) (.029)	-0.003 (-0.002) (.001)
Market constraint	0.383[b] (1.733) (.080)	0.366[a] (1.640) (.077)
Common stockholders	0.007 (0.016) (.001)	-0.026 (-0.054) (.005)
Indirect interlocks	0.763[b] (1.859) (.170)	0.734[b] (1.776) (.163)
Business Roundtable	0.321 (0.471) (.067)	0.220 (0.301) (.045)
Concentration	2.850[b] (1.803) (.598)	2.444[e] (1.284) (.541)
Size	–	0.002 (0.370) (.000)
X^2	16.193	16.335
d.f.	7	8

a. $p < .10$
b. $p < .05$
c. $p < .01$
d. $p < .001$
e. $p = .10$

Note: All probabilities are one-tailed. N=80 in all equations. Logit coefficients are reported on the first line, with T statistics in parentheses on the second line. The third line contains, in parentheses, the change in the probability of agreement (dP_a) due to a one-unit increase in the independent variable. See text for details.

with testimony agreement as the dependent variable. These equations contain the same predictors as those in Table 8.2.

Unlike the findings based on campaign contributions (Equation 1 of Table 8.2) the effects of headquarters proximity and common industries in Equation 1 of Table 8.4 are not significant. Both of these findings, however, correspond to those found for testimony agreement in all dyads in Chapter 7. The effects of the other variables in Equation 1 are similar to those in the analysis of campaign contributions.[5] Market constraint, indirect interlocks, and concentration are all significant predictors of agreement. It is difficult to compare the effects on the two dependent variables (campaign contributions and testimony) because of differences in scale, but the effect of concentration on testimony agreement is quite strong. A one-unit increase in concentration increases the probability of agreement by nearly 60 percent. The same increase in concentration in Equation 1 of Table 8.2 increases the predicted number of common contributions by more than 100 percent (from 22 to about 45). Since the maximum difference in concentration between two dyads is .700 (see the previous section), the probability of testimony agreement is about 42 percent higher for the most concentrated industry than for the least concentrated one. A "100-point" increase in concentration (for example, from .500 to .600) increases the probability of agreement by about six percent. An increase in one indirect interlock increases the probability of agreement by 17 percent.

Size is entered into the model in Equation 2. As in the analysis of campaign contributions, the insertion of size leads to a decline in the effect of concentration. In this case, the probability of the concentration coefficient increases to about .10, making it only marginal in terms of statistical significance. The size of the coefficient remains nearly as large, however. A one-unit increase in concentration increases the probability of agreement in Equation 2 by about 54 percent. The probability of agreement is thus about 38 percent higher for the most concentrated industry (tobacco) than for the least concentrated

---

[5] To facilitate interpretation of the effects in the logistic regression equations, I have included a computation for the change in the probability of agreement expected based on a one-unit change in the independent variable (Petersen, 1985). This is computed according to the formula $dP_a = [\exp(L_a)/(1 + \exp(L_a))] - [(\exp(L_o)/(1 + \exp(L_o))]$, where dP_a equals the change in the probability of agreement, L_o equals the logit (the natural logarithm of the odds) of agreement versus neutrality, and L_a equals the logit of agreement based on a one-unit increase in the variable.

one (printing and publishing). A "100-point" (.100) increase in concentration increases the probability of agreement by about 5.4 percent. In contrast, in the analysis of campaign contributions, the inclusion of size in Equation 2 of Table 8.2 drops the proportional increase in campaign contributions for an average dyad from more than 100 percent to about 44 percent (about 9.7 candidates). Size itself has no association with testimony agreement (a finding that echoes that presented in Chapter 7) nor does common Business Roundtable membership. Market constraint and indirect interlocks, however, remain as significant predictors, although the probability level of market constraint in Equation 2 increases to slightly above .05.

Overall, then, the effects of the key variables on agreement in testimony are similar to those on similarity of political contributions. For both similarity of contributions and testimony agreement, once size is controlled, the effect of concentration declines. The decline is considerably greater for similarity of contributions than for testimony agreement but the effect of concentration on the former was initially much higher. Still, the findings in both analyses are consistent with the suggestion that members of concentrated industries are likely to engage in similar political behavior.

Discussion

I began this chapter by raising a fundamental problem of collective action: How can major firms in industries that possess large amounts of resources achieve the unity of behavior that would enable them to exercise effective political power? I hypothesized that industry concentration would facilitate the achievement of similar political behavior among members of an industry. The findings support this hypothesis. Even when we control for the role of common secondary industries, market constraint relations, common stock ownership, director interlocks with the same financial institutions, and common membership on the Business Roundtable, members of concentrated industries are more likely to engage in similar political behavior. Only when size is controlled does the effect of concentration decline significantly and only in the analysis of campaign contributions. Even with size controlled, the effect of concentration on similarity of behavior remains evident.

Thus the first hypothesis of this chapter, whether members of concentrated industries are more likely to engage in similar political behavior than are members of less concentrated industries, is confirmed.

It is time now to see whether industries that behave similarly have higher rates of political success.

Concentration, Similarity of Behavior, and Political Success

In Chapter 3 I argued that a group's power was a function of the extent to which its members engaged in similar behavior. Most of the analyses in this book have examined the determinants of similar behavior. But I have not demonstrated empirically that groups that engage in similar political behavior are in fact more successful in achieving their goals. In this section I examine this hypothesis with data on industry political influence drawn from a study by Esty and Caves (1983).

The Problem of Political Outcomes

Pluralists have emphasized the need for examinations of actual political struggles in order to gauge a group's power. Unfortunately, although Dahl, Polsby, and others have provided explicit criteria for the determination of appropriate political issues, the possibility always remains that powerful elites can prevent issues that they view as fundamentally important from ever reaching the public arena (Bachrach and Baratz, 1962; Crenson, 1971; Lukes, 1974). For example, the debate over socialism versus capitalism has not been a salient political issue in the United States since early in the twentieth century. A pluralist might argue that a reason for this is a lack of public support for socialism. It is equally possible, however, that political and economic elites as well as the mass media have chosen, consciously or unconsciously, to keep this issue off the public agenda. One could argue, then, that the only issues that become public controversies are those that do not challenge the hegemony of societal elites. If so, then a tabulation of success rates across groups would be strongly biased toward making non-elite actors appear more powerful than they actually are.

Although I find this criticism persuasive when applied to comparisons of power among groups, I believe that success rates on public controversies can be a valid indicator of power when applied to a particular group. In other words, if business is more successful in securing or blocking legislation at one time than it is at another time, then it might be accurate to suggest that its power is greater during the former period than it is during the latter. This is admittedly not a perfect assumption. The business community may offer only token resistance to bills that it does not consider especially important. And bills that appear to be anti-business may in fact be supported by key sectors of the community (Kolko, 1963; Weinstein, 1968; Domhoff, 1970).

There is, in addition, a more fundamental issue. In Chapter 3 I argued that the power of a collectivity should be defined independent of the consciousness of its members. A group can be viewed as powerful, I suggested, if the actions of its members in the aggregate have significant objective consequences regardless of the intentions of the actors. Yet the idea of political success assumes the existence of conscious goals: a group can only be successful if its members have a vision of what they want and work, preferably in concert, to achieve it. Is it possible to reconcile these divergent perspectives and at the same time acknowledge the existence of latent power? The answer is a qualified yes. The key is to recognize that legislative success is only one indicator of a larger, multidimensional concept. Ideally, one would hope to be able to measure several different forms of power. As Lukes (1974) has noted, however, there is nothing in a behavioral, goal-oriented measure that guarantees a particular empirical outcome.

A study by Esty and Caves (1983) of industry lobbying activities and political success provides a useful example. The authors attempted to account for variation in political success among industries. Based on a study of thirty-five detailed (four-digit) industries, Esty and Caves searched through the congressional data base between 1976 and 1980 (years proximate to those analyzed in my study) to identify bills that were of concern to particular industries. They created three variables based on the success with which the bills were passed. In addition, from interviews with 150 Washington offices and trade associations tied to the 35 industries, they developed four more variables based on the significance that the industry officials attached to the particular bills.

The authors of the article have generously made their data available to interested parties. I was able to secure the data for all seven measures of political influence from Professor Caves. These measures form the basis of my analysis of political influence.[6] The match be-

---

[6] Earlier in this chapter I noted that corporate tax rates have also been employed as an indicator of business power. Salamon and Siegfried (1977) computed estimated tax rates for 110 industries in 1963. The enormous difficulties involved in attempting to reproduce the Salamon and Siegfried measures on my industries in 1980 (confirmed in a conversation with Professor Siegfried) have persuaded me not to use industry tax rates as an indicator here.

tween Esty and Caves's 35 four-digit industries and my 19 two-digit industries is far from perfect. I was able, however, to extract relevant Esty-Caves influence measures for 15 of my industries, accounting for 70 of my 80 within-industry dyads. In several cases (such as petroleum refining, steel, tires, and cigarettes), the Esty-Caves four-digit industries matched my two-digit industries almost perfectly. In other cases, such as autos (grouped with shipbuilding, aircraft, and tanks in the two-digit aggregated industry), in which the Esty-Caves four-digit industries were more detailed, I averaged the scores for all four-digit industries in their data that corresponded to two-digit industries in mine. It is important to emphasize that this procedure created measurement error that almost certainly increased the probability of Type II error. In other words, the results based on this analysis are likely to err on the side of conservatism.[7]

I employed six of the seven Esty-Caves variables (the seventh variable was virtually identical to the sixth). They were (Esty and Caves, 1983, pp. 27–28, based on quotes and paraphrase):

BILLS—the number of pieces of legislation filed between 1976 and 1980 deemed to affect the industry.

WTBILL—a weighted value of bills, given 4 if the bill was passed by both Houses of Congress, 3 if taken to a floor vote, 2 if a committee vote occurred, and 1 if introduced. This coding was reversed for bills opposed by the industry—3 if never reported out of committee, 2 if voted on by committee but prevented from reaching the floor, 1 if defeated in a floor vote, and 0 if the bill passed.

ZBILL—identical to *WTBILL* except that bills were given a weight of 1 if passed by both Houses of Congress and − 1 if adopted over the industry's opposition.

SCORE—a weighted sum of the number of bills that industry spokespersons viewed as having priority; success was given two points, compromise one, and failure zero.

ZSCORE—weighted sum of number of priorities claimed by the in-

---

[7] My fifteen industries, with corresponding Esty-Caves industries in parentheses, were food (cereal, milk, cookies and crackers, beer, sugar); tobacco (cigarettes); textiles (carpets); lumber and wood products (mobile homes); paper and allied products (paper boxes, stationery); printing and publishing (book publishing); chemicals and allied products (chemicals, plastics, soaps and detergents); petroleum and coal (petroleum refining); rubber and miscellaneous plastics (tires); stone, clay, and glass (gaskets); primary metals (steel, copper refining); fabricated metals (metal cans); machinery, except electrical (machine tools); electric and electronic equipment (semiconductors, vacuum cleaners); and transportation equipment (autos, shipbuilding, aircraft, tanks).

dustry, with a success receiving one point, compromise zero, and failure minus one.

AVE—SCORE divided by the number of priorities claimed by the industry.

Prior to analyzing these data, two statistical issues must be considered. First, the dependent variables in this analysis involve measures of the political effectiveness of an industry. The 70 dyads that include members of the corresponding Esty-Caves industries, however, involve more than one dyad per industry. This was not a problem in the analysis of similarity of political behavior since each dyad had a unique score on this variable regardless of industry. In the Esty-Caves data, each industry has one score for each variable. This means that if one knows the industry of the firms in a dyad, one automatically knows the dyad's influence score. It is therefore difficult to make the case that we have 70 observations, regardless of possible statistical controls. Indeed, attempts to compute the level of network autocorrelation with IRR revealed an excessive amount (nearly 1 in some cases). An alternative is to treat the industry itself (rather than the dyad) as the unit of analysis. This reduces the number of observations from 70 to 15 but it ensures that the observations are independent. To do this, for each variable I computed the mean score among all dyads involving members of that industry. The fact that the analysis is now based on only 15 observations does limit the number of variables that can be examined simultaneously. Despite the small number of observations, the results in general are consistent with theoretical expectations.

The second issue regards the multiple measures of the dependent variable. Table 8.5 presents correlations among the six Esty-Caves indicators for the 15 industries included in the analysis plus the two similarity of political behavior variables. Because five of the six Esty-Caves measures were highly correlated and because I prefer to focus the discussion on substantive issues rather than on detailed differences among particular indicators, I chose to create a composite measure of political influence from the Esty-Caves indicators.[8] To do this I performed a principal components analysis on the correlation matrix

---

[8] Separate analyses were performed using each of the six Esty-Caves indicators as dependent variables. Although some fluctuation did exist among the effects on particular variables, the overall substantive conclusions did not differ from those based on the composite measure.

Table 8.5. Means, standard deviations, and correlations among similarity of behavior and Esty-Caves political influence measures (N = 15)

Variable	Mean	SD	2	3	4	5	6	7	8
1. Similarity of behavior	.318	.107	627	685	-057	387	363	259	602
2. BILLS	55.40	68.65	–	967	155	792	732	657	272
3. WTBILL	54.33	83.20	–	–	001	708	634	535	260
4. ZBILL	.600	2.10	–	–	–	217	269	280	076
5. SCORE	9.27	6.84	–	–	–	–	914	876	248
6. ZSCORE	1.53	3.62	–	–	–	–	–	915	329
7. AVE	.515	.246	–	–	–	–	–	–	203
8. Testimony agreement	.298	.351	–	–	–	–	–	–	–

among those five variables (*ZBILL* was the one excluded variable). The first principal component accounted for about 82 percent of the variation (eigenvalue = 4.099), with loadings distributed as follows: *BILLS* .914, *WTBILL* .845, *SCORE* .951, *ZSCORE* .930, and *AVE* .883. Factor scores for this variable, hereafter referred to as *political influence*, were employed as the dependent variable.

Results

The model examined here is substantively identical to that described in Figure 3.1. To recapitulate, the argument was that power was a function of similarity of behavior, which itself was a function of cohesion and structural equivalence in market and social network relations among firms. Table 8.6 presents simple correlations between the two similarity of political behavior measures, the political influence factor score, and the exogenous variables examined earlier in the chapter.

The correlations between the Esty-Caves political influence measures and the two similarity of political behavior measures are, with one exception, positive. The correlations involving similarity of political contributions are generally stronger than those involving agreement in testimony, however. The political influence factor is correlated .509 with contribution similarity but only .290 with testimony agreement. Because the latter correlation is not statistically

Table 8.6. Means, standard deviations, and correlations among similarity of behavior, political influence, and exogenous variables (N = 15)

Variable	Mean	SD	2	3	4	5	6	7	8	9	10	11
1. Similarity of behavior	.318	.107	432	462	578	472	202	361	424	634	602	509
2. Proximity	.229	.261	–	502	854	-084	-473	122	-281	208	-212	321
3. Common industries	.549	.131	–	–	669	300	018	393	-333	183	-028	156
4. Market constraint[a]	.760	1.84	–	–	–	283	-337	352	-171	330	-034	492
5. Common stockholders[b]	1.29	.636	–	–	–	–	427	381	284	596	408	391
6. Indirect interlocks	.573	.502	–	–	–	–	–	229	381	473	348	001
7. Business Roundtable	.560	.409	–	–	–	–	–	–	-063	586	063	291
8. Concentration	.401	.190	–	–	–	–	–	–	–	455	548	482
9. Size	-95.24	82.08	–	–	–	–	–	–	–	–	313	678
10. Testimony agreement	.298	.351	–	–	–	–	–	–	–	–	–	290
11. Political influence[c]	0.00	1.00	–	–	–	–	–	–	–	–	–	–

a. Factor scores drawn from larger data set
b. In logarithms (base e)
c. Factor scores drawn from present data set

significant with only 13 degrees of freedom, I shall focus my attention on the political contributions variable as a measure of similarity of political behavior.

The first step in the analysis involved an examination of the extent to which variables found to influence similarity of political behavior in previous analyses also do so in this sample of 15 industries. This was not a straightforward task, since the inclusion of multiple variables with so few observations is likely to generate computational problems. I began by including the seven variables employed earlier in this chapter.

As is evident from Table 8.6, all of the exogenous variables are positively associated with similarity of contribution patterns among the 15 industries. Only the coefficient associated with indirect interlocks (.202) is below the level necessary for statistical significance. Many of these variables also have sizable correlations with one another, however. As a consequence, when all eight are combined into a regression equation (Equation 1 of Table 8.7), only industry concentration exhibits a significant positive effect on similarity of behavior.

Table 8.7. Determinants of similarity of political behavior within industries: Industry-level data (OLS estimates)

Independent variable	(1)	(2)	(3)	(4)
Constant	-11.796 (-0.400)	18.570[b] (1.948)	14.914[c] (3.215)	16.620[c] (3.530)
Proximity	25.016 (0.807)	–	–	–
Common industries	24.626 (0.855)	–	–	–
Market constraint	-0.479 (-0.112)	3.967[b] (2.749)	4.380[d] (4.122)	3.912[c] (3.680)
Common stockholders	3.587 (0.526)	–	–	–
Indirect interlocks	2.835 (0.365)	4.704 (0.879)	6.116[a] (1.476)	–
Business Roundtable	4.972 (0.507)	–	–	–
Concentration	35.623[a] (1.892)	22.507[b] (1.849)	24.958[b] (2.389)	30.338[c] (2.957)
Size	-0.014 (-0.193)	0.016 (0.444)	–	–
R^2	.749[e]	.685	.678	.615

a. $p < .10$
b. $p < .05$
c. $p < .01$
d. $p < .001$
e. Equation F is not statistically significant.

Note: All probabilities are one-tailed. $N = 15$ in all equations. Metric coefficients are reported, with T statistics in parentheses. Coefficients are multiplied by 100.

The tolerance levels of all eight variables are very low, however, which raises questions about the reliability of the results.[9]

At this stage, I removed variables one at a time on the basis of two criteria. First, I identified variables whose effects were near zero and whose correlations with the other independent variables played a major role in lowering their tolerance levels. Second, once these variables

[9] Tolerance is a measure of the proportion of variation in a variable that remains to affect the dependent variable once the effects of the other independent variables in the equation have been controlled. The highest tolerance level in Equation 1 of Table 8.7, that for concentration, is only .376 while those for market constraint and geographic proximity are .078 and .073 respectively. By comparison, the tolerance levels of the variables in Equation 2 of Table 8.2 ranged from .926 to .582 and those in Equation 1 of Table 8.2 (with size excluded) ranged from .972 to a low of .791.

were identified, I removed those that met the first set of criteria and that I deemed to be of relatively low substantive significance in this context. Two findings emerged. First, although mean firm size had the strongest bivariate association with similarity of contribution patterns, this variable was not a significant predictor when industry concentration, market constraint, and indirect interlocking were controlled (Equation 2). As shown in Equation 3 of Table 8.7, the latter three variables are all significant predictors of similarity of contribution patterns when examined simultaneously.

The model in Figure 3.1, which provides the basis of this analysis, suggests that various interfirm organizational and social network factors will increase the similarity of behavior among firms which in turn will increase the likelihood of the group's political success. Based on the findings in Equation 3 of Table 8.7, we can present the results of the model in a path diagram. This is done in Figure 8.1. Because the simple correlation of similarity of behavior and the political influence factor is .509, the figure reveals both a strong effect of interfirm organizational and social network factors on similarity of political behavior and a strong effect of similarity of behavior on political success. About 68 percent of the variation in similarity of behavior is accounted for by concentration, market constraint, and indirect interlocking and about 25 percent of the variation in political success is accounted for by similarity of behavior. This indicates that about 17 percent of the variation in political influence is accounted for indirectly by concentration, constraint, and interlocking.

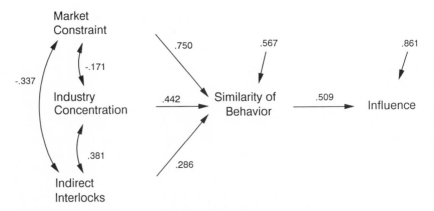

Figure 8.1. Path model of industry political influence

This analysis assumes, however, that the organizational and network variables play no direct role in political influence. Since these variables are expected to affect political influence indirectly, it would be useful to also examine the extent to which they affect it directly. To do this, I inserted concentration, market constraint, and indirect interlocking into an equation along with similarity of political behavior, with political influence as the dependent variable. This is presented in Equation 1 of Table 8.8.

The results are striking. Indirect interlocking, which, interestingly, had a non-significant (near zero) correlation with political influence (Table 8.6) is also not a significant predictor in the multivariate analysis. Concentration and market constraint, on the other hand, are strongly associated with political influence. When these variables are entered as controls, the effect of similarity of campaign contribution patterns on political influence is reduced to zero (the coefficient actually becomes negative, although not significantly so). The revised path model is presented in Figure 8.2.

What is the source of this finding? It is worth remembering that 68 percent of the variation in similarity of political behavior is accounted for by concentration, constraint, and interlocking. Concentration and constraint by themselves account for nearly 62 percent of the varia-

Table 8.8. Determinants of industry political influence (OLS estimates)

Independent variable	(1)	(2)	(3)
Constant	-1.141[a] (-1.599)	-1.729[b] (-2.252)	-1.784[b] (-2.348)
Market constraint	0.411[b] (2.193)	–	–
Indirect interlocks	0.073 (0.147)	-0.462 (-0.911)	–
Concentration	3.640[b] (2.559)	2.143[a] (1.480)	1.703 (1.256)
Similarity of behavior	-2.117 (-0.636)	3.573[a] (1.475)	3.466[a] (1.442)
R^2	.589	.391	.345

a. $p < .10$
b. $p < .05$
c. $p < .01$
d. $p < .001$

Note: All probabilities are one-tailed. N = 15 in all equations. Metric coefficients are reported, with T statistics in parentheses.

tion in similarity of behavior (see Equation 4 of Table 8.7). When these variables are inserted simultaneously into an equation containing similarity of behavior as a predictor, substantial multicollinearity is likely to occur. Indeed, the tolerance level of similarity of behavior in Equation 1 of Table 8.8 is only .321, which represents the variation in this variable that is unaccounted for by the other three. In other words, concentration, constraint, and, to a lesser extent, indirect interlocks are so successful in accounting for the variation in similar political behavior that there is little variation in the latter left with which to account for political influence. As a consequence, it falls on the other variables to explain the latter variable, which, to a considerable extent, they do.

Equation 2 of Table 8.8 illustrates the impact of one of the controls, market constraint, on the effect of similarity of political behavior. With this variable removed from the equation, similarity of political behavior becomes a significant positive predictor of political influence, even with industry concentration and indirect interlocking controlled. The tolerance of similarity of behavior increases to .819 with constraint removed from the equation. The effect of similarity of behavior remains significant when indirect interlocking is removed from the model (Equation 3) but the probability of the concentration coefficient increases to slightly above .10.

Before discussing the theoretical implications of these findings, one final point must be considered. In Chapter 3 I suggested that both cohesion and structural equivalence were sources of similar behavior

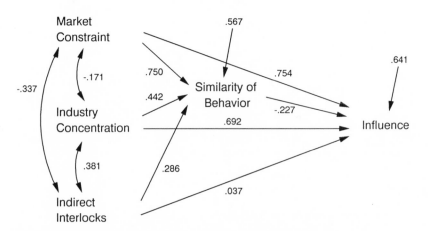

Figure 8.2. Revised path model of industry political influence

among members of a group. I have treated industries as my units of analysis in this chapter. To what extent did this affect whether the variables on which I focused in this chapter are indicative of either cohesion or structural equivalence? Interfirm market constraint, as discussed in Chapter 4 and operationalized in Chapter 5, constitutes a measure of economic interdependence. This concept, I have argued, represents a form of cohesion. Indirect interlocks through financial institutions, I have argued, represent a form of structural equivalence since they are based on a common set of ties to third parties. Industry concentration was not theorized as a form of either cohesion or structural equivalence but rather as a factor that, as with cohesion, could facilitate similar behavior among members of an industry. These variables, imperfect as they are, especially in an analysis with only 15 observations, do provide a rough approximation of measures of cohesion and structural equivalence. But what of the key measure of economic structural equivalence, membership in the same industry? This factor is not a variable in this chapter because primary industries are the units of analysis. But one possible substitute is available: the extent to which members of the same industry are diversified into the same other industries. This variable had a correlation of .462 with contributions to the same candidates among the 15 industries in this analysis. Indeed, common industries were a significant predictor of similarity of political behavior even when concentration and constraint were controlled (not shown here). Because common industries had a correlation with constraint of .669, the inclusion of both variables simultaneously depressed the effect of constraint considerably (its T statistic dropped to 1.882, while that of common industries was 1.625; that of concentration was 3.494). In other equations the substitution of common industries for constraint led to similar, although weaker, results. The high correlation between common industries and market constraint is not surprising, since, as I noted in Chapter 6, firms tend to acquire establishments in industries that exert market constraint over them (Burt, 1983a, pp. 72–74). The finding on common industries suggests that cohesion and structural equivalence are often closely related and may even be interchangeable as indicators in certain circumstances. Those interested in measurement issues surrounding the use of these concepts are referred to the discussion in Chapter 9 (see also Mizruchi, 1990c).

In Chapter 3 I proposed a model of political power in which the power of a collectivity was viewed as a function of similarity of behavior among its members, which in turn was viewed as a function of relations of cohesion and structural equivalence among them. The first part of the model, that similarity of behavior is a function of cohesion and structural equivalence, was relatively straightforward to test. This constituted the primary focus of the discussion in Chapter 4 and the analysis in Chapters 6 and 7 and the first part of this chapter. The second part of the model, that involving political power, is somewhat more elusive.

I have handled the issue first by limiting the type of power I examine to the success of a particular group in achieving its legislative agenda. I employed a measure of political influence based on several indicators proposed by Esty and Caves (1983) that deal with the ability of members of an industry to secure legislation favorable to its interests and to prevent legislation contrary to its interests. Based on an analysis of 15 industries, I found support for the argument that industries whose largest members behave similarly will be more successful politically than will industries whose largest members do not behave similarly. Because nearly 70 percent of the variation in similar behavior was accounted for by three organizational and social network variables, however, two of which were also strongly associated with political influence, similarity of behavior was not a significant predictor of political influence once these three variables were controlled.[10]

This finding does not negate the argument, however. First, for purely statistical reasons, the null effect of similarity of behavior might be a function of the exceedingly small number of observations in this analysis, which left little variation for the variable to explain. Second, and more important, the bivariate association between similarity of behavior and political success still exists. The findings in Figure 8.2 suggest only that a more complex explanation is necessary to account for that association. Similarity of behavior *is* correlated with political

---

[10] This finding has an interesting parallel with Burt's (1983a) analysis of the relations among market constraint, interlocking directorates, and profits. Burt found that industries that were in positions to exercise market constraint over other industries tended to have high profit margins. He also found a positive association between director interlocks and profits. The effect of market constraint on interlocks was so strong, however (establishments tended to interlock with members of industries that exercised market constraint over them), that once market constraint was controlled, the association between interlocks and profits disappeared. In a related study of Canada using the concept of "enterprise groups" developed by Berkowitz et al. (1979), Carrington (1981) found that interlocks played a significant intervening role in the association between concentration and profitability.

influence. Both variables, however, can be explained by the interfirm networks that characterize particular industries. In industries characterized by high levels of concentration, market constraint, and indirect interlocking, the leading firms are more likely to contribute to the same political candidates than are the leading firms in industries characterized by low levels of those three variables. Industries that have high levels of concentration and market constraint are also more likely to be politically influential. This finding provides further support for Jacobs' (1988) argument and evidence that economic concentration is a source of political influence. Although Jacobs suggested that it might be necessary to examine concentration at the level of the economy as a whole in order to identify this association, I have shown that it is possible to reproduce a similar finding based on an examination of variation across industries.

Similarity of political behavior does not necessarily play an independent role in enabling an industry to achieve political influence. But the factors that contribute to similar behavior also appear to contribute to influence, and similar behavior and political influence are highly correlated. Considering the debate over the meaning of political contribution data, the fact that similarity of behavior and influence are so highly correlated gives new and crucial meaning to studies employing campaign contribution data. That a group that has similar political contribution patterns is also likely to be politically influential is a finding of critical importance.

Finally, it is worth noting that the findings in this chapter lend additional support to a crucial aspect of Useem's (1984) inner circle argument. Classwide organization is facilitated, according to Useem (1982, p. 205), "to the extent to which there are relatively few economic actors joined in inclusive and diffusely structured networks . . . [ties that are simultaneously densely connected and wide-ranging]. A small number of corporate units in a network facilitates the evolution of a common culture and organization among those directing corporate activities." The findings presented here suggest that concentration facilitates not only classwide organization but industry organization, and political success as well.

9 · From Dyad to System: Multiple Networks of Organizational and Political Relations

In the previous chapter we moved to the industry level to examine the political influence of industries. But most of the analyses in this book have been conducted at the dyadic level. The dyadic approach has enabled us to identify the sources of unity and conflict between pairs of firms. But do the relations that we have identified between organizational and social networks and corporate political behavior hold at the level of the system as a whole? Can we glean additional information by turning our attention to the network level? This chapter represents an attempt to answer these questions. Using the concept of structural equivalence, I identify clusters of firms within each of several networks. Using the concept of prominence, I compute the centrality of firms in each of several networks. I then analyze two phenomena. First, I examine the extent to which firms that appear in the same positions in interfirm organizational and social networks also appear in the same positions in the political behavior network. That is, do firms that share similar positions in, for example, the network of market constraint relations also share similar positions in the network of similarity of campaign contributions? Second, I examine the extent to which a firm's centrality in interfirm organizational and social networks is associated with its centrality in the political behavior network. In other words, are firms that are in central positions in, for example, the network of interlocking directorates, also in central positions in the network of campaign contributions?

The Network and its Subgroups

Network analysts have spent considerable energy examining the structure of relations among firms. As I noted in Chapter 2, most of these studies have involved interlocking directorates. A major focus has been the extent to which the network is divided into clusters. An earlier work of mine (Mizruchi, 1982) provides an extensive review of these studies, most of which were done in the 1970s.

It was not until a study by Neustadtl and Clawson (1988), however, that an attempt was made to map corporate political groupings in network terms. Using a technique to identify what graph theorists call "maximal complete subgraphs," or groups of actors in which each actor is connected to every other actor (Harary, Norman, and Cartwright, 1965), Neustadtl and Clawson identified a number of "cliques," based on campaign contribution patterns, within a network of 230 firms.

Maximal complete subgraphs are normally derived from what are called "binary" networks, in which each relation between actors is dichotomous (it either exists or it does not). In the study of similarity of firm contribution patterns, however, the vast majority of firm pairs have non-zero similarity scores. That is, most pairs of firms have at least one contribution in common, rendering the use of a binary matrix infeasible. Neustadtl and Clawson handled this problem by computing correlation coefficients between firm contribution patterns, similar to those employed in the present study. They then defined a relation between firms as existent (coded 1) or non-existent (coded 0) on the basis of whether the interfirm correlation coefficient exceeded an arbitrarily defined cutpoint. The authors experimented with three different cutpoints, .6, .5, and .4. They found that as the size of the correlation at which the cutpoint was drawn was relaxed, one large clique of firms emerged, containing about one-half of the firms in their data set. Neustadtl and Clawson found that the firms in this large clique were characterized primarily by their conservatism. Members were less likely than non-members to depend on defense contracts, to operate in regulated industries, and to have direct interlocks with other firms.

Neustadtl and Clawson's pathbreaking study is limited by two factors. The first is the operationalization of the network itself. A contribution to a candidate by two firms is an example of similar behavior but it is not by itself a social relation between the two firms. On the contrary, the extent to which social relations such as interlocking directorates between the firms lead to common contribution patterns is precisely the hypothesis that needs to be examined.

Second, as with the studies of interlocking directorates discussed in

Chapter 2, Neustadtl and Clawson's study focuses on only one network. The relational variables examined in the present study enable us to study the relations among firms in several networks simultaneously. In addition, they enable us to examine the extent to which firms in similar positions in one network are also in similar positions in another network. The analysis that follows is based on these multiple network data.

Mapping the Networks

I begin with a global assessment of the relations among the 57 firms in the sample. Five networks are examined: the "dependent variable" network (similarity of political behavior) and four "independent variable" networks (market constraint, common stock ownership, direct interlocks, and indirect interlocks).

The primary object of this analysis will be to identify groups of firms in what Burt (1982) has called "jointly occupied positions." Joint occupants of a position in a social structure are actors who are roughly structurally equivalent; that is, they have similar relations to the other actors in the system. From there my objective will be to examine the extent to which joint occupancy of a position in the similarity of political behavior network can be predicted from joint occupancy of positions in the remaining four networks. Substantively, this analysis will test the same hypotheses as those tested in Chapters 6 and 7. The difference here is that rather than an exclusive focus on direct relations between pairs in dyads, the variables in this analysis will be derived from firms' positions in the network as a whole.

Neustadtl and Clawson chose to identify cliques using graph-theoretic techniques designed to detect cohesive actors. These techniques generate cliques by searching for maximal complete subgraphs or groups that approximate them (Alba, 1973). I shall identify clusters using techniques designed to detect structurally equivalent actors. In structural equivalence techniques, actors that have similar relations to other actors in the system are placed together into clusters, regardless of whether they have direct relations with one another. My reasons for focusing on structural equivalence as opposed to cohesion as a basis for detecting subgroups are both theoretical and empirical. Theoretically, although contributions to the same candidates could be a consequence of cohesion, there is little basis for defining such contributions as cohesive (a point recognized by Neustadtl and Clawson). There is a basis for defining such contributions in terms of structural equivalence, however, since they indicate common relations to the same actors, in this case political candidates. That is, firms that contribute to the same candidates are structurally equivalent with respect to the pool of candidates. Empirically, Neustadtl and Clawson, in a related cluster analysis based on structural equivalence techniques, found results virtually identical to those found in their cohesion analysis. This conforms to findings and arguments made by Burt (1983b) and myself (1984). Burt argued that techniques based on cohesion could be viewed as a subset of structural equivalence techniques. I argued that because groups of structurally equivalent actors are likely (if not guaranteed) to have direct relations with one another, subgroups identified by the two approaches will tend to be similar.

Operationalization of Structural Equivalence

The decision to employ structural equivalence criteria in a network analysis, however, raises the issue of how structural equivalence is to be operationalized. Structural equivalence has been measured in two primary ways. White, Boorman, and Breiger (1976) correlated the columns of the relation matrix. The higher the correlation coefficient between the columns associated with a pair of actors, the more structurally equivalent they are. For example, two firms that have strong, weak, and null relations to the same other firms will tend to have high correlations. Burt (1982) has employed Euclidean distance as a measure of structural equivalence. The computation of distances involves summing the squared differences between the column entries for each actor. The larger the differences between column entries, the greater the distances between actors. Conversely, the smaller the differences between columns, the "closer" (that is, the more structurally equivalent) are two actors. Two firms with identical relations with other firms would have distances of zero.

Under most conditions, the correlation and Euclidean distance measures should yield similar results. Actors whose column entries are similar should also have small distances and high correlations. Consider the example in Figure 9.1. In this five-person network, actors A and B are friends with C and D but not friends with E or with each other. Following convention, self-relations (in the diagonal of the matrix) are ignored. Notice that the first and second columns of the matrix are identical. Columns A and B have a perfect correlation (1.0) and a Euclidean distance of zero.

The situation in which the correlation and distance measures are

	A	B	C	D	E
A	-	0	1	1	0
B	0	-	1	1	0
C	1	1	-	x	x
D	1	1	x	-	x
E	0	0	x	x	-

An 'x' in a cell indicates that
the size of the relation is not
of interest in this example and
thus is arbitrary.

Figure 9.1. Hypothetical five-actor network

most likely to differ is one in which wide discrepancies exist in the strength of the relations in which the firms are involved (Faust and Romney, 1985).[1] For example, if two firms are both tied and not tied to the same other firms, their column entries will be highly correlated. Using correlation as a measure, they will have a high level of structural equivalence. If firm B has strong relations with the firms with which it is tied (for example, with large numbers of interlocks) while firm A has weaker relations (small numbers of interlocks), then the Euclidean distance between them may be high even if they are tied to the same firms. Using Euclidean distance as a measure, firms A and B will have a low level of structural equivalence. This process is illustrated in Figure 9.2.

In this six-firm network, firms A and B are both tied to C and D (and not to any others) while E is tied only to F. But A's ties to C and D are both of strength 1 while B's ties are of strength 4. Firm E is tied only to firm F (also strength 1). Based on their ties and absence of ties to the same other firms, firms A and B have a perfect (1.0) correlation. By this criterion, they are completely structurally equivalent. Actors A and E, which share not a single tie in common, have a correlation of $-.577$, indicating that they are far from structurally equivalent. Because of the large difference in the strength of their relations with C and D, the standardized Euclidean distance between A and B is 2.121, while the

[1] Both Faust and Romney (1985) and Burt (1988b) have demonstrated that the correlation between two actors is equal to their Euclidean distance controlling for the actors' means and variances (that is, their tendency to be involved in relations and the variation in the strength of the relations).

	A	B	C	D	E	F
A	0	0	1	1	0	0
B	0	0	4	4	0	0
C	1	4	0	0	0	0
D	1	4	0	0	0	0
E	0	0	0	0	0	1
F	0	0	0	0	1	0

Pearson correlation
between A and B: 1.000
between A and E: -.577

Euclidean distance
between A and B: 2.121
between A and E: 0.866

Figure 9.2. Hypothetical six-actor network

distance between A and E is only 0.866. In other words, based on their Euclidean distances, firms A and E are more similar than are firms A and B, even though A and E have not a single tie in common while A and B are tied to the same other firms!

Before we assume that Euclidean distance is a misleading measure, however, it is worthwhile to ask what the difference between A and B means. The fact that B is intensely involved with C and D while A is only casually involved with them may be of considerable importance. If one employs correlation coefficients to measure equivalence, then one assumes that this difference is irrelevant.

Whether one employs correlations or Euclidean distances is an issue that is best decided by the substantive problem being addressed (Burt, 1986). In my analysis, there is no automatic basis for choosing one measure over the other. There is reason to believe, however, that the correlation measure is preferable in this context. The reason has to do with the role of isolates, actors with few ties in the system.

In Burt's (1987b) reanalysis of the Coleman, Katz and Menzel (1966) study of innovation adoption, two physicians who do not adopt tetracycline are viewed as behaving similarly. Since isolated physicians tended not to adopt and since they also tended to be structurally equivalent based on Euclidean distance (because of their zero relations to most other actors), there was a tendency for structurally equivalent actors to behave similarly. With my political contribution data, however, behavior is defined as similar only to the extent that firms contribute to particular candidates. Isolated firms, which tend to be relatively inactive, are less likely to contribute to the same candidates, even though (because of their zero relations to most other actors) they may be structurally equivalent by Euclidean distance criteria.

This suggestion was confirmed in an analysis of the effect of direct interlocks on similarity of campaign contributions (Mizruchi, 1990c). I found that structural equivalence based on Euclidean distance was *negatively* related to similarity of contribution patterns. Structural equivalence based on the correlation measure, however, was, as expected, positively related to similarity of contribution patterns. In the present study I identified clusters based on both correlation and Euclidean distance criteria. The clusters identified by the correlation measures yielded considerably stronger results. The presentation that follows is based on the correlation measure.

The Mechanics of Clustering

Clusters were identified using Burt's network analysis program, STRUCTURE. The program employs a hierarchical clustering routine in which firms are initially grouped together only if they are highly similar. Those of greater distances are then grouped together in successive iterations. The researcher must decide where to draw the boundaries. Input data for the analysis consist of raw matrices of relations among firms on a particular variable. The five separate networks were examined using the correlation measure of structural equivalence.

Firms were placed into clusters on the basis of cluster definition figures and spatial maps. The cluster definition figure provides a description of actors at varying "distances." Firms with high levels of structural equivalence are relatively close together in the figure. For example, Figure 9.3 contains the cluster definition figure for the similarity of political behavior network. Abbreviations of firm names are listed at the top of the figure (see Table A.1 or A.3 for the list of firm names). Euclidean distances standardized by the mean and variance of each firm (to make them inversely related to correlation coefficients) are presented in the left-hand margin.[2] Firms whose modified dis-

---

[2] These distances can be derived from correlation coefficients with the formula $d_{ij} = [2(1 - r_{ij})]^{1/2}$, where d_{ij} equals the modified distance between i and j and r_{ij} equals the correlation coefficient (Burt, 1988b, p. 13). Correlation coefficients can be derived from

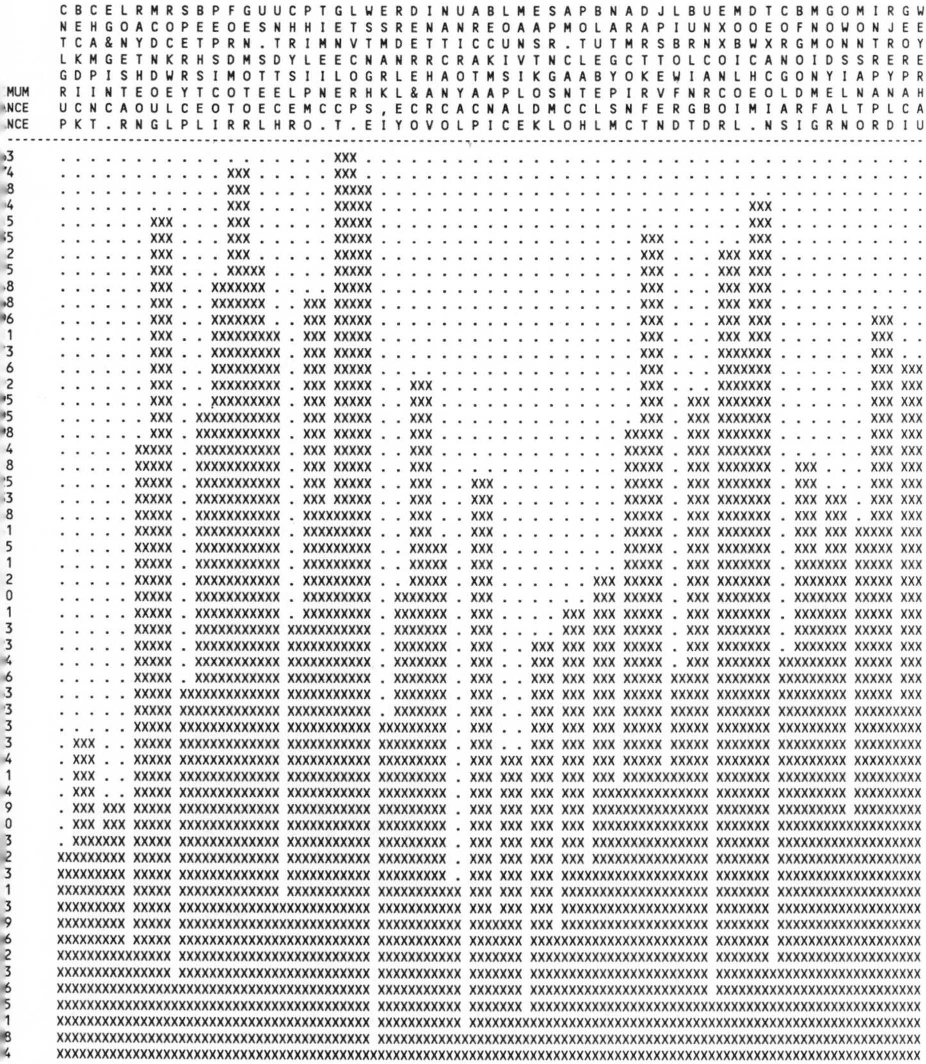

```
      C B C E L R M R S B P F G U U C P T G L W E R D I N U A B L M E S A P B N A D J L B U E M D T C B M G O M I R G W
      N E H G O A C O P E E O E S N H H I E T S S R E N A N R E O A A P M O L A R A P I U N X O O E O F N O W O N J E E
      T C A & N Y D C E T P R N . T R I M N V T M D E T T I C C U N S R . T U T M R S B R N X B W X R G M O N N T R O Y
      L K M G E T N K R H S D M S D Y L E E C N A N R R C R A K I V T N C L E G C T T O L C O I C A N O I D S S R E R E
      G D P I S H D W R S I M O T T S I I L O G R L E H A O T M S I K G A A B Y O K E W I A N L H C G O N Y I A P Y P R
MUM   R I I N T E O E Y T C O T E E L P N E R H K L & A N Y A A P L O S N T E P I R V F N R C O E O L D M E L N A N A H
NCE   U C N C A O U L C E O T O E C E M C C P S , E C R C A C N A L D M C C L S N F E R G B O I M I A R F A L T P L C A
NCE   P K T . R N G L P L I R R L H R O . T . E I Y O V O L P I C E K L O H L M C T N D T D R L . N S I G R N O R D I U
```

Figure 9.3. Similarity of political behavior network cluster definition figure

tances are less than this value are grouped together. At the most similar level, listed in the first row, only General Electric and LTV form a cluster. A second cluster containing Ford and General Motors emerges in the second row. As we move to less stringent levels of

the modified distance scores by the formula $r_{ij} = 1 - d_{ij}/2$. For those interested in Burt's article, note that in his equation for this latter computation, the parentheses are misplaced.

inclusion, increasing numbers of firms are grouped into the same clusters. By the last row, all firms are grouped together into a single cluster. A decision must be made about the appropriate level to define the clusters. A choice that is too restrictive (as in the top rows of the figure) may provide little information beyond that derived from consideration of each firm individually. A choice that is too inclusive (as in the bottom rows of the figure) leads to clusters with an unacceptable level of internal variation. Ideally, we would like to include as many firms as possible within a cluster while at the same time maintaining a high degree of similarity among the group's members. To do this, I attempted to maximize simultaneously the number of firms and the "reliability" of each cluster. Reliability was computed based on the proportion of variation accounted for by the first principal component of the matrix of identified firms. It is a measure of the similarity of the firms in the cluster. Table A.3 lists the membership of all 57 firms in each of the five networks. All clusters in the five networks can be reproduced from this table.

Figure 9.4 presents a two-dimensional spatial map of the political contributions network, derived with the multidimensional scaling routine in SYSTAT. The stress coefficient is .135, indicating that the map provides a good fit with the data.

The political contributions network was divided into five clusters. These are outlined on the spatial map in Figure 9.4. The shape of the figure suggests that the political contribution network is characterized by a core-periphery structure with a fairly dense concentration of firms in the center and more widely spaced firms in the outer areas. The clusters are distinct in that they do not overlap on the spatial map. On the other hand, there is no evidence of clearly discrete groups. Firms that appear very close together on the map are not necessarily in the same cluster. This indicates the absence of oppositional groups in the system.

The members of each of the five clusters in the similarity of political behavior network are listed in Table 9.1. The network is dominated by one group with 21 members. This group includes the three auto companies, three military aircraft firms (McDonnell-Douglas, Rockwell International, and United Technologies), the three electrical equipment firms (General Electric, Raytheon, and Westinghouse), the two tobacco companies (R. J. Reynolds and Philip Morris), two instruments firms (Becton Dickinson and E G & G), and individual representatives of several other industries. This cluster appears to be

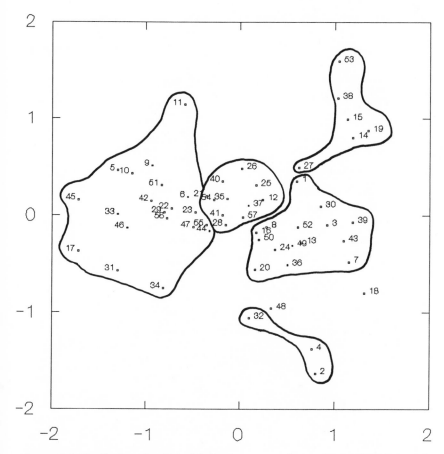

Figure 9.4. Similarity of political behavior network two-dimensional spatial map

heavily dominated by defense contractors. Of the 13 firms with known defense contracts in 1980, ten were members of this cluster. Only one-fourth of the non-defense firms (11 out of 44) were members of this group (chi-square = 11.63 with 1 d.f., $p < .001$).

The second largest similarity of political behavior cluster consists of 15 members. This group includes the three oil companies and two members from several industries including textiles (Burlington Industries and J. P. Stevens), lumber and wood products (Georgia-Pacific and Potlatch), chemicals (Dow and Union Carbide), and stone, clay, and glass (Libbey-Owens-Ford and National Gypsum). But other members of these four industries are not in this cluster. The third group (with

Table 9.1. Clusters of firms with similar political behavior

Group 1: reliability = .782[a]	*Group 4*: reliability = .723
Deere R. R. Donnelley Esmark International Harvester National Can Uniroyal	American Can Armco Blue Bell Burlington Industries Dart & Kraft Dow Chemical Exxon Georgia-Pacific
Group 2: reliability = .762	Libbey-Owens-Ford Mobil
Beckton, Dickinson & Co. Bethlehem Steel Champion International Chrysler The Continental Group EG & G Ford General Electric General Motors LTV Lone Star Industries McDonnell-Douglas Manville Philip Morris R. J. Reynolds Raytheon Rockwell International Sperry Time, Inc. United Technologies Westinghouse	National Gypsum Potlach J. P. Stevens Texaco Union Carbide *Group 5*: reliability = .811 Arcata Beckman Instruments Louisiana-Pacific Isolates: Eastman Kodak Springs Mills
Group 3: reliability = .776	
Corning Glass B.F. Goodrich Goodyear Tire & Rubber International Paper Minnesota Mining & Manufacturing Monsanto Owens-Illinois Pepsico United States Steel Weyerhaeuser	

a. Reliability equals the proportion of variation in relations among firms in the cluster accounted for by the first principal component.

ten members) includes three paper and allied products firms, two rubber companies, Goodyear and Goodrich (but not Uniroyal), and Corning Glass and Owens-Illinois (but not the other stone, clay, and glass firms). The final two groups contain only Deere and International Harvester as members of the same industry. In short, although distinct groups do exist, there is little, beyond certain industry clustering, that is immediately apparent about them.

This finding, based on just one of the five networks for which cluster analyses were conducted, illustrates the need for a theoretical foundation with which to make sense of the data. To reiterate, my concern here is not with the specific firms that behave similarly, but rather with the extent to which the structure of interfirm relations on similar political behavior can be accounted for by the structure of interfirm organizational and social relations. This issue is examined in the following section.

Relations Among Relations

The analysis involved an attempt to predict common cluster membership in the similarity of political behavior network on the basis of common cluster membership in the market constraint, common stockholding, and direct and indirect interlock networks. For each network, a binary firm-by-firm (57 × 57) matrix was created with the cell entries defined as one if the firms were members of the same group and zero if they were not. Because the matrices are symmetric, it was necessary to employ only one-half of the off-diagonal elements, that is, the 1,596 firm-to-firm relations. This process led to the creation of five dichotomous, dyadic variables, one for each of the five networks. The analyses were conducted using quadratic assignment.[3]

In addition to the four independent network variables, controls for common headquarters location, membership in the same primary industry, and common membership in the same industries (primary and/ or secondary) were included. Network analyses were not conducted on these variables because the variables already represented clusters by definition. For example, a cluster analysis of an interfirm common industry matrix would cluster firms together when they were members of the same industry. The same holds for common headquarters location. The network of market constraint relations will also tend to cluster firms together based on participation in the same industries, since members of the same industries are by definition subject to the same market constraint forces. Not surprisingly, therefore, common group position in the market constraint network is strongly (although not perfectly) correlated with common industry membership.

---

[3] As noted in Chapter 5, because it is a nonparametric technique, quadratic assignment may proceed without any assumptions about the distribution of the dependent variable. The presence of a dichotomous dependent variable thus poses no problems for the analysis.

Table 9.2 presents means, standard deviations, and correlations for the variables in the analysis, including several of the dyadic measures employed in previous chapters. The correlations between the common positions variables and their dyadic counterparts, although strongly positive, are far from perfect. They range from a low of .271 for direct interlocks to a high of .495 for indirect interlocks.

Table 9.3 presents the results of three multiple regression equations with quadratic assignment probabilities. Equation 1 contains common group membership in the similarity of contributions network as the dependent variable. The coefficients in Equation 1 indicate the change in the probability of being in the same cluster in the similarity of political behavior network as a result of being in the same cluster in the particular independent variable network. For example, being in the same market constraint cluster increases the probability of being in the same political behavior cluster by an average of 14.8 percent. The effects of same industry and common industries in Equation 1

Table 9.2. Means, standard deviations, and correlations among raw dyadic and cluster variables $(N = 1596)$

Variable	Mean	SD	2	3	4	5	6	7	8	9	10	11	12	13
1. Similarity (raw)	.233	.107	<u>273</u>	119	086	083	153	175	281	200	098	020	264	123
2. Similarity (corr)	.237	.425	–	109	095	109	088	153	071	-004	-031	016	088	088
3. Proximity	.081	.274	–	–	079	018	058	023	118	089	084	053	142	083
4. Same primary ind.	.050	.218	–	–	–	358	110	400	045	044	-045	034	003	-037
5. Common industries	.174	.222	–	–	–	–	274	442	034	044	-036	-019	054	029
6. Constraint (raw)[a]	.000	1.000	–	–	–	–	–	<u>399</u>	047	042	001	-033	059	018
7. Constraint (corr)	.142	.349	–	–	–	–	–	–	064	020	-006	014	079	-002
8. Stockholders (raw)[b]	1.160	.665	–	–	–	–	–	–	–	<u>483</u>	060	-007	175	082
9. Stockholders (corr)	.209	.407	–	–	–	–	–	–	–	–	045	005	121	040
10. Direct ilks (raw)	.048	.241	–	–	–	–	–	–	–	–	–	<u>271</u>	237	156
11. Direct ilks (corr)	.125	.331	–	–	–	–	–	–	–	–	–	–	027	096
12. Indirect ilks (raw)	.403	.719	–	–	–	–	–	–	–	–	–	–	–	<u>495</u>
13. Indirect ilks (corr)	.130	.336	–	–	–	–	–	–	–	–	–	–	–	–

a. Factor scores.
b. In logarithms (base e).

Note: 'Raw' variables are dyadic measures employed in Chapter 5; 'corr' variables are dummy variables indicating whether firms are members of the same cluster in structural equivalence analyses based on correlations. Means of 'corr' variables indicate proportion of dyads in network in which the firms belong to the same cluster. Correlations among different measures of same variables are underlined.

Table 9.3. Determinants of same position within campaign contribution network—correlation position measure

Independent variable	(1)#	(2)	(3)
Constant	0.178^c (.001)	20.889^c (.001)	17.547^c (.001)
Proximity	0.153^c (.004)	3.485^b (.024)	1.977 (.107)
Same primary industry	0.053 (.174)	0.515 (.364)	1.197 (.209)
Common industries	0.081 (.130)	-0.374 (.431)	-0.778 (.383)
Same position market constraint network	0.148^c (.003)	5.148^c (.002)	3.300^b (.036)
Same position common stockholders network	-0.022 (.262)	4.831c (.006)	1.859 (.136)
Same position direct interlocks network	0.002 (.455)	0.018 (.462)	0.124 (.417)
Same position indirect interlocks network	0.102^b (.018)	3.464^b (.024)	-0.050 (.473)
Market constraint dyadic measure	–	–	0.910 (.126)
Common stockholders dyadic measure	–	–	3.100^b (.032)
Direct interlocks dyadic measure	–	–	1.473 (.181)
Indirect interlocks dyadic measure	–	–	2.886^c (.001)
R^2	.043	.093	.164

a. $p < .10$
b. $p < .05$
c. $p < .01$

Note: OLS estimates with QAP probabilities. All probabilities are one-tailed. # - Dependent variables: Equation 1, same position in similarity of political behavior network, correlation measure of structural equivalence; Equations 2 and 3, raw measure of similarity of political behavior. Metric coefficients are reported, with quadratic assignment probabilities in parentheses. N = 1596 in both equations. Coefficients in Equations 2 and 3 are multiplied by 100.

were virtually zero. Both of the same industry variables overlapped considerably with same position in the market constraint network (the correlations were .400 for same primary industry and .442 for the standardized number of common industries). This is not unexpected since firms that jointly occupy positions in the market constraint network are likely to be members of the same industries. This may account for the relative strength of the constraint coefficient, since same industry has been a strong predictor of similar political behavior in most of the previous analyses. Among the three remaining network variables, only joint occupancy of positions in the indirect interlock network was a significant predictor of common positions in the contribution network.

Equation 2 of Table 9.3 includes the same independent variables as those in Equation 1 but substitutes the raw common contributions score employed in Chapters 6 and 8 as the dependent variable. The interpretation of coefficients in Equation 2 is the same as that in the similarity of contribution analyses in Chapters 6 and 8. Being in the same market constraint cluster, for example, increases the number of common contributions by an average dyad (with 100 contributions each) by slightly more than five. As in Equation 1, the common industry variables have null effects. Interestingly, the effects of the common cluster variables are as strong or even stronger in Equation 2 than in Equation 1. Especially noteworthy is the stronger effect of common stockholding relations, which was not a significant predictor of joint occupancy in the contribution network. In both cases, consistent with the findings in Chapter 6, the indirect interlocks variable was a significant predictor of similar political behavior while the direct interlocks variable had a null effect.

The fits of the models in Equations 1 and 2 are not directly comparable because of the different scales on which the dependent variables are measured. But when we compare Equation 2 with the findings in Chapter 6, we find that the direct dyadic analyses of common contributions yield results considerably stronger than those presented here based on common positions in network clusters.

The correlations between the dyadic variables and their common cluster counterparts are low enough that we can simultaneously compare their effects on similar political behavior. Equation 3 of Table 9.3 contains all of the variables in Equation 2 plus the four dyadic network variables (market constraint, common stockholders, and direct and indirect interlocks).

Of the three significant network predictors of similarity of political behavior, two (common stockholders and indirect interlocks) are the dyadic measures while one (market constraint) is the common cluster variable. As noted above, the finding on market constraint may be a result of the fact that joint occupants of positions in the market constraint network are likely to be members of the same industries. The effects of both the common stockholders and indirect interlocks common cluster variables disappear when their dyadic counterparts are examined simultaneously.

Overall, the variables based on direct dyadic measures of the relations between firms appear to provide a stronger set of predictors than do the variables based on the identification of common positions in the network as a whole. Still, the inclusion of the positional variable for market constraint does provide additional predictive value even after the dyadic measures are included in the equation.

Discussion

The measures based on common positions within the network as a whole enable us to predict similarity of political behavior among firms. But their predictive capacity is less than that of the measures based on direct dyadic relations between firms. By themselves, membership in the same position within the market constraint and indirect interlock networks increases the probability that a pair of firms will be occupants of the same position in the political contributions network. Common membership in the market constraint and indirect interlock networks as well as in the common stockholders network increases the general level of similar political behavior between firms. But the common cluster variables as a group do not provide as good a fit with the measure of similar political behavior (common campaign contributions) as do the direct dyadic relations between the firms. Why is this the case?

It is important to remember what the dyadic measures actually represent. Network analyses normally begin with the depiction of relations among actors in matrix form. The representation of relations among actors in a single network is normally presented in a square actor-by-actor matrix. Depending on the nature of the relation being examined, the matrix may be symmetric or asymmetric. Regardless, except for those techniques based exclusively on the use of directed graphs, most of the common network analytic techniques, including clustering routines, factor analyses, blockmodels, and the computation of centrality scores, involve operations on these square actor-by-actor matrices. It is crucial to remember that the cells of these matrices are the dyadic relations between actors.

When data reduction techniques are employed to provide simplified representations of the relations among actors, they necessarily involve some loss of information. In the construction of blockmodels,[4] for example, the benefits that accrue from a simple representation of

---

[4] Blockmodels are binary representations of social structures based on relations among actors. See White, Boorman, and Breiger (1976) and Arabie, Boorman, and Levitt (1978) for definitive treatments.

the group's social structure are viewed as worth the loss of information that occurs as a result of the blocking procedure. The identification of clusters of structurally equivalent actors by any technique requires some loss of information precisely because few actors in complex networks are likely to be purely structurally equivalent. The reduction of data matrices into clusters or blocks, therefore, is similar to the collapsing of variables into categories to facilitate tabular analysis. A certain amount of richness in the data will be sacrificed by such procedures, which is one reason that social scientists over the past three decades have turned toward regression-based techniques and away from tabular ones. In the cluster analyses, firms are either "in" or "not in" the same cluster. Firms that are not in the same cluster are treated as equally different, despite the fact that some pairs of firms may be more different than others. One important benefit of dyadic analysis, then, is that the use of dyads preserves in total the information in the original relation matrix. The units of analysis are the actual cells of the matrix rather than approximations of those cells.

One criticism of dyadic analysis, raised initially by Simmel ([1917] 1950), is that dyadic relations cannot be understood apart from the larger social structures within which they are embedded. This point is valid, however, only to the extent that the variables employed to account for dyadic relations fail to take these social structural factors into account. Of the four key network variables employed as independent variables in my analysis, three have built-in mechanisms to account for factors beyond the two firms themselves. The measure of market constraint by definition involves an account of the social structures of the industries within which firms operate. A dyad will have a higher level of market constraint to the extent that the industries in which the firms operate are concentrated. The measure of common stockholders involves the extent to which other firms, most of which are institutional investors, own stock in the two firms in the dyad. And the measure of indirect interlocks involves the extent to which firms share directors with the same third parties, in this case financial institutions. Only the measure of direct interlock ties does not have a built-in means of accounting for relations beyond the two firms. Even here it is possible for firms to interlock through what are called "incidental" ties, in which an officer of a bank, for example, sits on the board of two nonfinancial firms, creating an interlock between the two nonfinancials. Interestingly, direct interlock ties (alone among the network variables) more often than not have a null association with similarity of political behavior.

In short, it may be unfair to assume that analyses of dyads fail to take the structure of the network into account. It is true that dyadic analyses do not provide a graphic presentation of the character of the network as a whole. If pictorial representation of the entire network is one's purpose, then blockmodels, graphs (in small networks), or multidimensional scaling plots provide far more information. If one is concerned with making inferences about the effects of several types of social relations on other social relations, dyadic analyses provide an effective mechanism.

Although we have found that an analysis based on the grouping of firms into jointly occupied positions fails to approach the analytical power of the dyadic analysis presented in Chapters 6 and 7, one additional approach remains to be examined: the effect of a firm's centrality in the network. In the following section I address the question of whether a firm's centrality in the networks of market constraint, common stockholdings, and direct and indirect interlocks is associated with its centrality in the network of common campaign contributions.

Prominence and Centrality

Centrality has been a crucial concept since the emergence of network analysis in the 1950s. Dating back to the small group experiments at MIT beginning in the late 1940s, centrality in a social network has been assumed to be associated with an actor's power, influence, and leadership qualities (see Hopkins, 1964, for a review of this literature). Controversy has raged over the extent to which centrality and power are correlated (Cook et al., 1983; Bonacich, 1987). Virtually all observers agree, however, that network centrality is an important component of social differentiation.

Centrality has been defined and operationalized in several different ways (Bonacich, 1972; 1987; Freeman, 1979; Knoke and Burt, 1983; Mizruchi, Mariolis, Schwartz, and Mintz, 1986). In its most general usage, however, an actor is viewed as central when he or she is tied, both directly and indirectly, to a large number of other actors in a network. This is often operationalized as the ability to reach a large number of other actors in a small number of steps. Freeman (1979) has presented the most sophisticated conceptual development, distinguishing three types of centrality, *connectedness* (the number of actors with whom one has direct ties), *closeness* (the ability to reach large numbers of others in a small number of steps), and *betweenness* (the extent to which others must pass through an actor to reach additional actors). Burt (see Knoke and Burt, 1983) has developed the more general concept of "prominence" to distinguish centrality from prestige, the latter a product of relations that are not necessarily symmetric. And I, along with Mariolis, Schwartz, and Mintz (Mizruchi et al., 1986), have decomposed centrality into two components, which we call "reflected" and "derived" centrality. As we point out in that paper, the latter concept has parallels with Freeman's concept of betweenness.

The literature on centrality is enormous and, with the emergence of the journal *Social Networks* during the 1980s, has grown geometrically. It is not my intent here to discuss the issue of the most "appropriate" measure of centrality. Instead, I note only that I shall employ the commonly used measure based on extraction of the largest eigenvector of the matrix of relations among actors (Bonacich, 1972; Knoke and Burt, 1983). The measure itself will be described briefly below.

One theoretically appealing aspect of the concept of centrality is that the centrality of a firm in a particular network cannot be understood without knowledge of the positions of all firms in the network. Unfortunately, because many studies of relations among corporations have focused on only one network, these analyses have tended to take on a descriptive character. This was one of the problems of the studies of interlocking directorates described in Chapter 2. The authors of many works on interlocks were content to describe the centrality of various firms in networks without consideration of the sources and consequences of this centrality. More sophisticated analysts, such as Mintz and Schwartz (1985), theorized the sources of firm centrality in the roles played by firms in various sectors of the economy, especially banks. But despite a considerable amount of anecdotal data, Mintz and Schwartz provided no systematic evidence of the sources or consequences of bank centrality.

In the context of the present study, centrality can be seen as an indicator of the extent to which a firm is integrated into the network. My aim is to determine whether a high level of integration, or closeness to other firms, in interfirm organizational and social networks is associated with the firm's level of integration in the political behavior network. In the analysis that follows, I reexamine the model presented in Chapter 4 (and tested in Chapters 6 through 8 and earlier in this chapter) using a centrality analysis. Rather than viewing the similarity of firm contribution patterns as a function of their organizational and social network ties, I examine the extent to which a firm's centrality in the contribution network is a function of its centrality in various organizational and social networks. Centrality scores are computed for the 57 firms in each of five networks: common campaign contributions with other firms, market constraint relations, common stockholding, and direct and indirect interlocks. The firms' centrality scores in the common contributions network are then regressed on their centrality scores in the other four networks. If a systemic approach yields more complete information than a focus only on dyads, then the results of this analysis should be stronger than the results of the dyadic analysis.

Measure of Centrality

The measure of centrality employed in this analysis is based on extraction of the first principal component from the raw firm-by-firm relation matrix. The loadings on this component, standardized so that the largest score receives a value of 1, represent the centrality scores. Bonacich, (1972), Knoke and Burt (1983), and Mizruchi et al. (1986) provide details of the mathematical operations. From the point of view of the individual firm, a firm's centrality is based on the number of firms to which it is directly tied; the intensity, or strength, of the ties; and the centrality of the firms to which it is tied. Other things being equal, a firm with ties to highly central firms will be more central than a firm with the same number of ties to more peripheral firms.[5]

Results

Table 9.4 presents means, standard deviations, and correlations among the centrality measures for the five networks. A list of centrality scores for the 57 firms on all five networks is presented in Table A.4. Notice in Table 9.4 that the firms themselves are the units of analysis so that, unlike with the dyadic analyses, the number of observations

---

[5] Specifically, centrality scores are computed by solving the matrix equation $\lambda C = RC$, where R is the $N \times N$ matrix of associations among the actors, C is the $N \times 1$ vector of centrality scores, and λ is the largest eigenvalue of R. See Knoke and Burt (1983), Mizruchi et al. (1986), or standard matrix algebra texts for solutions to this equation. Centrality scores were computed here using the default network indices routine in STRUCTURE.

Table 9.4. Means, standard deviations, and correlations among firm centrality variables (N = 57)

Variable	Mean	SD	2	3	4	5	6
1. Similarity	.671	.181	108	383	328	434	424
2. Constraint[a]	.495	.225	–	-083	172	258	090
3. Stockholders[b]	.612	.206	–	–	249	323	261
4. Direct ilks	.157	.221	–	–	–	542	244
5. Ind. ilks	.308	.257	–	–	–	–	293
6. Size[c]	.165	.169	–	–	–	–	–

a. Factor scores drawn from larger data set
b. In logarithms (base e)
c. Square root of reciprocal of firm's *Fortune* 500 rank.

here is 57. As with the cluster analyses presented earlier in the chapter, the five networks include common political contributions (the dependent variable), market constraint, common stockholdings, and direct and indirect interlocks. Centrality in all four independent variable networks is positively associated with centrality in the political behavior network, although the correlation of market constraint centrality is somewhat lower than the others.

Table 9.5 presents the results of four multiple regression equations, with centrality in the political contributions network as the dependent variable and centrality in the four other networks as independent variables. Because the units of analysis are the 57 firms, these analyses are computed with ordinary least squares regression. Equation 1 contains the effects of the four network variables. In Equation 2, the square root of the reciprocal of the firm's *Fortune* 500 rank is inserted to ensure that the associations observed in Equation 1 are not spurious effects of large size.[6] The reciprocal is taken so that larger firms will have larger values on the measure. Because of the high correlation between centrality in the direct and indirect interlock networks, I examined equations (3 and 4) with each of the two variables excluded.

It is difficult to compare the regression results in Table 9.5 with

---

[6] As I noted in Chapter 6, whether the effect of size can render the effects of other variables spurious is questionable. Market constraint, in particular, is as likely to be a cause of large size as it is a consequence of it. This should be kept in mind while examining Equations 2 through 4.

Table 9.5. Effects of centrality in organizational networks on centrality in similarity of political behavior network (OLS estimates)

Independent variable	(1)	(2)	(3)	(4)
Constant	0.435^d (5.008)	0.432^d (5.170)	0.429^d (5.178)	0.422^d (4.990)
Market constraint centrality	0.033 (0.323)	0.023 (0.233)	0.026 (0.264)	0.059 (0.608)
Common stockholders centrality	0.238^b (2.104)	0.192^b (1.738)	0.198^b (1.803)	0.234^b (2.137)
Direct interlocks centrality	0.083 (0.713)	0.061 (0.540)	–	0.144^a (1.408)
Indirect interlocks centrality	0.198^b (1.872)	0.165^a (1.605)	0.191^b (2.094)	–
Size	–	0.298^b (2.264)	0.304^b (2.336)	0.019^c (2.459)
R^2	.263	.330	.327	.297

a. $p < .10$
b. $p < .05$
c. $p < .01$
d. $p < .001$

Note: All probabilities are one-tailed. N=57 in all equations. Metric coefficients are reported, with T statistics in parentheses.

those of the cluster analysis earlier in the chapter and the dyadic analysis in Chapter 6. The primary difficulties involve the large disparity in the number of observations (57 versus 1,596) and the fact that the dyadic variables involve relations between firms while the firm variables involve characteristics (albeit network-based) of particular firms. As is evident in Equation 1 of Table 9.5, the four variables in the centrality analysis account for a greater portion of the variation in the dependent variable than do the same variables in the dyadic analysis. On the other hand, if statistical significance levels are employed, only two of the four variables are statistically significant in the centrality analysis, compared with three of the four in the dyadic analysis. Whether significance tests are necessary or appropriate in either analysis is a difficult question to resolve. It is clear from the equations in Table 9.5 that the centrality analysis produces results in line with the theoretically expected outcomes.

What exactly do these results suggest? Knowledge of the extent to which firms are central in networks of common stockholdings, indirect interlock ties, and, to a lesser extent, market constraint and direct interlock ties enables us to account for about one-fourth of the variation in the firms' centrality in the political contributions network. The insertion of firm size as a control variable increases the explained variance to about one-third, but the presence of size does not significantly affect the predictive capacities of the network variables. Because firm size has itself been employed as an indicator of a firm's economic power, its strong effect on centrality in the political contributions network is consistent with the arguments developed in Chapter 4 and the findings in Chapters 6 through 8. Even when size is controlled, however, firms that are centrally located in interfirm economic and social networks are likely to find themselves centrally located in terms of their similarity of political behavior with other firms.[7]

As with the dyadic findings in Chapter 6, indirect interlocks again emerge, along with common stockholders, as the most important predictor of similarity of political behavior. This finding provides further evidence of the importance of financial institutions as integrating mechanisms within the community of large American corporations.

Dyadic Ties and Centrality

Both the dyadic analysis in Chapter 6 and the centrality analysis in the previous section demonstrated that to varying degrees, network variables are positively associated with similar political behavior. But which is more important in generating this similarity, the firms' positions in the entire network or their relations with one another? In other words, does simultaneous location in the center of a network lead firms to behave similarly even if they are neither cohesive nor structurally equivalent?

Because of differences in levels of analysis and number of observations, it is difficult to compare directly the results in Table 9.5 with those based on the dyadic analyses. There are two ways to proceed. One approach is to adjust the dyadic network variables to account for the firms' level of centrality. The second approach is to create measures of joint centrality for the network variables and insert them into

---

[7] When the equations presented in Table 9.5 are recomputed using centrality in the network of political opposition as the dependent variable, the results are similar but stronger. The effect of market constraint yields a statistically significant T statistic even when size is controlled.

equations already containing the dyadic variables. This would enable us to determine whether dyads in which the firms are highly central behave more similarly than dyads in which only one or neither firm is central.

Both approaches are employed here. The focus was on the four network variables (market constraint, common stockowners, and direct and indirect interlocks). Two variations on the raw dyadic measures were computed. In the first, the variables for common stockholders and direct and indirect interlocks were standardized by the centrality of each firm in the network. For each of the three variables, the number of ties is divided by the geometric mean of the total number of ties in which each of the two firms is involved. For example, American Can and Armco Steel had one indirect interlock. American Can had 17 indirect interlocks within the 57-firm network while Armco had 26. The standardized indirect interlock score between the two firms was $1 / (17 \times 26)^{\frac{1}{2}}$, or .048. It was not necessary to standardize the measure of market constraint because the firms' prominence in the system is already taken into account in the raw measure (see Chapter 5).

Another approach to controlling for centrality involves creating measures of joint centrality by computing the geometric mean of the two firms' centrality scores in each of the four networks. The problem with the use of joint dyadic centrality scores, however, is that it is impossible to distinguish dyads that contain one highly central firm and one peripheral firm from dyads with two moderately central firms. For example, consider the centralities of four firms in the market constraint network: General Electric (.807), International Harvester (.282), LTV (.509), and Dow Chemical (.445). The joint centrality of the GE-Harvester dyad (.477) is virtually the same as that of the LTV-Dow dyad (.476), despite the wide variation in centrality between GE and Harvester. A solution to this problem is to create separate dummy variables for each network, one for pairs in which both firms have high centrality and one for pairs in which one firm is central and the other peripheral. These two types can then be distinguished from dyads in which neither firm is central. I created separate variables for "high-high" and "high-low" dyads, where "high" was defined as greater than or equal to the mean centrality for that variable. A high-high dyad, therefore, contains firms with centrality at or above the mean for that network. This approach is imperfect, since it collapses some dyads with large differences in centrality into the same category. It fails, for example, to distinguish dyads with very high centralities from those with centralities only slightly above the mean. Nevertheless, the use of dummy variables is preferable on substantive grounds to the use of the geometric mean of the firms' centralities.

For this analysis, three of the four network variables (common stockholdings and direct and indirect interlocks) have three measures each: the raw dyadic score used in previous analyses; the raw dyadic score standardized by each firm's total number of ties in the network; and the joint centrality score (reflected by the centrality dummy variables). Market constraint is measured by the raw dyadic score (which is already standardized) and the joint centrality dummies. Table 9.6 presents correlations between similarity of political behavior and the four dyadic network measures (in the columns), and the dyadic centrality variables. The first three rows include the dyadic network variables standardized by the centrality of the firms in the dyad. The following eight rows contain the dummy variables for dyads in which both firms are at or above the mean in centrality and those in which one firm is at or above the mean and the other is below the mean.

Table 9.6. Correlations among similarity of political behavior, dyadic network variables, and joint centrality variables.

Variable	Mean	SD	(1)	(2)	(3)	(4)	(5)
Common stockholders[a]	.962	.468	212	039	888	055	105
Direct interlocks[a]	.013	.069	065	013	041	844	186
Indirect interlocks[a]	.014	.025	169	052	102	228	835
High-high constraint[b]	.254	.436	042	370	-076	022	145
High-low constraint[b]	.509	.500	-059	-298	-027	-003	-039
High-high stockholders[b]	.331	.471	294	-032	670	099	208
High-low stockholders[b]	.496	.500	-103	008	-300	-056	-089
High-high direct ilks[b]	.075	.264	145	025	190	319	247
High-low direct ilks[b]	.411	.492	114	036	134	-059	035
High-high indirect ilks[b]	.188	.391	291	105	269	191	543
High-low indirect ilks[b]	.501	.500	008	014	027	-068	-164

Key: (1) similarity of behavior; (2) market constraint; (3) common stockholders; (4) direct interlocks; (5) indirect interlocks.

a. value standardized by geometric mean of firms' centrality
b. dummy variable; see text for explanation

Table 9.7 presents three multiple regression equations with quadratic assignment probabilities. Equation 1 contains the effects of the standardized dyadic independent variables on the raw measure of similarity of political behavior. Also included are the variables for common headquarters location, same primary industry, and the standardized number of common industries. Except for the adjustments made to the common stockholders and direct and indirect interlocks variables, this equation is equivalent to Equation 2 in Table 5.2. The results demonstrate that standardizing the relational variables for the centrality of each firm does not negate the significant effects of common stockholders and indirect interlocks. The effect of direct ties was not statistically significant when controls were introduced in earlier equations so its non-significance here is not surprising.

Equation 2 contains the effects of the interfirm joint centrality dummy variables on the raw measure of similarity of political behavior, with controls inserted for headquarters proximity and membership in the same primary and secondary industries. The key variables are the "high-high" dummies, which include dyads in which both firms are at or above the mean centrality in the particular network. This equation is the closest dyadic equivalent to Equation 1 of Table 9.5, and the results are similar. The effects of high centrality in the common stockholders and indirect interlocks networks are positive, although their probabilities are slightly above .05. The effects of high centrality in the market constraint and direct interlocks networks are slightly positive, but neither coefficient even approaches statistical significance. The results in Equation 2 are roughly equivalent to those in Equation 1 of Table 9.5, but those in Table 9.5 are considerably stronger. Equation 1 of Table 9.7 indicates that the effects of the dyadic network variables hold even when the firms' centrality in the network is controlled. Equation 2 suggests that firm centrality by itself is associated with similarity of political behavior, although only for common stockholdings and indirect interlocks. But which effect is stronger, the direct dyadic relations between firms or their network centrality?

If one is interested in comparing the effects of joint network centrality with those of direct relations between firms, the solution is to enter both sets of variables simultaneously into an equation. This is rendered difficult by the high correlations between common stockholders and high joint centrality in the common stockowners network (.670) and between indirect interlocks and high joint centrality in the indirect interlocks network (.543). Nevertheless, I attempted to

Table 9.7. Determinants of similarity of campaign contributions controlling for network prominence dummy variables

Independent variables	(1)	(2)	(3)
Constant	17.902[d] (.001)	16.196[c] (.007)	16.034[b] (.010)
Proximity	2.577[a] (.060)	2.347[a] (.080)	1.709 (.141)
Same Primary Industry	2.540[b] (.034)	3.180[c] (.010)	3.239[c] (.010)
Common Industries	0.769 (.413)	3.138 (.147)	1.620 (.304)
Market Constraint	1.331[b] (.027)	–	1.276[b] (.034)
Common Stockholders*	4.288[c] (.006)	–	1.015 (.281)
Direct Interlocks*	3.656 (.135)	–	1.034 (.163)
Indirect Interlocks*	56.214[d] (.001)	–	1.818[b] (.019)
High-High Constraint	–	0.341 (.456)	-0.736 (.432)
High-Low Constraint	–	-0.436 (.412)	-0.264 (.434)
High-High Stockholders	–	6.556[a] (.054)	5.523 (.116)
High-Low Stockholders	–	2.911[a] (.068)	2.519 (.126)
High-High Direct Ilks	–	1.130 (.417)	0.436 (.454)
High-Low Direct Ilks	–	0.542 (.417)	0.596 (.393)
High-High Indirect Ilks	–	6.657[a] (.064)	4.221 (.150)
High-Low Indirect Ilks	–	2.393 (.129)	1.847 (.182)
R^2	.099	.172	.196

a. $p < .10$
b. $p < .05$
c. $p < .01$
d. $p < .001$

Note: OLS estimates with QAP probabilities. All probabilities are one-tailed. *Equation 1, standardized by centrality. N = 1596 in all equations. Unstandardized coefficients are reported, with quadratic assignment probabilities in parentheses. Coefficients are multipled by 100.

combine the raw dyadic network measures from Equation 1 (minus the standardization for centrality, which would be redundant) with the joint centrality scores from Equation 2. This is done in Equation 3. The dyadic market constraint effect, which was significant in Equation 1, remains significant in the presence of the dummy variables for centrality in the constraint network. High joint centrality in the constraint network, meanwhile, again has no effect on similarity of contribution patterns. In fact, the coefficient is slightly negative. The dyadic measure for indirect interlocking also remains strongly significant in Equation 3. But the effect of high joint centrality in the indirect interlock network, which was significant in Equation 2, drops below statistical significance when the dyadic measure is taken into account. The common stockholders variables, meanwhile, are both non-significant in Equation 3, although both joint centrality variables approach statistical significance. This finding may be a result of the high correlation between the dyadic measure of common stockholders and the joint centrality measure. The effect of direct interlocks remains non-significant in both the dyadic and joint centrality measures.

Except for the effect of common stockholdings, the results in Equation 3 of Table 9.7 indicate that the strength of dyadic relations between firms is a stronger predictor of similarity of political behavior than their common positions in the centers of various networks. Firms that are simultaneously in central positions within the common stockholdings and indirect interlocks networks have relatively high levels of similar political behavior. These effects decline, however, when the strength of dyadic relations between firms is controlled.

An Interpretation of the Role of Network Centrality

What should we make of these findings? It may be premature to assume that firms' centrality is less important than their direct relations. First, the firm-level analysis in Table 9.5 revealed a strong effect of centrality. Firms that were central in various networks, especially those based on common stockholdings and indirect interlocks, were likely to be central in the political behavior network. Second, the dummy variables in Table 9.7 are relatively crude measures that do not take into account the wide range of variation in firm centralities both above and below the means. But why would we expect central firms to behave similarly in the first place?

Unless a network is highly balkanized (that is, characterized by discrete groups with few cross-group ties), central actors will, in the aggregate, be "closer" to one another than will peripheral actors. This is true by definition and it accounts for the high correlations between joint centrality and dyadic ties. If we assume that a network is both hierarchical (with centrality unequally distributed) and not balkanized (an accurate assumption in this study), then we can envision a structure with a core of central actors and a periphery of less central actors. Although it is possible for peripheral actors to have direct relations with one another, the probability of this occurring is considerably lower than the probability for central actors. Within this core, which corresponds to what Zeitlin (1974) called the "inner group," Alba and Moore (1983) called the "central circle," and Useem (1984) called the "inner circle," information is likely to pass among actors even if they do not directly interact. Furthermore, it is possible that firms that are centrally located in interfirm networks are likely to see the world in similar ways, independent of their communications with one another. If this is true, however, it is their positions within interfirm networks that condition these worldviews, independent of the firms' individual attributes. It is not simply that firms are large, for example, that leads them to have similar contribution patterns. It is that firms have ties to other firms through which they communicate information and opinions; that firms, even without direct ties to one another, have ties to similar third parties; and firms, even without ties to one another or to similar third parties, are involved in similar *types* of relations.

This latter concept, involvement in similar types of relations, even if not with the same alters, has received several different labels by network analysts, including *automorphic, regular, positional,* and, most recently, *role* equivalence (Sailer, 1978; White and Reitz, 1983; Winship, 1988; Burt, 1990). Two actors are role equivalent when they are involved in identical types of relations with other actors. As an example, consider the network in Figure 9.5. Firms 7, 8, and 9 share ties with firm 10. Otherwise, however, each firm is tied to different actors. Therefore, these actors have a low level of structural equivalence. All three, however, are in broker positions between firm 10 and two peripheral firms. The three firms thus play identical roles in the system. They are involved in the same types of ties.

Although existing operationalizations of role equivalence do not take into account the unique circumstances of highly prominent actors, it is plausible to suggest that central actors are likely to be in-

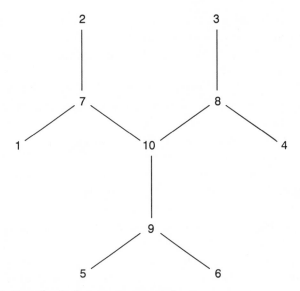

Figure 9.5. Hypothetical ten-actor network

volved in similar types of relations with others, regardless of whether those others are the same actors. The findings presented here suggest that central firms are likely to relate both to one another and to the same others. They also suggest that highly central firms are likely to engage in similar political behavior.

As with the cluster analyses presented earlier in this chapter, the findings based on the centrality analysis provide broad support for the thesis that organizational and social networks play a role in the determination of corporate political behavior. The analysis of the effects of joint centrality on similarity of behavior yielded qualified support for the suggestion that firms with similar locations in interfirm networks are likely to engage in similar political behavior. The cluster analyses described in the first part of the chapter provided results that were consistent with the theoretical model presented in Chapter 4, but they did not significantly increase our understanding of these processes beyond that gleaned from the dyadic analyses presented in the previous chapters. The analysis of firms' joint centrality in the network yielded interesting insights about the possible effects of role equivalence. Overall, however, the results based on the inclusion of joint centrality scores as separate variables were not strong enough to override the results based on the analysis of direct dyadic relations. My conclusion with regard to the cluster analysis thus applies to the centrality analysis as well: both are useful tools, but for testing causal hypotheses, neither provides a level of empirical grounding equal to that of the dyadic analysis.

This conclusion should not be interpreted to mean that analyses of larger networks are less useful than analyses of dyadic relations within those networks. The key issue is the unit of analysis. When the data are cross-sectional and are drawn from a single source (such as one country), cluster and centrality analyses provide useful descriptions of the network as a whole, but they are less useful as inferential hypothesis testing techniques. If the units of analysis are entire networks at different points in time or across nations, then cluster and centrality analyses of different networks will yield variation that can form the basis of falsifiable hypothesis formulation. The next step in research on corporate political behavior will be to conduct analyses in which system-level hypotheses can be examined. This will ultimately be necessary for a complete understanding of the extent of unity and conflict within the business community as a whole.

10 · The Conditional Nature of Business Unity

I began this volume with a discussion of the broad debates in theoretical and political sociology that led me into the study of corporate political behavior. As the book progressed, I considered in increasing detail the role of social and economic networks in the behavior and political success of firms and industries. In this chapter I return to my initial themes. My aim is to summarize and synthesize the most important findings and to suggest future directions for the study of corporate political behavior.

This study has its roots in the debate over the structure of power in industrialized capitalist societies. The rise of the large corporation at the turn of the twentieth century presented a challenge to democratic theory. Theorists ranging from conservatives to Marxists have agreed that big business is potentially powerful. The major source of controversy has been the extent to which business is politically unified. This debate has been couched at a high level of abstraction, however. It is possible to view business as both unified and divided: unified in its support for the political system; but divided on day-to-day issues.

I have argued for a different approach. Rather than asking *whether* business is unified or divided, I have suggested that business unity must be treated as a conditional phenomenon. The business community in the United States, both large and small firms, is undoubtedly unified in its belief in the legitimacy of the American political order. In terms of specific political issues, however, business is capable of disunity as well as unity. The task of social scientists interested in the political behavior of business is to identify the conditions under which either unity or conflict occurs within business.

Part of the problem with such a task is to define exactly what is

meant by the term "unity." I argued, in Chapter 3, that power structure researchers and even classical sociologists have not always explicitly defined the term. The first step in conceptualizing the term is
to recognize why business unity is such a critical issue. In a seminal
statement, Robert Dahl (1958) argued that unity was crucial because
a unified group is more powerful. If we focus on the behavioral manifestations of power, then a unified group is powerful, I argued, because
its members behave similarly.[1] Since actors may behave similarly for
reasons other than cohesive within-group relations, cohesion is not a
necessary condition for a group to exercise power. Actors in similar
positions in a social structure may also behave similarly. Even those
who might otherwise oppose one another, if they have similar relations to the same actors, may behave similarly. Such behavior may
increase the power of both actors.

But under what specific conditions does similar behavior occur?
And in the study of business unity, who are the relevant actors? In
Chapter 4 I attempted to answer both questions. I argued that a transformation of American capitalism occurred early in the twentieth
century in which the system moved from one dominated by a small
number of powerful individuals to one dominated by the institutions
that these individuals had created. By the late twentieth century, the
key actors in the business community were organizations, specifically
large corporations, rather than individuals.

But under what conditions do large corporations exhibit similar
political behavior? To answer this question, I turned to two approaches to the study of intercorporate relations, the resource dependence, or organizational, model and the social class model. Based on
a synthesis of these two models, I argued that there were several "mediating mechanisms" that served as sources of similar political behavior among firms. The two most important, however, were
economic interdependence and the social network ties that linked
firms to one another and to larger interfirm networks. The organizational model suggested that interfirm ties (such as director interlocks)
were formed in response to the uncertainty that firms faced in acquir-
ing resources from their environments. The class model suggested
that these ties were a reflection of the cohesion among members of a
dominant social class. The organizational model predicted that interlocks resulted from interdependence between firms. The class model

[1] See Chapter 3 for a discussion of situations in which power is not measured
behaviorally.

suggested that similarity of political behavior between firms was a partial function of the extent to which they were interlocked.

To this I added an additional point. The economic interdependence between firms that, according to organizational theorists, led to interlocking could also be an independent source of similar political behavior. The bases for this suggestion are twofold. First, firms will attempt to either placate or avoid antagonizing those on whom they depend for resources, especially when there are few alternative firms with which to do business. Second, even when the dependence is mutual, both actors will have an interest in maintaining a smooth relationship.

In addition to the role of economic interdependence and director interlocks in producing similar political behavior, I examined the effects of common stockholdings by financial institutions and several variables intended to capture common interests among firms, including membership in the same primary and secondary industries, geographic proximity of headquarters location, and similar interests toward labor, government regulation, and defense spending.

System and Dyad

Although my topic is political unity among large corporations, I have analyzed unity primarily at the level of dyadic relations between firms. I discussed this problem in Chapter 5 but it warrants further attention here. In commenting on an earlier draft of this book, a friendly critic asked whether the use of dyads "tells us anything about business political unity as that term is ordinarily (and reasonably) understood." In other words, can one study business unity at the level of pairs of firms? Does this represent a major shift in emphasis?

It does not. Remember that I am interested in locating where and under what conditions business unity occurs. Unity and the factors hypothesized to influence it are, by definition, relational variables. Although the business community is itself a collection of many firms, the most basic unit in which relations between firms can be examined is the dyad. As long as the larger context within which the relations occur is taken into account, the use of dyads represents the most direct way to test hypotheses involving relational variables. The dyadic approach shifts the focus from the system as a whole to parts within the system. But this focus enables us to identify, without loss of information, the specific points at which business unity occurs and the sources of this unity.

An additional problem remains, however. To quote the same critic, "What concerns me is that similar patterns of results based on dyads seem consistent with widely varying patterns of uniformity of behavior." The reviewer's point is correct, but his concern is unwarranted. The existence of unity among dyads is indeed consistent with several different levels of unity in the system as a whole. This is not a problem for my analysis, however. To illustrate this, consider a system that is divided into two hostile camps, such as that in Figure 10.1. Each group has four members, all of whom are interlocked with one another. There are no interlocks across the two groups. Suppose that all dyads within each group engage in similar political behavior while the two groups themselves are in direct opposition to one another. In this situation, there are many interlocked dyads (12 out of a possible 28) and all interlocked dyads have high levels of similar political behavior. Yet the unity at the system level is low because of the two warring factions. Notice, however, that there are no interlocks between the two factions. In other words, the absence of interlocks at the dyadic level is associated with dissimilar political behavior at the dyadic level and this has direct implications at the system level. If interlocks and similarity are associated, then the establishment of interlocks among the dyads in the two factions should increase their level of similarity. The factions would disappear.

This does not mean that a focus on dyads tells us everything we need to know about the system as a whole. Figure 10.2 presents an eight-firm network with the same number of interlocks as in Figure 10.1. Despite the same number of ties, this network is far more unified. It is theoretically possible for the relation between interlocking and similar political behavior at the dyadic level to be the same in Figure 10.2 as in Figure 10.1. Although the network in Figure 10.2 is not divided into two distinct camps, it could still contain the same number of

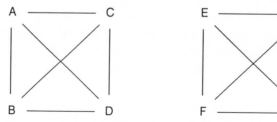

Figure 10.1. Eight-actor network with polarized structure

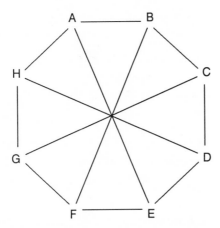

Figure 10.2. Eight-actor network with unified structure

politically unified, interlocked dyads and non-unified, non-interlocked dyads as does Figure 10.1.

On the other hand, it is unlikely that the non-interlocked firms in Figure 10.2 would have levels of political similarity as low as those in Figure 10.1. Consider the ties among firms A, B, and C. Firm A is tied to firm B and firm B is tied to firm C. Firms A and B and B and C have similar political behavior. Unless there is zero transitivity (that is, unless the components of B's behavior that correspond with A and C are completely orthogonal), there will be some overlap in behavior between A and C. In fact, A and C are indirectly interlocked, and indirect interlocks in this study were a stronger predictor of similar behavior than were direct interlocks.

This discussion suggests that the dyadic association between interlocking and similarity of behavior is likely to be higher in oppositional structures such as Figure 10.1 than in unified structures such as Figure 10.2. The five networks that I examined in Chapter 9 had structures that were much more similar to Figure 10.2 than to Figure 10.1. Were the structures more similar to Figure 10.1, the effects of the network variables on similarity of political behavior would likely have been even stronger.

Three Key Findings

The analyses in Chapters 6 through 9 involved a large number of variables, several different data sets, and three different levels of analysis. Rather than review all of the findings in detail, I shall focus here on three general conclusions. They can be summarized as follows:

1. Networks of interfirm relations have a significant impact on the similarity of political behavior.
2. Similar interests lead to similar political behavior. But the effect of similar interests on similarity of political behavior is not as strong as is the effect of network variables.
3. Unified groups are more politically effective than less unified groups. A group whose members behave similarly exercises more power than a group whose members' similarity of behavior is low.

After the extensive analyses that led to these conclusions, these findings may appear unsurprising. When placed in the context of the prevailing theories and evidence, however, they are far from obvious. In the following sections I describe the findings and show how they require a shift in our approach to the study of corporate political behavior.

Behavioral Consequences of Interfirm Relations

According to critics of network analyses of intercorporate relations, the existence of network ties among firms is not sufficient to generate political unity. If anything, in this view, interdependent firms will tend to be politically *opposed* to one another. Neither of these claims is supported by the data, however. Firms that are tied together, including those that are interdependent, are more likely to engage in similar political behavior.

The analyses dealt with four independent variables (market constraint, common stockholders, and direct and indirect interlocks) that were operationalized in explicit network terms plus five similarity of behavior variables: campaign contributions to the same candidates; contributions to candidates of similar ideology; contributions to candidates of the same party; contributions to opposing candidates; and agreement in congressional testimony. Not all types of ties were equally associated with all types of similar behavior, but taken as a whole, the network effects were consistent and strong. Three of the four network variables (all except direct interlocks) were positively associated with contributions to the same candidates and negatively associated with contributions to opposing candidates. All four network variables were associated with agreement in corporate testimony. The findings on contributions to candidates of similar ideologies and the same party were not as strong (perhaps a result of the pragmatic character of most campaign contributions [see Chapter 6]), but even here, indirect interlocks had a positive effect.

Market Constraint

The two most important findings on the network variables are those involving market constraint and indirect interlocks. Market constraint, the extent to which members of one industry constrain the ability of members of another industry to realize profits, is a key indicator of economic interdependence, which forms the basis for the model of business unity developed in Chapter 4. Traditional pluralists such as Galbraith (1952), as well as more recent ones such as Pfeffer (1987), suggest that interdependent firms will tend to be on opposite sides of political issues. This is a plausible argument, since what is good for one partner in a business transaction is often bad for the other. I argued, however, that firms on which others were dependent might be able to use their positions as a source of leverage to induce similar behavior. Even when firms do not actively seek to induce others to comply, firms that are constrained by others may "go along," I suggested, to prevent possible repercussions.

The findings support my argument. The greater the level of market constraint between firms, the more likely are the firms to engage in similar political behavior. This finding holds regardless of whether the interfirm constraint relation was mutual or one-way. This supports both my argument in Chapter 4 and an argument in Emerson's (1962) classic paper on power-dependence relations. The market constraint effect was epitomized in a comment made by a San Francisco banker to Whitt (1982, p. 116) about why the bank had reversed its position supporting the diversion of money from the California Highway Trust Fund to mass transit:

> Standard Oil and the other oil companies are extremely important customers and they have a lot of clout in many ways, and I think a lot of people are unhappy about being in opposition. You take a banker, and Standard Oil, Union Oil, Shell, you name it, Mobil, Atlantic-Richfield are good customers, and if they say "we're opposed to this," it's awfully hard for the banker to say, "Well, we're in favor of it."

In the California mass transit case, the bank may have avoided taking a position out of fear that its major customers would object. But economic interdependence can encourage as well as discourage certain types of behavior. Neustadtl, Scott, and Clawson (1991) report a case in which a corporate PAC that had contributed overwhelmingly to staunch conservatives contributed to a liberal in its district in response to pressure from its lead bank, despite the fact that a PAC official reported that the contribution "made me sick." My suspicion is that cases such as this, in which direct pressure is applied, are relatively rare. More often, constraint probably affects political behavior by limiting the boundaries of what is considered acceptable decision making. Corporate officials decide whom to support and what positions to take on issues. Their positions are likely to be influenced by the positions of others. Once these views are formed, we can expect that corporate officials will take precautions to ensure that their actions will not offend salient alters, and will know which actions will curry favor with such alters. The findings of this study suggest that corporate political behavior is patterned along these lines. If we assume that direct pressure of the kind identified by Neustadtl, Scott, and Clawson is relatively rare, it would explain why the constraint effect does not account for a larger portion of the variation in similarity of contribution patterns. The effects of constraint may be operating at all times even if they do not generate observable behavioral consequences. The findings indicate, however, that constraint produces statistically non-negligible behavioral effects. To the extent that there are additional non-observable effects, constraint would play an even greater role than the findings indicate.

Indirect Interlocking

As we saw in the Introduction and in Chapter 2, numerous studies have demonstrated that corporations are heavily interlocked, both with one another and, especially, with financial institutions. But critics have asked, justifiably, "So what?" Evidence that interlocking affects corporate political behavior has been fragmented and contradictory (Koenig, 1979; Mizruchi and Koenig, 1986; Burris, 1987; Clawson and Neustadtl, 1989). I have exhaustively examined the association between interlocks and similar political behavior between firms. The findings are complex but they provide strong support for the view that interlocks matter.

The key, I have shown, is to distinguish direct interlocks between firms from indirect interlocks, in which firms are tied to the same financial institutions. Direct interlocks between firms was a significant positive predictor of agreement in congressional testimony but it was only a marginally significant predictor of contributions to the same political candidates. The number of ties that firms shared with the same financial institutions, however, was the most consistently significant predictor of similar political behavior across different measures of the variable. In other words, direct interlocks between firms were only modestly related to similar political behavior. But indirect ties between firms through financial institutions were a strong predictor of similar behavior. Firms tied to the same financial institutions were more likely to engage in similar political behavior than were firms tied to one another. Why should this be the case?

There are at least three possible, and compatible, interpretations of this finding (see Chapters 6 and 7). The first, consistent with Mintz and Schwartz's (1985) argument, is that financial institutions influence the behavior of the nonfinancial firms with whom they have formal relations. The second, also consistent with Mintz and Schwartz as well as with the arguments of Zeitlin (1974), Domhoff (1983), and Useem (1984), is that financial institutions serve as meeting places for the leading representatives of the business community, among whom information is circulated. In Useem's words, one's presence on multiple boards increases one's "business scan," or scope, breadth, and sheer number of sources of information. Common membership on financial boards of directors ensures a wide range of common business scan. Third, there is the view that the effect of indirect interlocks demonstrates the tendency of structurally equivalent actors (those tied to the same alters) to behave similarly (White, Boorman, and Breiger, 1976; Burt, 1987b). The sources of this similar behavior are twofold. In one suggestion (Friedkin, 1984), structurally equivalent actors behave similarly because they are influenced simultaneously by the same alters. Two firms with ties to the same other firms will have similar sources of information. Another interpretation (Burt, 1987b) is based on the idea that actors, due to their competitive relations with those with whom they share positions in a social structure, attempt to mimic one another to prevent the other from gaining an advantage with respect to third parties. In this view, if one firm believes that its competitor will gain an advantage with a financial institution by contributing to a particular candidate or taking a certain policy position, the firm will follow suit by also contributing to that candidate or expressing the same position. There is no reason to assume that these interpretations are incompatible. In fact, the idea that structurally equivalent actors compete for the favor of the same third parties is consistent with the suggestion that they are simultaneously influenced by the same actors. Most important, however, is the fact that interlocking directorates are clearly associated with similar political behavior between firms.

A Theoretical Convergence

The findings on market constraint and indirect interlocking also suggest a convergence between network analysis and institutional theory. I have already described the role played by the concepts of cohesion and structural equivalence in the interpretation of these findings. But the effects of market constraint and indirect interlocks on similar political behavior are also consistent with two processes described by DiMaggio and Powell (1983) in their well-known discussion of institutional isomorphism.[2] By "isomorphism" DiMaggio and Powell mean a process by which the structures of different organizations come to resemble one another. This can occur either as a result of the pressure of one organization on another (coercive isomorphism) or as a result of one organization copying another in response to environmental uncertainty (mimetic isomorphism). The concept of similar political behavior described in this book is not identical to the concept of institutional isomorphism. Political behavior is considerably more fluid and has fewer sunk costs (it is much easier for firms to change their political strategies than to restructure their organizations). The focus in the concept of similar political behavior is more on what organizations do than on what organizations are. On the other hand, DiMaggio and Powell's discussion includes examples of organizational behaviors as well as structures, and the concepts of isomorphism and similar political behavior are, whatever their differences in emphasis, fully compatible.

Let us refer to the process of similar political behavior as one of *strategic convergence* between firms. The process by which market constraint leads to similar political behavior between firms can then be referred to as *coercive strategic convergence*. The processes by which indirect interlocking leads to similar political behavior can be referred to as both coercive strategic convergence (when firms are

---

[2] I have referred to DiMaggio and Powell's discussion briefly in Chapters 4 and 6.

subject to common sources of influence) or as *mimetic strategic convergence* (when firms follow the behavior of those with which they are structurally equivalent in order to curry favor with the same third parties).[3] DiMaggio and Powell (ibid., p. 150) note that it is not always possible to distinguish the operation of coercive and mimetic processes. As the findings presented here suggest, this is certainly the case in the production of similar political behavior. It is clear, however, that both concepts (coercive and mimetic strategic convergence) are useful in increasing our understanding of the mechanisms by which similar political behavior is generated.

Interests or Networks?

The prevailing view among students of corporate political behavior, derived from interest group pluralism (Truman, 1951), is that corporations act in accordance with their interests.[4] If the behavior of firms coalesces, in this view, it must be because the firms have similar interests. This argument is fine as far as it goes. But there is much more to corporate political unity than the coalescence of firms with similar interests.

Firms do not always act in accordance with their interests if they can achieve the same result by free riding (Olson, 1965). If firms do act when free riding is an alternative, then there must be social structural factors that induce or pressure them to get involved. Still, not all benefits from political action are public goods. A firm might receive the full benefit of a candidate's election only if it makes its own campaign contribution. Even if Mobil benefits, in terms of legislation, from the reelection of a pro–oil company senator, the firm might benefit even more from the access that a contribution to the senator may provide. Viewed in this light, it is plausible to suggest that firms act in accordance with their interests.

Let us assume for the moment that we can equate true preferences, as reflections of interests, with revealed preferences, as indicated by

[3] The concept of strategic convergence does not necessarily indicate the existence of a conscious collective strategy between firms. Consistent with the position that I have taken throughout this book, it is possible for two firms' strategies to resemble one another without direct communication between them.

[4] Truman's formulation has received considerable attention, although most of it is focused on non-business groups. More recent studies by political scientists include Moe (1980), Walker (1983), and Salisbury (1984); see Knoke (1988) for a sociological treatment. Moe's work contains an analysis of business organizations.

what firms actually do. Convergence in firms' true preferences, in this view, would be expected to occur among firms with similar interests. Several such common interests have been suggested. They include geographic proximity of headquarters location, membership in the same primary and/or secondary industries, and common interests in labor policy, regulation, and defense spending.

These factors are, to varying degrees, positively associated with similar political behavior among firms. Members of the same primary industries were more likely to contribute to the same candidates and express similar positions in congressional testimony than were members of different primary industries. The same finding held for dyads in which both firms were defense contractors. Dyads in which both firms had primary operations in newly regulated industries were more likely to contribute to the same candidates than were dyads in which one or both firms were not in newly regulated industries. Dyads whose firms had similar levels of capital intensity were more likely to agree in their congressional testimony than were those whose firms had different levels of capital intensity. Geographic proximity was significantly associated with contributions to candidates of similar ideologies and party affiliations and was positively, although not always significantly, associated with contributions to the same candidates. Overall, common interests do appear to contribute to similar political behavior between firms, just as interest group pluralism suggests.

Yet even when all of these factors are controlled, the network variables described above continue to play important roles in the convergence of firm political behavior. Economic interdependence, as indicated by market constraint relations, common stockholdings by financial institutions, and shared director interlocks with the same financial institutions generate convergence of political behavior above and beyond that created by conventional measures of common interests.

In fact, these three network factors play a more powerful role in predicting similar behavior than do the common interests variables. In Chapter 6 I presented an equation (#3 in Table 6.2) that included six common interests variables (geographic proximity of headquarters, same primary and secondary industries, similar levels of capital intensity, and common interests in regulation and defense spending) and four network variables (market constraint, common stockholdings, and direct and indirect interlocks). The equation accounted for 19.7 percent of the variation in similar behavior among interfirm dyads.

With only the six common interests variables, the equation accounts for 9.1 percent of the variation in similarity of political behavior. The addition of the four network variables increases the explained variance by 10.6 percent. The four network variables by themselves account for 14.4 percent of the variation. The addition of the six common interests variables increases the explained variance by only 5.3 percent.

This finding suggests that the network variables are more important than the common-interests variables. But even this understates the strength of the network effects. Common geographic location is indicative in part of social ties among inhabitants of the same region. And common industry membership is indicative of common relations of interdependence with other industries, a form of structural equivalence. We cannot separate the common-interest component from the social network component in these two variables. But it is possible, even plausible, that the location of firms in similar network positions creates similar interests.

How strong are these network effects in substantive terms? As noted in Chapter 6, two firms with 100 contributions each (the mean for all dyads), 22 of which are to the same candidates, will on average contribute to nine additional candidates in common on the basis of a one-unit increase in each of the four network variables. The combined impact of these additional common contributions across several firms is enough to have made the difference in several hotly contested races during the 1980 elections. In short, mediating mechanisms, as indicated by network variables, make a substantial difference in corporate political behavior.

The Inner Circle?

Is there an inner circle within the corporate community that is politically unified, as Useem suggests? The analyses in Chapters 6 and 8 clearly support this claim.

In the early part of the century, Hilferding and others spoke of the importance of finance capital in the centralization of business decision making. This idea was updated in the 1970s by Maurice Zeitlin (1974; 1976). Zeitlin identified a small group of business leaders, whom he termed "finance capitalists," who sat at the apex of the corporate community and whose decisions had ramifications throughout the business world:

Neither "financiers" extracting interest at the expense of industrial profits nor "bankers" controlling corporations, but finance capitalists on the boards of the largest banks *and* corporations preside over banks' investments as creditors and shareholders organizing production, sales, and financing, and appropriating the profits of their integrated activities. (Zeitlin, 1976, p. 900).

Zeitlin argued that this group constituted an "inner group" of the capitalist class. Subsequent theorists, including Moore (1979) and Ratcliff (1980) also produced analyses of elites that suggested the existence of a core of central actors. This idea later formed the basis of Useem's "inner circle" thesis. An important difference exists between Zeitlin's and Useem's arguments, however. For Zeitlin, members of the inner group are part of a capitalist class that exists independent of one's organizational position. As we saw in Chapter 4, Zeitlin argued that both banks and nonfinancial corporations were tools for the general accumulation of capital by this class. For Useem, membership in the inner circle is a function primarily of one's position in organizations rather than one's social class background. To the extent that inner circle members are integrated into elite social circles, as they tend to be, it is a result rather than a source of their inner circle membership.

I argued in Chapter 4 that during the first two decades of the twentieth century, a transformation occurred in American capitalism from a system dominated by a few powerful individuals to one dominated by the institutions that those individuals had created. This suggests that the key source of power in the contemporary business world is one's organizational (or, more accurately, interorganizational) position. In this sense, Useem's argument that the inner circle is based in interorganizational networks is consistent with mine.

Several findings from my analysis lend support to the inner circle thesis. First, although I employed a measure of similarity of contribution patterns that was independent of the number of contributions made by each firm, larger firms were still more likely to contribute to the same candidates than were smaller firms. Second, dyads in which both firms were members of the Business Roundtable were more likely to contribute to the same candidates than were dyads in which only one or neither firm was a member. In addition to these two findings, the fact that indirect interlocks were a consistently strong predictor of similar political behavior is consistent with the notion that interfirm networks serve as a source of business unity.

Based on an analysis of dyads in which both firms were members of the same primary industry (Chapter 8), I found that dyads that included large firms, firms in concentrated industries, and firms with indirect interlocks were more likely to contribute to the same candidates than were dyads without such characteristics.

The analyses in Chapter 9 revealed that the networks among the 57 firms in the study could be viewed as core-periphery structures, in which a relatively small number of firms were highly central while a relatively large number were peripheral. The analyses in both chapters suggested that firms in the center of the network were more likely to behave similarly politically than were firms on the periphery. Location in the center was found to contribute to similar political behavior, although this effect appeared to be a function of the already existing ties among central firms.

Do the leaders of these central firms constitute a self-conscious elite that looks out for the long-term interests of the business community as a whole? This question is more difficult to answer. Most observers of corporate PACs have found the behavior of large firms to be more pragmatic (concerned with furthering the firms' specific interests) than ideological (concerned with furthering class interests). If we limit consideration of the inner circle thesis to the issue of business unity, however, the findings presented here clearly support the view that firms in the center of intercorporate networks will be more likely to behave similarly politically than will firms on the periphery of such networks. This is precisely what the thesis would predict.

Unity and Power

"When business has been unified," writes David Vogel, "its political power has often been extremely impressive" (1989, p. 12). This explains my focus on business unity. I have also examined the effects of business unity on an industry's political power. I have emphasized the behavioral aspects of power, where power is operationalized in terms of a group's ability to achieve its goals.[5] Several studies at both the local and the national level have examined groups' success in achieving desired outcomes on political issues (see Liebert and Imershein, 1977; Stone, 1984; Mollenkopf, 1989 for reviews of studies at the local level; Domhoff, 1979; 1990; Kingdon, 1984, pp. 54–57; Laumann and

---

[5] My theoretical definition of power is somewhat broader. See Chapter 3.

Knoke, 1987; and Vogel, 1989 for studies at the national level). Despite the extensive work in this area, there is little systematic, as opposed to anecdotal or implicit, evidence of a correlation between similar behavior and political success.

The analysis of power in this book should be viewed as an effort to open up research into a hitherto neglected area. Still, my results suggest that a unified group is more politically powerful than a less unified group. As we saw in Chapter 8, industries whose leading firms behave similarly politically are more likely to get their way, both in terms of passing legislation favorable to their interests and in preventing legislation unfavorable to their interests. The impact of similar behavior on political success occurs primarily because of the forces that lead to similar behavior in the first place. Once the effects of industry concentration, interfirm market constraint, and indirect interlocks among the industry's largest firms are controlled, the effect of similar behavior on political success disappears.

The analysis in Chapter 8 was based on only 15 industries, drawn from another study (Esty and Caves, 1983), some of which were not perfectly matched with the industries in my study. In addition, the measures of power (success on bills studied by Esty and Caves) and similar behavior (common campaign contributions and congressional testimony) were based on very different indicators. The fact that such strong results were nevertheless observed is remarkable considering the small number of observations and the inevitable measurement error. By showing, systematically, that unity increases a group's power, we have reaffirmed the status of business unity as a critical theoretical and substantive problem. But have we solved it?

Pluralism, Class, or Contingency?

Is big business unified or divided? Is the pluralist model of atomistic firms competing for influence an accurate portrayal of business in politics, or does the class model of a unified corporate elite more effectively capture the essence of corporate political behavior? Are mediating mechanisms effective in forging unity out of disagreement, as class theorists argue, or are they largely irrelevant, as pluralists suggest?

The level of unity among the 57 large firms in my study far exceeds the level of conflict. As noted in Chapter 6, the average pair of firms in my study contributed to 24.1 candidates in common but opposed each other only 2.65 times. Figure 10.3 shows the distribution of similarity of campaign contributions using a Pearson correlation (see Chapter 5). If two firms' contributions were entirely random, the expected correlation between their contribution patterns would be zero. The observed mean is .205 with a standard deviation of .100. Only ten of the 1,596 dyads had correlations below zero (that is, they contributed to fewer candidates than would be expected by chance). The lowest score, − .022, was less than one-fourth of a standard deviation below the random figure. Nearly half of the dyads were more than two standard deviations above the expected correlation of zero.

Figure 10.4 shows the distribution of Pearson correlations for levels of contributions to opposing candidates (O_{ij} in Chapter 6). Again, if all contributions were random, the expected opposition correlation would be zero. The mean correlation for opposing contributions is − .072 with a standard deviation of .054. More than 94 percent of the dyads had correlations of less than zero (the correlation expected by chance). More than half were more than one standard deviation below zero.

The findings on congressional testimony were similar, if not as overwhelming. Firms were approximately four times as likely to agree with one another as they were to oppose one another. If we remove the big three auto companies, which had high levels of both agreement and opposition, the ratio of agreed to opposing appearances increases to five to one.

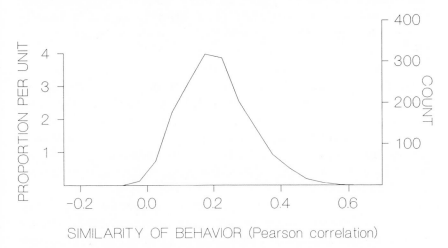

Figure 10.3. Frequency distribution of similarity of political behavior

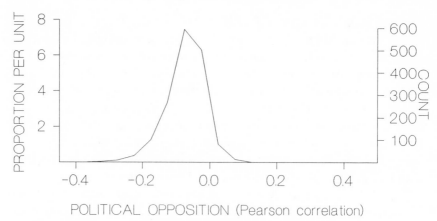

POLITICAL OPPOSITION (Pearson correlation)

Figure 10.4. Frequency distribution of political opposition

In addition to the high level of unity relative to opposition, unity is likely to be highest in the presence of network ties. This finding is consistent with the argument of class theorists that mediating mechanisms exist that facilitate business political unity. The finding is especially important because the 57 firms in this study are the largest in their industries and are all members of the *Fortune* 500. As a result, the ranges of both interfirm relations and similarity of behavior are lower than they would be if smaller firms were included in the study. Since smaller firms tend to have fewer intercorporate relations and lower levels of interfirm political unity than do larger firms, the relations between network ties and political unity would be even stronger had smaller firms been included. Still, both the high level of unity relative to opposition and the unifying effect of the mediating mechanisms lend support to the class model.

On the other hand, although the level of direct opposition is low, there certainly are firms that have little to do with one another. This is especially true of firms in industries that have little contact, in terms of economic transactions or director ties. Variation exists even among firms within particular industries, however. Moreover, although unity tends to be higher where mediating mechanisms exist, considerable unexplained variance remains. If the presence of mediating mechanisms enables us to predict where business unity will be highest, the predictions are imperfect ones. Even among the 57 large firms on which this study is based, the patterns of political behavior reveal a capitalist class that is far from monolithic. Had smaller firms been included, the effects of the network variables on business unity between firms might have been stronger, but the overall level of unity would probably have been lower.

The findings, then, reveal a high ratio of unity compared to opposition, but the degree of unity is variable. The presence of mediating mechanisms is associated with higher levels of unity but the fit between the two is far from perfect. In short, some findings are consistent with the class model while other findings are consistent with pluralism. Which model is superior?

This question is equivalent to asking whether a glass is half-full or half-empty. As I have suggested repeatedly, however, the important question is not whether business is unified or divided but when, and under what conditions, unity and conflict occur. Once we pose the question of business unity as a conditional one, our answers become far more specific.

Conditional thinking has existed in the social sciences for some time. In the mid-1960s, a group of theorists argued that organizational structures varied based on the tasks that the organization performed (Lawrence and Lorsch, 1967; Perrow, 1967). Although this approach, labeled "contingency theory," has since given way to several alternative perspectives within organizational theory, its emphasis on the conditional nature of organizational structures has had a lasting impact. Meanwhile, conditional thinking has increasingly become the norm in the study of organizations and politics. Vogel (1989) has responded to the question, "Is business powerful?" by saying that sometimes it is and sometimes it is not. Others have examined, longitudinally, the conditions that have led to changes in corporate tax rates (Jacobs, 1988; Quinn and Shapiro, 1991) and government expenditures (Griffin, Devine, and Wallace, 1982; Hicks, 1984; Devine, 1985). Mann (1986) has presented an impressive example of a conditional approach to different sources of power during the course of human history. In collective action theory, Oliver and Marwell (1988) have argued that it is time to move beyond the question of "do people free ride?" toward a focus on the conditions under which free riding is likely to occur.

Nowhere is the need for conditional thinking more obvious than in the study of corporate political unity. I have attempted such an analysis here, but this study represents only a beginning. My focus has been on variations in corporate political unity within a single population at a particular point in time. Longitudinal and cross-national research on corporate political behavior is the next major order of business.

I began this book with a discussion of corporate power and its effect on American democracy. The work was informed by questions such as "Is there a power elite, or a cohesive ruling class?" and "Is business politically unified?"

I have argued that these are the wrong questions. By doing so, I lay myself open to the charge that I have ducked the "big issues" with which I opened the book. I plead innocent. To explain why, let us consider the questions in the preceding paragraph. For more than a century, both American and European analysts have been puzzled by the absence of strong anti-corporate and working-class movements in the United States. The existence of a powerful and unified capitalist class has been proposed as one source of this absence. At the same time, liberal thinkers, from Thomas Jefferson to recent critics such as Robert Dahl and Charles Lindblom, have expressed concern that concentrated economic power would lead to concentrated political power. But concentrated political power is not in itself a problem, according to pluralists, as long as there are multiple centers of counteracting influence that neutralize one another (Schumpeter, 1942; Galbraith, 1952). Concentrated political power is a problem when the powerful are unified. In this case, concentration is viewed as providing unfair advantages for the groups within which power is concentrated.

The issues of business unity and political power remain every bit as relevant today as they have been in the past. The problem is how to approach the topic, theoretically, empirically, and in practice. My argument is that to locate the sources of corporate political power, we should identify firms that are tied together by economic interdependence, common ownership ties, and interlocking directorates. Many of these firms, of course, will be the largest in the most concentrated industries. But it is not size or concentration *per se*, but rather corporations' economic, organizational, and social interaction that unify and empower them. Whether this unity is produced by economic leverage and implicit threat, or as a result of the social cohesion that emerges from interaction among corporate directors, the result is the same: an increased potential for concentrated political power.

For decades, social scientists debated the role of business elites in industrialized capitalist societies. By 1980, attention to this issue appeared to be in decline. But the past few years have witnessed a revival of interest in the topic of corporations and politics. Research on corporate political behavior has proliferated not only in sociology and political science departments but in business schools as well. This is a positive development for practical as well as academic purposes.

Regardless of the course of international events, as the American economy continues its long-term decline, conflicts over the allocation of domestic resources are likely to become ever more critical. Whether and how federal policy makers are willing to deal seriously with the casualties of this decline are likely to become increasingly volatile political issues. What role will corporations play in this process? Will large firms continue to avoid the issues of the environment, housing, education, and poverty? Will they attempt to coopt them through public relations measures? Will the many industries that stand to benefit from increased attention to domestic needs have the willingness and the capability to stand up to those that continue to benefit from huge military expenditures? Who will oppose these changes and for what reasons? Understanding the social organization of the business community will increasingly become a requirement for researchers, policy makers, and activists who share concerns about the nation's well-being.

Appendix:
Data on Firms and Candidates

Table A.1. Distribution of firm contributions by candidate ideology and party

Firm	SIC	Can	Hea	LiD	LaD	MoD	MoR	MCR	CoD	CoR	PctD	Ideo
American Can	34	69	4	9.8	8.2	3.3	13.1	4.9	6.6	54.1	27.9	2.689
Arcata	27	19	1	.0	5.3	5.3	10.5	.0	.0	78.9	10.5	1.789
Armco	33	62	15	.0	1.6	3.3	14.8	3.3	6.6	70.5	11.5	1.787
Beckman Instruments	38	24	1	8.3	.0	.0	12.5	.0	.0	79.2	8.3	1.875
Beckton Dickinson	38	33	2	22.6	9.7	9.7	22.6	.0	9.7	25.8	51.6	4.000
Bethlehem Steel	33	104	25	18.9	17.9	3.2	7.4	3.2	5.3	44.2	45.3	3.495
Blue Bell	23	48	0	.0	.0	.0	.0	2.1	12.5	85.4	12.5	1.167
Burlington Industries	22	118	8	2.7	3.5	5.3	8.8	1.8	19.5	58.4	31.0	2.044
Champion International	26	55	13	22.9	8.3	6.3	4.2	4.2	20.8	33.3	58.3	3.458
Chrysler	37	130	58	33.1	20.3	8.5	4.2	2.5	6.8	24.6	68.6	4.585
Continental Group	34	26	1	10.0	15.0	5.0	15.0	.0	25.0	30.0	55.0	3.250
Corning Glass Works	32	38	8	2.7	10.8	5.4	16.2	.0	10.8	54.1	29.7	2.514
Dart & Kraft	20	132	4	.8	1.7	.0	6.7	1.7	4.2	84.9	6.7	1.412
Deere	35	35	17	.0	6.5	3.2	9.7	3.2	.0	77.4	9.7	1.806
R. R. Donnelley	27	43	1	.0	8.6	2.9	11.4	11.4	.0	65.7	11.4	2.114
Dow Chemical	28	234	19	1.0	5.0	.5	5.5	3.0	14.9	70.1	21.4	1.701
EG & G	38	37	1	25.0	19.4	2.8	16.7	.0	11.1	25.0	58.3	4.194
Eastman Kodak	38	24	5	.0	4.2	4.2	8.3	.0	8.3	75.0	16.7	1.708
Esmark	20	20	0	.0	10.0	5.0	10.0	5.0	20.0	50.0	35.0	2.300
Exxon	29	105	54	6.1	4.0	2.0	8.1	2.0	12.1	65.7	24.2	2.051
Ford	37	120	75	8.0	11.6	6.3	5.4	4.5	11.6	52.7	37.5	2.679
General Electric	36	284	84	15.8	11.3	5.7	8.5	2.4	13.4	42.9	46.2	3.178
General Motors	37	242	84	8.3	8.8	3.4	7.8	2.0	13.7	56.1	34.1	2.483
Georgia-Pacific	24	120	5	4.7	3.8	5.7	9.4	.9	13.2	62.3	27.4	2.132
B. F. Goodrich	30	91	5	3.5	2.4	3.5	7.1	4.7	11.8	67.1	21.2	1.894
Goodyear	30	81	23	1.4	1.4	2.9	10.0	2.9	18.6	62.9	24.3	1.814
International Harvester	35	81	2	6.3	10.1	2.5	7.6	2.5	7.6	63.3	26.6	2.342
International Paper	26	170	11	6.5	6.5	6.5	7.7	2.6	16.8	53.5	36.1	2.419
LTV	33	286	15	16.7	13.8	7.5	5.9	1.3	16.7	38.1	54.8	3.364
Libbey-Owens-Ford	32	56	0	3.8	1.9	1.9	11.3	.0	9.4	71.7	17.0	1.830
Lone Star Industries	32	32	3	25.8	6.5	6.5	9.7	.0	16.1	35.5	54.8	3.581
Louisiana-Pacific	24	56	22	7.8	15.7	2.0	2.0	3.9	13.7	54.9	39.2	2.608
Mc Donnell-Douglas	37	116	32	8.7	16.3	3.8	3.8	1.0	20.2	46.2	49.0	2.827
Manville	32	59	13	20.8	7.5	1.9	5.7	.0	7.5	56.6	37.7	2.943
Minnesota Mining & Mfg	26	112	13	6.9	4.9	6.9	12.7	2.0	9.8	56.9	28.4	2.451
Mobil	29	92	23	4.5	4.5	.0	4.5	3.4	13.6	69.3	22.7	1.841
Monsanto	28	96	43	6.0	9.5	7.1	8.3	3.6	16.7	48.8	39.3	2.607
National Can	34	24	0	4.3	4.3	.0	13.0	4.3	4.3	69.6	13.0	2.000
National Gypsum	32	33	4	.0	.0	.0	6.9	6.9	6.9	79.3	6.9	1.414
Owens-Illinois	32	92	4	4.9	7.3	3.7	8.5	1.2	14.6	59.8	30.5	2.232
Pepsico	20	192	9	7.4	3.4	4.0	10.3	1.7	8.0	65.1	22.9	2.200
Philip Morris	21	166	8	26.2	12.1	9.2	6.4	1.4	14.9	29.8	62.4	3.915
Potlach '	24	38	8	5.6	8.3	.0	16.7	.0	.0	69.4	13.9	2.250
R. J. Reynolds	21	167	5	9.4	6.7	7.4	7.4	2.0	21.5	45.6	45.0	2.671
Raytheon	36	84	2	20.8	15.3	4.2	6.9	.0	16.7	36.1	56.9	3.556
Rockwell International	37	95	33	12.8	18.6	5.8	5.8	1.2	16.3	39.5	53.5	3.291
Sperry	35	98	13	10.6	2.1	1.1	6.4	1.1	10.6	68.1	24.5	2.106
Springs Mills	22	39	1	2.7	.0	8.1	8.1	2.7	29.7	48.6	40.5	2.081
J. P. Stevens	22	90	0	.0	.0	2.3	4.5	2.3	4.5	86.4	6.8	1.318
Texaco	29	135	32	.8	3.2	2.4	7.2	2.4	12.8	71.2	19.2	1.696
Time	27	152	3	23.1	13.1	9.2	6.9	.8	13.1	33.8	58.5	3.762
Union Carbide	28	65	42	6.5	4.8	6.5	6.5	3.2	12.9	59.7	30.6	2.274

Table A.1. (continued)

Firm	SIC	Can	Hea	LiD	LaD	MoD	MoR	MCR	CoD	CoR	PctD	Ideo
Uniroyal	30	10	3	22.2	.0	.0	.0	.0	.0	77.8	22.2	2.333
U.S. Steel	33	194	27	10.1	7.7	5.3	8.3	1.8	12.4	54.4	35.5	2.609
United Technologies	37	226	34	8.1	6.2	3.8	10.0	1.4	10.4	60.2	28.4	2.374
Westinghouse	36	201	64	16.4	14.1	4.0	9.0	1.1	11.3	44.1	45.8	3.254
Weyerhaeuser	26	117	16	8.7	9.6	2.9	3.8	3.8	19.2	51.9	40.4	2.500
Mean (unweighted)		99.3	17.5	9.1	7.6	4.0	8.5	2.2	11.7	56.9	32.4	2.505

Key: **SIC**, two-digit code of firm's primary industry (see below); **Can**, number of candidates to whom firm contributed; **Hea**, number of hearings at which firm representative presented testimony; **LiD**, proportion of candidates to whom firm made contributions who were liberal Democrats; **LaD**, labor Democrats; **MoD**, moderate Democrats; **MoR**, moderate Republicans; **MCR**, moderate-conservative Republicans; **CoD**, conservative Democrats; **CoR**, conservative Republicans; **PctD**, proportion of contribution recipients who were Democrats; **Ideo**, weighted ideology score (higher score indicates more contributions to liberals).

SIC codes: 20, food; 21, tobacco; 22, textiles; 23, apparel and other textile products; 24, lumber and wood products; 26, paper and allied products; 27, printing and publishing; 28, chemicals and allied products; 29 petroleum and coal; 30, rubber and miscellaneous plastics; 32, stone, clay, and glass; 33, primary metals; 34, fabricated metals; 35, machinery, except electrical; 36, electric and electronic equipment; 37, transportation equipment; 38, instruments and related products.

Table A.2.   Ideological classifications of general election candidates

1 2 3	4	5 6	1 2 3	4	5 6
s ak	murkowski, frank h	c CoR	h ca21	corman, james c.	i LiD
s al	denton, jeremiah a	c CoR	h ca21	fiedler, bobbi	c CoR
s al	folsom, jim jr	c CoD	h ca22	moorhead, carlos j.	i CoR
h al 1	edwards, jack	i CoR	h ca23	winckler, robert mitchell patrick	c CoR
h al 2	dickinson, hon. william l.	i CoR	h ca26	rousselot, john h	i CoR
h al 3	nichols, hon. bill	i CoD	h ca27	dornan, robert k.	i CoR
h al 4	bevill, tom	i CoD	h ca28	dixon, julian c.	i LiD
h al 5	flippo, ronnie gene	i CoD	h ca29	hirt, michael arthur	c CoR
h al 6	clifford, wesley bryant "pete"	c CoD	h ca29	hawkins, augustus	i LiD
h al 6	smith, albert lee jr	c CoR	h ca30	platten, john arthur	c CoR
h al 6	buchanan, john h.	i MCR	h ca30	danielson, george e	i LaD
h al 7	shelby, richard craig	i CoD	h ca31	dymally, mervyn m	c LiD
s ar	clark, william penn	c CoR	h ca32	anderson, glenn m.	i LaD
s ar	bumpers, dale	i MoD	h ca33	grisham, wayne richard	i CoR
h ar 1	alexander, bill	i CoD	h ca34	lungren, daniel e	i CoR
h ar 2	bethune, ed	i CoR	h ca35	dreier, david t	c CoR
h ar 3	hammerschmidt, john paul	i CoR	h ca35	lloyd, jim	i LaD
h ar 4	anthony, beryl f. jr.	i CoD	h ca36	stark, john paul	c CoR
s az	goldwater, barry m	i CoR	h ca37	lewis, jerry	i CoR
h az 1	rhodes, john	i CoR	h ca38	patterson, jerry m.	i MoD
h az 2	huff, richard h	c CoR	h ca39	dannemeyer, william edwin	i CoR
h az 2	udall, morris king	i LiD	h ca40	badham, robert e	i CoR
h az 3	stump, bob	i CoD	h ca41	wilson, bob	o CoD
h az 4	rudd, eldon	i CoR	h ca41	lowery, bill	o CoR
s ca	cranston, alan	i LiD	h ca42	van deerlin, lionel mc	i LiD
s ca	rousselot, john h	c CoR	h ca43	burgener, clair w	i CoR
s ca	gann, paul	c CoR	s co	hart, gary w	i LiD
h ca 1	chappie, eugene	c CoR	s co	buchanan, mary estill	c MCR
h ca 1	johnson, hon. harold t.	i LaD	h co 1	bradford, naomi l	c CoR
h ca 2	clausen, donald h.	i CoR	h co 1	schroeder, pat	i LiD
h ca 3	matsui, robert t.	i LiD	h co 2	mcelderry, john r	c CoR
h ca 4	fazio, vic	i LiD	h co 2	wirth, timothy e	i LiD
h ca 5	mcquaid, john dennis	c CoR	h co 3	kogovsek, ray	i LaD
h ca 7	st clair, giles jr	c CoR	h co 3	mccormick, harold l	c CoR
h ca 8	hughes, charles v.	c CoR	h co 4	brown, hank	o CoR
h ca 9	stark, fortney h.	i LiD	h co 4	barragan, polly baca	o LiD
h ca10	lutton, john m.	c CoR	h co 5	kramer, kenneth bentley	i CoR
h ca11	royer, william h.	o CoR	s ct	buckley, james lane	c CoR
h ca11	lantos, thomas p	c LiD	s ct	dodd, christopher john	o LiD
h ca12	mccloskey, paul n jr	i MoR	h ct 1	cotter, william r.	i MoD
h ca13	mineta, norman y	i LiD	h ct 2	guglielmo, d anthony	o CoR
h ca14	shumway, norman	i CoR	h ct 3	lieberman, joseph	o LiD
h ca15	coelho, anthony lee	i MoD	h ct 3	denardis, lawrence j	o MoR
h ca16	panetta, leon e	i MoD	h ct 4	mckinney, stewart b.	i MoR
h ca17	pashayan, charles s jr	i CoR	h ct 5	ratchford, william r	i LiD
h ca18	thomas, william m	i CoR	h ct 5	donahue, edward m	c MCR
h ca19	lagomarsino, robert j	i CoR	h ct 6	moffett, anthony toby	i LiD
h ca20	goldwater, barry m jr	i CoR	h dc	fauntroy, walter	i LiD

Table A.2.   (continued)

1 2 3	4	5 6	1 2 3	4	5 6
h de	evans, thomas beverley jr	i MCR	h id 1	symms, steve	i CoR
s fl	gunter, bill	c CoD	h id 1	nichols, glenn w	o LiD
s fl	hawkins, paula	c CoR	h id 2	hansen, george	i CoR
h fl 1	briggs, warren marshall	c CoR	s il	dixon, alan j	o MoD
h fl 1	hutto, earl dewitt	i CoD	s il	o'neal, david c	o CoR
h fl 2	fuqua, don	i CoD	h il 3	russo, martin a.	i LaD
h fl 3	bennett, charles e	i CoD	h il 4	derwinski, edward j	i CoR
h fl 4	chappell, william v jr	i CoD	h il 6	hyde, henry j.	i CoR
h fl 5	mccollum, bill	c CoR	h il 7	collins, cardiss	i LiD
h fl 5	best, david ryan	c CoD	h il 8	rostenkowski, dan	i LaD
h fl 6	young, c w	i CoR	h il 9	yates, sidney r	i LiD
h fl 7	gibbons, sam m	i CoD	h il10	porter, john edward	o MoR
h fl 8	ireland, andy	i CoD	h il11	zanillo, michael r	c CoR
h fl 9	nelson, bill	i CoD	h il11	annunzio, frank	i LaD
h fl10	bafalis, l a skip	i CoR	h il12	crane, philip m.	i CoR
h fl11	mica, daniel andrew	i CoD	h il13	mcclory, robert	i CoR
h fl12	shaw, eugene clay jr	c CoR	h il14	erlenborn, john n	i CoR
h fl13	lehman, william mc	i LiD	h il15	corcoran, thomas j.	i CoR
h fl14	pepper, claude	i LaD	h il16	aurand, douglas r	o LiD
h fl15	fascell, dante b.	i LaD	h il16	martin, lynn	o MoR
s ga	talmadge, herman eugene	i CoD	h il17	o'brien, george m	i CoR
s ga	mattingly, mack f	c CoR	h il18	knuppel, joh linebaugh	c LaD
h ga 1	ginn, ronald "bo"	i CoD	h il18	michel, robert h	i CoR
h ga 2	hatcher, charles floyd	o CoD	h il19	railsback, tom	i MoR
h ga 3	brinkley, jack thomas	i CoD	h il20	robinson, david l	c LiD
h ga 4	levitas, elliot h.	i CoD	h il20	findley, paul	i MCR
h ga 5	fowler, w wyche jr	i MoD	h il21	madigan, edward	i CoR
h ga 6	gingrich, newton leroy	i CoR	h il22	crane, dan	i CoR
h ga 7	mcdonald, lawrence patton	i CoD	h il23	price, melvin	i LaD
h ga 8	evans, billy lee	i CoD	h il24	simon, paul	i LiD
h ga 9	jenkins, edgar l.	i CoD	s in	quayle, dan	c CoR
h ga 9	ashworth, david g.	c CoR	s in	bayh, birch e. jr.	i LiD
h ga10	barnard, druie douglas jr.	i CoD	h in 1	benjamin, adam jr.	i LaD
s hi	inouye, daniel k	i MoD	h in 2	fithian, floyd j.	i MoD
h hi 1	heftel, mr. cecil landau	i MoD	h in 3	hiler, john patrick	c CoR
h hi 2	akaka, daniel k.	i MoD	h in 3	brademas, john	i LiD
s ia	culver, john c.	i LiD	h in 4	coats, daniel r	o CoR
s ia	grassley, charles e	c CoR	h in 5	ackerson, nels	c MoD
h ia 1	leach, james a s	i MoR	h in 5	hillis, elwood h	i CoR
h ia 2	tauke, tom	i CoR	h in 6	evans, david walter	i CoD
h ia 3	evans, thomas cooper	o MoR	h in 6	crane, david goodrich	c CoR
h ia 3	grassley, charles e.	i CoR	h in 7	myers, john t	i CoR
h ia 4	young, donald carter	c CoR	h in 8	snider, kenneth charles	c MoD
h ia 4	smith, neal	i LaD	h in 8	deckard, h joel	i CoR
h ia 5	hultman, calvin oscar	c CoR	h in 9	hamilton, lee herbert	i MoD
h ia 5	harkin, tom	i LiD	h in10	sharp, philip r.	i MoD
h ia 6	carney, clarence s	c CoR	h in10	frazier, wiiliam g	c CoR
s id	symms, steve	c CoR	h in11	suess, sheila s	c CoR
s id	church, frank	i LiD	h in11	jacobs, andrew jr.	i MoD
h id 1	craig, larry e	o CoR	s ks	dole, robert	i CoR

Table A.2.   (continued)

1 2 3	4	5 6	1 2 3	4	5 6
h ks 1	roberts, c patrick	o CoR	h me 2	snowe, olympia j.	i MCR
h ks 2	jeffries, jim	i CoR	h mi 1	conyers, john j.	i LiD
h ks 3	winn, larry jr.	i CoR	h mi 2	pursell, carl d	i MoR
h ks 4	glickman, daniel r.	i MoD	h mi 3	gilmore, jim	c CoR
h ks 5	whittaker, robert russell	i CoR	h mi 3	wolpe, howard e	i LiD
s ky	ford, wendell h.	i LaD	h mi 4	stockman, david allen	i CoR
h ky 1	hubbard, carroll jr	i CoD	h mi 5	sawyer, harold s	i CoR
h ky 3	mazzoli, romano l.	i LaD	h mi 6	dunn, james w jr	c CoR
h ky 3	cesler, richard paul	c CoR	h mi 6	carr, m robert	i LiD
h ky 4	snyder, gene	i CoR	h mi 7	kildee, dale e.	i LiD
h ky 5	rogers, harold	o CoR	h mi 8	traxler, bob	i LaD
h ky 5	rogers, john d	o CoR	h mi 9	vanderjagt, guy	i CoR
h ky 6	hopkins, larry jones	i CoR	h mi10	allen, richard john	c CoR
s la	long, russell b	i CoD	h mi10	albosta, donald joseph	i LaD
h la 1	livingston, robert l.	i CoR	h mi11	davis, robert w	i MCR
h la 2	couhig, robert e jr	c CoR	h mi12	walsh, kirk	c CoR
h la 2	boggs, lindy (mrs hale)	i MoD	h mi12	bonior, david e.	i LiD
h la 3	tauzin, w j "billy"	i CoD	h mi14	caputo, victor d	o CoR
h la 3	donelon, james j	o CoR	h mi14	hertel, dennis m	o LiD
h la 4	roemer, charles e "buddy" iii	c CoD	h mi15	ford, william david	i LiD
h la 4	leach, claude "buddy"	i CoD	h mi16	dingell, john d.	i LaD
h la 5	huckaby, thomas jerald	i CoD	h mi17	brodhead, william m	i LiD
h la 6	moore, henson w.	i CoR	h mi18	blanchard, james johnston	i LaD
h la 7	breaux, john	i CoD	h mi19	broomfield, william s	i CoR
h la 8	long, gillis w	i MoD	h mn 1	erdahl, arlen	i MoR
h ma 1	conte, silvio o.	i MoR	h mn 2	hagedorn, tom	i CoR
h ma 2	boland, edward p	i LiD	h mn 3	frenzel, bill	i CoR
h ma 3	early, joseph d.	i LaD	h mn 4	berg, john r	c CoR
h ma 4	frank, barney	o LiD	h mn 4	vento, bruce f	i LiD
h ma 5	shannon, james	i LiD	h mn 5	sabo, martin olav	i LiD
h ma 6	trimarco, thomas m	c CoR	h mn 6	weber, vin	o CoR
h ma 6	mavroules, nicholas	i LaD	h mn 7	stangeland, arlan	i CoR
h ma 7	markey, edward j.	i LiD	h mn 8	oberstar, james l.	i LiD
h ma 8	o'neill, thomas	i LiD	s mo	eagleton, thomas f.	i LiD
h ma 9	moakley, john joseph	i LaD	s mo	mcnary, gene	c CoR
h ma10	heckler, margaret	i MoR	h mo 1	clay, william l	i LiD
h ma11	donnelly, brian j	i LaD	h mo 2	young, robert a.	i LaD
h ma12	studds, gerry e.	i LiD	h mo 3	gephardt, richard	i LaD
s md	mathias, charles mcc. jr.	i MoR	h mo 4	skelton, ike	i CoD
h md 1	bauman, robert e	i CoR	h mo 5	bolling, richard	i LaD
h md 2	long, clarence dickinson	i LiD	h mo 6	coleman, e thomas	i CoR
h md 2	bentley, helen delich	c CoR	h mo 7	taylor, gene	i CoR
h md 3	mikulski, barbara ann	i LiD	h mo 8	bailey, wendell	o CoR
h md 4	holt, marjorie	i CoR	h mo 8	gardner, steven m	o LiD
h md 5	spellman, gladys noon	i LiD	h mo 9	turner, john wayne	c CoR
h md 6	byron, goodloe e.	c CoD	h mo 9	volkmer, harold	i CoD
h md 6	byron, beverly butcher	i CoD	h mo10	burlison, bill d.	i LaD
h md 7	mitchell, parren j.	i LiD	h mo10	emerson, william (bill)	c CoR
h md 8	barnes, michael d	i LiD	h ms 1	moffett, t k	c CoR
h md 8	steers, newton i jr	c MoR	h ms 1	whitten, jamie lloyd	i CoD

Table A.2.   (continued)

1 2 3	4	5 6	1 2 3	4	5 6
h ms 2	bowen, david r	i CoD	h nj14	guarini, frank j.	i LaD
h ms 3	montgomery, gillespie v	i CoD	h nj15	o'sullivan, william j	o CoR
h ms 4	hinson, jon c.	i CoR	h nj15	dwyer, bernard j	o LiD
h ms 4	singletary, britt r	c CoD	h nm 1	lujan, manuel jr	i CoR
h ms 5	lott, trent	i CoR	h nm 2	skeen, joseph r	o CoR
h mt 1	williams, pat	i LiD	s nv	laxalt, paul	i CoR
h mt 2	marlenee, ronald charles	i CoR	h nv	santini, james david	i CoD
s nc	morgan, robert b.	i CoD	s ny	holtzman, elizabeth	c LiD
s nc	east, john p.	c CoR	s ny	javits, jacob k	i MoR
h nc 1	jones, walter	i CoD	s ny	d'amato, alfonse m	c CoR
h nc 2	fountain, l. h.	i CoD	h ny 1	carney, william	i CoR
h nc 3	whitley, charles o	i CoD	h ny 2	downey, thomas j.	i LiD
h nc 4	andrews, ike	i CoD	h ny 3	carman, gregory w	c CoR
h nc 4	hogan, thurman	c CoR	h ny 3	ambro, jerome a.	i LaD
h nc 5	neal, stephen l.	i CoD	h ny 4	lent, norman frederick	i CoR
h nc 5	bagnal, anne	c CoR	h ny 5	mcgrath, raymond j	o CoR
h nc 6	johnston, walter eugene iii	c CoR	h ny 6	leboutillier, john	c CoR
h nc 6	preyer, richardson	i MoD	h ny 6	wolff, lester l	i LiD
h nc 7	rose, charles g iii	i MoD	h ny 7	addabbo, joseph p congressman	i LiD
h nc 8	hefner, w g (bill)	i CoD	h ny 9	ferraro, geraldine a	i LiD
h nc 9	martin, james g	i CoR	h ny10	biaggi, mario	i LaD
h nc10	broyhill, james t.	i CoR	h ny11	scheuer, james h	i LiD
h nc11	hendon, william m	c CoR	h ny13	solarz, stephen j.	i LiD
h nc11	gudger, lamar	i CoD	h ny14	richmond, frederick w	i LiD
s nd	andrews, mark	o CoR	h ny15	atanasio, paul m	c CoR
h nd	smykowski, james george	o CoR	h ny15	zeferetti, leo c	i LaD
h nd	dorgan, byron l	o LiD	h ny17	molinari, guy v	c CoR
h ne 1	bereuter, douglas k	i CoR	h ny17	murphy, john m.	i LaD
h ne 2	daub, harold john jr (hal)	o CoR	h ny18	green, sedwick william	i MoR
h ne 3	smith, virginia d.	i CoR	h ny19	rangel, charles b.	i LiD
s nh	rudman, warren b	c CoR	h ny21	garcia, robert	i LiD
s nh	durkin, john anthony	i LiD	h ny24	ottinger, richard l	i LiD
h nh 1	d'amours, norman e.	i LaD	h ny25	fish, hamilton jr.	i MoR
h nh 1	cobleigh, marshall w	c CoR	h ny26	gilman, benjamin a	i MoR
h nh 2	gregg, judd alan	o CoR	h ny27	wallace, neil tyler	c CoR
h nh 2	arel, maurice l	o LiD	h ny27	mchugh, matthew f.	i LiD
h nj 1	florio, james j	i LiD	h ny28	stratton, samuel s	i LaD
h nj 3	muhler, marie sheehan	c MCR	h ny29	solomon, gerald b h	i CoR
h nj 3	howard, james j.	i LiD	h ny30	martin, david o'b	o CoR
h nj 4	smith, christopher h	c CoR	h ny31	mitchell, donald j.	i CoR
h nj 5	fenwick, millicent	i MoR	h ny32	wortley, george c	o CoR
h nj 6	forsythe, edwin b.	i MoR	h ny33	lee, gary a.	i CoR
h nj 7	roukema, margaret	c MoR	h ny34	horton, frank	i MoR
h nj 7	maguire, andrew	i LiD	h ny35	conable, barber benjamin jr	i CoR
h nj 8	roe, hon. robert a.	i LaD	h ny36	lafalce, john j.	i LaD
h nj 9	hollenbeck, harold c	i MoR	h ny36	feder, h william	c CoR
h nj10	rodino, peter w. jr	i LiD	h ny37	nowak, henry j.	i LiD
h nj11	minish, joseph george	i LaD	h ny38	kemp, jack	i CoR
h nj12	rinaldo, matthew j.	i MoR	h ny39	abdella, james	c CoR
h nj13	courter, james a	i CoR	h ny39	lundine, stanley n.	i LiD

Table A.2.   (continued)

1 2 3	4	5 6	1 2 3	4	5 6
s oh	glenn, john	i LaD	h pa 4	dougherty, charles f	i MoR
s oh	betts, james e	c CoR	h pa 5	schulze, richard t	i CoR
h oh 1	gradison, willis d jr	i CoR	h pa 6	yatron, gus	i LaD
h oh 2	atkins, tom	c CoR	h pa 7	rochford, dennis j	c CoR
h oh 2	luken, thomas a	i MoD	h pa 7	edgar, robert w.	i LiD
h oh 3	sealy, albert h	c CoR	h pa 8	coyne, james k	c CoR
h oh 3	hall, tony p.	i LiD	h pa 8	kostmayer, peter houston	i LiD
h oh 4	guyer, tennyson	i CoR	h pa 9	shuster, e. g. bud	i CoR
h oh 5	latta, delbert l.	i CoR	h pa10	mcdade, joseph m.	i MoR
h oh 6	mcewen, bob	o CoR	h pa11	musto, raphael	i LiD
h oh 7	brown, clarence j.	i CoR	h pa11	nelligan, james l	o CoR
h oh 8	kindness, hon. thomas n.	i CoR	h pa12	getty, charles a	c CoR
h oh 9	weber, edward f	c CoR	h pa12	murtha, john p.	i LaD
h oh 9	ashley, thomas l.	i LaD	h pa13	coughlin, lawrence	i MoR
h oh10	miller, clarence e.	i CoR	h pa14	thomas, stan	o CoR
h oh12	devine, samuel leeper	i CoR	h pa14	coyne, william j	o LiD
h oh13	pease, donald james	i LiD	h pa15	ritter, donald lawrence	i CoR
h oh14	mangels, louis arthur	c CoR	h pa16	walker, robert s	i CoR
h oh15	wylie, chalmers	i CoR	h pa17	seiverling, daniel s	c CoR
h oh17	ashbrook, john m.	i CoR	h pa17	ertel, allen e.	i LaD
h oh18	applegate, e douglas	i LaD	h pa18	walgren, doug	i LiD
h oh19	meshel, harry	c LiD	h pa20	gaydos, joseph m.	i LaD
h oh19	williams, lyle	i MoR	h pa21	bailey, donald allen	i LaD
h oh20	oakar, ms. mary rose	i LaD	h pa22	murphy, austin j.	i LaD
h oh21	stokes, louis	i LiD	h pa23	clinger, william f jr	i CoR
h oh22	nahra, joseph j	o CoR	h pa24	dicarlo, david c	c LaD
h oh23	mottl, ronald a.	i CoD	h pa24	marks, marc lincoln	i MoR
s ok	edwards, mickey	o CoR	h pa25	morris, robert henry	c CoR
s ok	coats, andy	o CoD	h pr	corrada, baltasar	i LiD
s ok	nickles, donald lee	o CoR	h ri 1	st germain, fernand j	i LiD
h ok 1	jones, james r.	i CoD	h ri 2	beard, edward p	i LiD
h ok 2	synar, michael lynn	i MoD	h ri 2	schneider, claudine cmarada	c MoR
h ok 2	richardson, gary lloyd	c CoR	s sc	hollings, ernest f.	i MoD
h ok 3	watkins, wesley wade	i CoD	h sc 1	hartnett, thomas forbes sr	o CoR
h ok 4	mccurdy, david k	o CoD	h sc 1	ravenel, charles d	o LiD
h ok 4	rutledge, howard elmer	o CoR	h sc 2	spence, floyd d.	i CoR
h ok 5	edwards, marvin h. mickey	i CoR	h sc 3	derrick, butler	i MoD
h ok 6	english, glenn	i CoD	h sc 3	parker, marshall j	c CoR
s or	packwood, bob	i MoR	h sc 4	campbell, carroll ashmore jr.	i CoR
h or 1	engdahl, lynn	c CoR	h sc 5	holland, kenneth l	i CoD
h or 1	aucoin, les	i LiD	h sc 6	jenrette, john w jr	i MoD
h or 2	smith, dennis alan	c CoR	h sc 6	napier, john l.	c CoR
h or 2	ullman, al	i LiD	s sd	mcgovern, george	i LiD
h or 3	wyden, ronald lee	c LiD	s sd	abdnor, james	c CoR
h or 4	fitzgerald, michael	c CoR	h sd 1	daschle, thomas andrew	i LiD
s pa	specter, arlen	o MoR	h sd 1	kull, bart	c CoR
s pa	flaherty, pete	o LiD	h sd 2	roberts, clint	o CoR
h pa 1	burke, robert r	c CoR	h tn 1	quillen, james	i CoR
h pa 2	gray, william h iii	i LiD	h tn 2	duncan, john j	i CoR
h pa 3	lederer, raymond f	i LiD	h tn 3	bouquard, marilyn lloyd	i CoD

able A.2.   (continued)

2 3	4	5 6	1 2 3	4	5 6
tn 5	boner, william hill	i LaD	h va 6	butler, m caldwell	i CoR
tn 5	adams, michael f	c CoR	h va 7	robinson, j. kenneth	i CoR
tn 6	beard, robin	i CoR	h va 8	harris, herbert e ii	i LiD
tn 7	jones, ed	i CoD	h va 8	parris, stanford e	c CoR
tn 8	ford, harold e.	i LiD	h va 9	wampler, william creed	i CoR
tx 1	hall, sam b jr	i CoD	h va10	fisher, joseph l	i LiD
tx 2	wilson, charles nesbitt	i CoD	h va10	wolf, frank r	c CoR
tx 3	collins, james m	i CoR	s vt	leahy, patrick j.	i LiD
tx 4	hall, ralph moody	o CoD	s vt	ledbetter, stewart	c CoR
tx 4	wright, john hairston	o CoR	h vt	jeffords, james	i MoR
tx 5	pauken, thomas w	c CoR	s wa	magnuson, warren g	i LiD
tx 5	mattox, james	i MoD	s wa	gorton, slade	c MCR
tx 6	gramm, william phillip	i CoD	h wa 1	pritchard, joel	i MoR
tx 7	archer, william	i CoR	h wa 2	snider, neal	c CoR
tx 8	fields, jack m jr	c CoR	h wa 2	swift, allan byron	i LiD
tx 8	eckhardt, robert	i LiD	h wa 3	bonker, donald l	i LiD
tx 9	brooks, jack	i MoD	h wa 4	morrison, sideney wallace	c CoR
tx10	pickle, james jarrell	i CoD	h wa 4	mccormack, mike	i LaD
tx11	leath, james marvin	i CoD	h wa 5	sonneland, john edward	c CoR
tx12	bradshaw, james e	c CoR	h wa 5	foley, thomas s.	i LaD
tx12	wright, jim	i LaD	h wa 6	dicks, norman d.	i LaD
tx13	hightower, jack	i CoD	h wa 7	dunlap, ronald w	c CoR
tx14	patman, william n (bill)	o MoD	h wa 7	lowry, michael e.	i LiD
tx14	concklin, charles lewis md	o CoR	s wi	nelson, gaylord a.	i LiD
tx15	garza, e (kika) dela	i CoD	s wi	kasten, robert jr	c CoR
tx16	white, richard c.	i CoD	h wi 1	aspin, les	i LiD
tx17	stenholm, charles	i CoD	h wi 1	canary, kathryn h	c CoR
tx18	leland, george thomas	i LiD	h wi 1	petrie, william w	c MoR
tx19	hance, kent	i CoD	h wi 2	wright, james a	c CoR
tx20	gonzalez, henry b	i LaD	h wi 2	kastenmeier, robert w	i LiD
tx21	loeffler, tom	i CoR	h wi 3	baldus, alvin	i LiD
tx22	andrews, michael allen	c CoD	h wi 3	gunderson, steven craig	c CoR
tx22	paul, ron	i CoR	h wi 4	zablocki, clement j.	i LaD
tx23	kazen, abraham	i CoD	h wi 5	reuss, henry s	i LiD
tx24	smothers, claiborne w	c CoR	h wi 6	goyke, gary r	c LiD
tx24	frost, martin	i LaD	h wi 6	petri, thomas	o MoR
s ut	garn, e. j. jake	i CoR	h wi 7	obey, david	i LiD
h ut 1	hansen, james v	c CoR	h wi 8	roth, toby	i CoR
h ut 1	mckay, gunn k.	i CoD	h wi 9	sensenbrenner, f. james jr.	i CoR
h ut 2	marriott, dan	i CoR	h wv 1	mollohan, robert	i LaD
h va 1	trible, paul seward jr	i CoR	h wv 2	benedict, cleveland keith	o CoR
h va 2	whitehust, g william	i CoR	h wv 3	staton, david michael "mick"	c CoR
h va 3	bliley, thomas j jr	o CoR	h wv 3	hutchinson, john g	i MoD
h va 4	daniel, robert w jr	i CoR	h wv 4	rahall, nick joe ii	i LaD
h va 5	daniel, dan (w c "dan" daniel)	i CoD	h wy	cheney, richard bruce	i CoR

Key: (1) s=Senate; h=House; (2) state; (3) House district (blank if Senate race or state has only one House seat);(4) candidate name; (5) i=incumbent, c=challenger, o=open seat; (6) ideology code (see Table A.1)

Table A.3. Firm membership in five network clusters

Firm	Si	Mc	St	Di	Ii
1. American Can	4	1	4	6	5
2. Arcata	5	0	2	0	6
3. Armco	4	3	1	6	4
4. Beckman Instruments	5	2	7	1	1
5. Beckton, Dickinson	2	4	7	3	8
6. Bethlehem Steel	2	3	1	2	3
7. Blue Bell	4	6	3	1	1
8. Burlington Industries	4	2	3	5	5
9. Champion International	2	4	2	7	4
10. Chrysler	2	2	1	0	7
11. Continental Group	2	0	4	2	4
12. Corning Glass Works	3	3	5	2	2
13. Dart & Kraft	4	2	2	5	3
14. Deere	1	2	1	4	4
15. R. R. Donnelley	1	4	2	4	6
16. Dow Chemical	4	2	3	0	6
17. EG & G	2	4	4	7	1
18. Eastman Kodak	0	2	7	2	3
19. Esmark	1	2	6	4	1
20. Exxon	4	2	8	5	5
21. Ford	2	1	1	7	2
22. General Electric	2	2	1	2	4
23. General Motors	2	3	1	2	3
24. Georgia-Pacific	4	2	5	0	5
25. B. F. Goodrich	3	1	3	6	6
26. Goodyear	3	3	3	2	4
27. International Harvester	1	1	1	4	4
28. International Paper	3	3	2	6	3
29. LTV	2	5	1	3	1
30. Libbey-Owens-Ford	4	1	4	3	8
31. Lone Star Industries	2	4	5	0	0
32. Louisiana-Pacific	5	4	5	1	1
33. Mc Donnell-Douglas	2	0	1	1	1
34. Manville	2	3	4	1	1
35. Minnesota Mining & Mfg	3	2	7	2	3
36. Mobil	4	2	8	7	1
37. Monsanto	3	2	3	6	2
38. National Can	1	5	4	3	1
39. National Gypsum	4	3	5	0	1
40. Owens-Illinois	3	1	4	2	4
41. Pepsico	3	2	2	2	3
42. Philip Morris	2	2	6	6	2
43. Potlach	4	0	2	0	6
44. R. J. Reynolds	2	6	6	2	6
45. Raytheon	2	2	1	7	2
46. Rockwell International	2	5	1	2	7
47. Sperry	2	2	1	2	5
48. Springs Mills	0	0	0	0	5

Table A.3. (continued)

Firm	Si	Mc	St	Di	Ii
49. J. P. Stevens	4	6	0	1	5
50. Texaco	4	2	8	2	2
51. Time	2	2	2	3	2
52. Union Carbide	4	3	3	2	7
53. Uniroyal	1	0	3	7	1
54. U.S. Steel	3	3	1	2	3
55. United Technologies	2	2	1	5	7
56. Westinghouse	2	2	1	2	6
57. Weyerhaeuser	3	2	2	4	3

Key: Si = similarity of political behavior network; Mc = market constraint network; St = common stockholdings network; Di = direct interlocks network; Ii = indirect interlocks network. Numbers in cells represent arbitrary cluster numbers. Zeros indicate isolates.

Table A.4. Centrality in five networks

Firm	Si	Mc	St	Di	Ii
American Can	.697	.684	.333	.048	.268
Arcata	.403	.170	.237	.023	.011
Armco	.703	.853	.625	.390	.401
Beckman Instruments	.464	.498	.681	.000	.000
Beckton, Dickinson	.404	.531	.607	.000	.135
Bethlehem Steel	.674	1.000	.785	.233	.354
Blue Bell	.535	.468	.639	.000	.000
Burlington Industries	.808	.427	.658	.234	.278
Champion International	.597	.009	.700	.078	.343
Chrysler	.508	.749	.852	.012	.276
Continental Group	.357	.622	.059	.534	.677
Corning Glass Works	.457	.397	.743	.041	.515
Dart & Kraft	.787	.494	1.000	.684	.448
Deere	.584	.576	.823	.270	.185
R. R. Donnelley	.569	.000	.586	.079	.165
Dow Chemical	.939	.560	.745	.016	.126
EG & G	.270	.484	.517	.000	.024
Eastman Kodak	.562	.445	.824	.664	.575
Esmark	.527	.367	.520	.000	.180
Exxon	.719	.263	.780	.231	.362
Ford	.802	.988	.407	.001	.428
General Electric	.980	.709	.872	.139	.891
General Motors	1.000	.807	.654	1.000	.749
Georgia-Pacific	.849	.431	.675	.111	.090
B. F. Goodrich	.779	.648	.354	.147	.342
Goodyear	.740	.589	.718	.382	.441
International Harvester	.739	.694	.356	.074	.231
International Paper	.905	.282	.880	.439	.486
LTV	.891	.731	.455	.000	.207
Libbey-Owens-Ford	.660	.548	.324	.000	.153
Lone Star Industries	.356	.509	.578	.026	.093
Louisiana-Pacific	.601	.328	.417	.000	.000
Mc Donnell-Douglas	.644	.696	.433	.000	.000
Manville	.553	.467	.568	.000	.000
Minnesota Mining & Mfg	.733	.400	.837	.398	.208
Mobil	.828	.343	.763	.000	.152
Monsanto	.730	.526	.873	.068	.442
National Can	.442	.685	.404	.000	.173
National Gypsum	.514	.278	.667	.000	.033
Owens-Illinois	.670	.459	.538	.090	.297
Pepsico	.890	.336	.620	.284	.591
Philip Morris	.675	.291	.781	.000	.408
Potlach	.597	.184	.351	.069	.180
R. J. Reynolds	.850	.182	.739	.362	.649
Raytheon	.550	.613	.693	.119	.095
Rockwell International	.524	.765	.460	.153	.297
Sperry	.698	.663	.863	.404	.578
Springs Mills	.620	.355	.159	.019	.025
J. P. Stevens	.758	.394	.564	.068	.000

Table A.4. (continued)

Firm	Si	Mc	St	Di	Ii
Texaco	.898	.344	.695	.046	.329
Time	.703	.085	.673	.007	.324
Union Carbide	.606	.565	.831	.069	.956
Uniroyal	.307	.575	.185	.000	.102
U.S. Steel	.918	.687	.529	.722	.758
United Technologies	.964	.749	.800	.012	.489
Westinghouse	.861	.629	.671	.093	1.000
Weyerhaeuser	.844	.089	.769	.115	.042

Key: Si = similarity of political behavior network; Mc = market constraint network; St = common stockholdings network; Di = direct interlocks network; Ii = indirect interlocks network.

References

Alba, Richard D. 1973. "A graph-theoretic definition of a sociometric clique." *Journal of Mathematical Sociology* 3:113–126.

Alba, Richard D., and Gwen Moore. 1983. "Elite social circles." Pp. 245–261 in Ronald S. Burt, Michael J. Minor, and Associates, *Applied Network Analysis: A Methodological Introduction.* Beverly Hills: Sage.

Alchian, Armen A., and Harold Demsetz. 1972. "Production, information cost, and economic organization." *American Economic Review* 62:777–795.

Aldrich, Howard E. 1979. *Organizations and Environments.* Englewood Cliffs, N.J.: Prentice-Hall.

Aldrich, Howard E., and Jeffrey Pfeffer. 1976. "Environments of organizations." *Annual Review of Sociology* 2:79–105.

Alexander, Herbert E. 1976. *Financing the 1972 Election.* Lexington, Mass.: Lexington Books.

—— 1981. "Corporate political behavior." Pp. 33–47 in Thornton Bradshaw and David Vogel, eds., *Corporations and Their Critics.* New York: McGraw-Hill.

—— 1983. *Financing the 1980 Election.* Lexington, Mass.: Lexington Books.

Alford, Robert R., and Roger Friedland. 1985. *Powers of Theory.* New York: Cambridge University Press.

Allen, Frederick Lewis. 1935. *The Lords of Creation.* New York: Harper & Row.

Allen, Michael P. 1974. "The structure of interorganizational elite cooptation: Interlocking corporate directorates." *American Sociological Review* 39:393–406.

—— 1978. "Economic interest groups and the corporate elite structure." *Social Science Quarterly* 58:597–615.

Allen, Michael P., and Philip Broyles. 1989. "Class hegemony and political finance: Presidential campaign contributions of wealthy capitalist families." *American Sociological Review* 54:275–287.

Amenta, Edwin, and Sunita Parikh. 1991. "Capitalists did not want the Social Security Act: A critique of the 'capitalist dominance' thesis." *American Sociological Review* 56:124–129.

Arabie, Phipps, Scott A. Boorman, and Paul R. Levitt. 1978. "Constructing blockmodels: How and why." *Journal of Mathematical Psychology* 17:21–63.

Axelrod, Robert. 1984. *The Evolution of Cooperation.* New York: Basic Books.

Bachrach, Peter, and Morton S. Baratz. 1962. "The two faces of power." *American Political Science Review* 56:947–952.

—— 1970. *Power and Poverty: Theory and Practice.* New York: Oxford University Press.

Baker, Frank B., and Lawrence J. Hubert. 1981. "The analysis of social interaction data: A nonparametric technique." *Sociological Methods and Research* 9:339–361.

Baker, Wayne E. 1984. "The social structure of a national securities market." *American Journal of Sociology* 89:775–811.

Balbus, Isaac. "Ruling elite theory vs. Marxist class analysis." *Monthly Review* 23:36–46.

Baran, Paul A., and Paul M. Sweezy. 1966. *Monopoly Capital.* New York: Monthly Review Press.

Barone, Michael, and Grant Ujifusa. 1982. *The Almanac of American Politics.* Washington: National Journal.

Barton, Allen H. 1980. "Fault lines in American elite consensus." *Daedalus* 109 (Summer):1–24.

—— 1985. "Determinants of economic attitudes in the American business elite." *American Journal of Sociology* 91:54–87.

Bauer, Raymond A., Ithiel de Sola Pool, and Lewis Anthony Dexter. [1963] 1972. *American Business and Public Policy: The Politics of Foreign Trade.* New York: Atherton Press.

Bell, Daniel. 1960. *The End of Ideology.* New York: Collier.

Berk, Richard A. 1983. "An introduction to sample selection bias in sociological data." *American Sociological Review* 48:386–398.

Berkowitz, S. D. 1982. *An Introduction to Structural Analysis.* Toronto: Butterworths.

Berkowitz, S. D., Peter Carrington, Yehuda Kotowitz, and Leonard Waverman. 1979. "The determination of enterprise groupings through combined ownership and directorship ties." *Social Networks* 1:391–413.

Berle, Adolf A., and Gardiner C. Means. [1932] 1968. *The Modern Corporation and Private Property.* New York: Harcourt, Brace & World.

Blalock, Hubert M., Jr. 1979. *Social Statistics.* Second Edition. New York: McGraw-Hill.

Blau, Peter M. 1964. *Exchange and Power in Social Life.* New York: John Wiley and Sons.

—— 1977. *Inequality and Heterogeneity.* New York: Free Press.

—— 1982. "Structural sociology and network analysis: An overview." Pp. 273–279 in Peter V. Marsden and Nan Lin, eds., *Social Structure and Network Analysis.* Beverly Hills: Sage.

Blau, Peter M., and Joseph E. Schwartz. 1984. *Crosscutting Social Circles.* Orlando, Fla.: Academic Press.

Block, Fred. 1977. "The ruling class does not rule: Notes on the Marxist theory of the state." *Socialist Revolution* 7, no. 3:6–28.

———— 1987. *Revising State Theory: Essays in Politics and Postindustrialism.* Philadelphia: Temple University Press.

Blin, Jean-Marie and Claude Cohen. 1977. "Technological similarity and aggregation in input-output systems: A cluster-analytic approach." *Review of Economics and Statistics* 59:82–91.

Boies, John L. 1989. "Money, business, and the state: Material interests, *Fortune* 500 corporations, and the size of political action committees." *American Sociological Review* 54:821–833.

Bonacich, Phillip. 1972. "Technique for analyzing overlapping memberships." Pp. 176–185 in Herbert Costner, ed., *Sociological Methodology 1972.* San Francisco: Jossey-Bass.

———— 1987. "Power and centrality: A family of measures." *American Journal of Sociology* 92:1170–1182.

Bowman, John R. 1989. *Capitalist Collective Action.* New York: Cambridge University Press.

Budde, Bernadette. 1980. "The practical role of corporate PACs in the political process." *Arizona Law Review* 22:555–567.

Bunting, David. 1976a. "Corporate interlocking: Part II—The modern money trust." *Directors and Boards* 1 (Summer):27–37.

———— 1976b. "Corporate interlocking: Part III—Interlocks and return on investment." *Directors and Boards* 1 (Fall):4–11.

Burnham, Walter Dean. 1970. *Critical Elections and the Mainsprings of American Politics.* New York: W. W. Norton and Co.

Burris, Val. 1987. "The political partisanship of American business: A study of corporate political action committees." *American Sociological Review* 52:732–744.

Burt, Ronald S. 1975. "Corporate society: A time series analysis of network structure." *Social Science Research* 4:271–328.

———— 1982. *Toward A Structural Theory of Action: Network Models of Social Structure, Perception, and Action.* New York: Academic Press.

———— 1983a. *Corporate Profits and Cooptation: Networks of Market Constraints and Directorate Ties in the American Economy.* New York: Academic Press.

———— 1983b. "Cohesion versus structural equivalence as a basis for network subgroups." Pp. 262–282 in Ronald S. Burt, Michael J. Minor, and Associates, *Applied Network Analysis: A Methodological Introduction.* Beverly Hills: Sage.

———— 1986. "A cautionary note." *Social Networks* 8:205–211.

———— 1987a. "Broken ties and corporate markets." Unpublished manuscript. Department of Sociology, Columbia University.

———— 1987b. "Social contagion and innovation: Cohesion versus structural equivalence." *American Journal of Sociology* 92:1287–1335.

———— 1988a. "The stability of American markets." *American Journal of Sociology* 94:356–395.

———— 1988b. "Some properties of structural equivalence measures derived from sociometric choice data." *Social Networks* 10:1–28.

———— 1990. "Equivalence conditions for social contagion." Paper presented at the Annual Sunbelt Social Network Conference. San Diego.

Burton, Michael G., and John Higley. 1987a. "Invitation to elite theory: The basic contentions reconsidered." Pp. 219–238 in G. William Domhoff and Thomas R. Dye, eds., *Power Elites and Organizations*. Beverly Hills: Sage.

—— 1987b. "Elite settlements." *American Sociological Review* 52:295–307.

Business Week. 1970. "Why the big traders worry industry." July 25:53–61.

Carosso, Vincent P. 1970. *Investment Banking in America*. Cambridge: Harvard University Press.

Carrington, Peter J. 1981. "Horizontal co-optation through corporate interlocks." Ph.D. dissertation, Department of Sociology, University of Toronto.

Cartwright, Dorwin, and Frank Harary. 1956. "Structural balance: A generalization of Heider's theory." *Psychological Review* 63:277–293.

Caswell, Julie A. 1984. "Direct stockholding and network interlocking directorates: Control of firms in the agribusiness sector." Ph.D. dissertation, Department of Agricultural Economics, University of Wisconsin, Madison.

Chandler, Alfred D., Jr. 1962. *Strategy and Structure*. Cambridge: The MIT Press.

—— 1977. *The Visible Hand*. Cambridge: Harvard University Press.

Chappel, Henry W., Jr. 1982. "Campaign contributions and congressional voting: A simultaneous probit-tobit model." *Review of Economics and Statistics* 64:77–83.

Chase, Ivan D. 1980. "Social process and hierarchy formation in small groups: A comparative perspective." *American Sociological Review* 45:905–924.

Clawson, Dan, Alan Neustadtl, and James Bearden. 1986. "The logic of business unity: Corporate contributions in the 1980 election." *American Sociological Review* 51:797–811.

Clawson, Dan, and Alan Neustadtl. 1989. "Interlocks, PACs, and corporate conservatism." *American Journal of Sociology* 94:749–773.

—— 1990. "What corporate PAC directors say about politics." Unpublished manuscript, Department of Sociology, University of Massachusetts, Amherst.

Clawson, Dan, and Tie-ting Su. 1990. "Was 1980 Special? A comparison of 1980 and 1986 corporate PAC contributions." *Sociological Quarterly* 31:371–387.

Clegg, Stewart. 1989. *Frameworks of Power*. London: Sage.

Cliff, Andrew, and Keith Ord. 1981. *Spatial Processes: Models and Applications*. London: Pion.

Clinard, Marshall B., Peter C. Yeager, J. M. Brissett, D. Petrashek, and E. Harries. 1979. *Illegal Corporate Behavior*. Washington: U.S. Government Printing Office.

Cochran, Thomas C., and William Miller. [1942] 1961. *The Age of Enterprise*. New York: Harper & Row.

Coleman, James S. 1974. *Power and the Structure of Society*. New York: W. W. Norton and Co.

———— 1982. *The Asymmetric Society.* Syracuse, N.Y.: Syracuse University Press.

———— 1990. *Foundations of Social Theory.* Cambridge: Harvard University Press.

Coleman, James S., Elihu Katz, and Herbert Menzel. 1966. *Medical Innovation.* New York: Bobbs-Merrill.

Cook, Karen S. 1977. "Exchange and power in networks of interorganizational relations." *Sociological Quarterly* 18:62–82.

Cook, Karen S., and Richard M. Emerson. 1978. "Power, equity, and commitment in exchange networks." *American Sociological Review* 43:721–739.

Cook, Karen S., Richard M. Emerson, Mary R. Gillmore, and Toshio Yamagishi. 1983. "The distribution of power in n-person exchange networks: Theory and experimental results." *American Journal of Sociology* 89:275–305.

Cook, Karen S., and Margaret Levi, eds. 1990. *The Limits of Rationality.* New York: Cambridge University Press.

Corey, Lewis. 1930. *The House of Morgan.* New York: G. Howard Watt.

Corporate Data Exchange. 1981. *Stock Ownership Directory: Fortune 500.* New York: Corporate Data Exchange.

Crenson, Matthew A. 1971. *The Un-Politics of Air Pollution: A Study of Non-Decisionmaking in the Cities.* Baltimore: The Johns Hopkins University Press.

Dahl, Robert A. 1957. "The concept of power." *Behavioral Science* 2:201–215.

———— 1958. "A critique of the ruling elite model." *American Political Science Review* 52:463–469.

———— 1961. *Who Governs?* New Haven: Yale University Press.

———— 1970. *After the Revolution?* New Haven: Yale University Press.

———— 1982. *Dilemmas of Pluralist Democracy.* New Haven: Yale University Press.

Dahl, Robert A., and Charles E. Lindblom. [1953] 1976. *Politics, Economics, and Welfare.* Chicago: University of Chicago Press.

Dahrendorf, Ralf. 1959. *Class and Class Conflict in Industrial Society.* Stanford: Stanford University Press.

Davis, James A. 1963. "Structural balance, mechanical solidarity, and interpersonal relations." *American Journal of Sociology* 68:444–463.

Deutscher, Irwin. 1973. *What We Say/What We Do.* Glenview, Ill.: Scott, Foresman, and Co.

Devine, Joel A. 1985. "State and state expenditure: Determinants of social investment and social consumption spending in the postwar United States." *American Sociological Review* 50:150–165.

DiMaggio, Paul J., and Walter W. Powell. 1983. "The iron cage revisited: Institutional isomorphism and collective rationality in organizational fields." *American Sociological Review* 48:147–160.

DiTomaso, Nancy. 1980. "Organizational analysis and power structure research." Pp. 255–268 in G. William Domhoff, ed., *Power Structure Research.* Beverly Hills: Sage.

Domhoff, G. William. 1967. *Who Rules America?* Englewood Cliffs, N.J.: Prentice-Hall.

——— 1970. *The Higher Circles.* New York: Vintage.

——— 1974. *The Bohemian Grove and Other Retreats.* New York: Harper & Row.

——— 1979. *The Powers That Be.* New York: Vintage.

——— 1983. *Who Rules America Now?* Englewood Cliffs, N.J.: Prentice-Hall.

——— 1990. *The Power Elite and the State.* New York: Aldine de Gruyter.

Dooley, Peter C. 1969. "The interlocking directorate." *American Economic Review* 59:314–323.

Doreian, Patrick. 1981. "Estimating linear models with spatially distributed data." Pp. 359–388 in Samuel Leinhardt, ed., *Sociological Methodology 1981.* San Francisco: Jossey-Bass.

Dow, Malcolm M., Michael L. Burton, Douglas R. White, and Karl P. Reitz. 1984. "Galton's problem as network autocorrelation." *American Ethnologist* 11:754–770.

Durkheim, Emile. [1893] 1933. *The Division of Labor in Society.* New York: Free Press.

——— [1897] 1951. *Suicide.* New York: Free Press.

——— [1895] 1966. *The Rules of Sociological Method.* New York: Free Press.

Dye, Thomas R. 1983. *Who's Running America? The Reagan Years.* Englewood Cliffs, N.J.: Prentice-Hall.

Eismeier, Theodore J., and Philip H. Pollock III. 1984. "Political action committees: Varieties of organization and strategy." Pp. 122–141 in Michael J. Malbin, ed., *Money and Politics in the United States: Financing Elections in the 1980s.* Chatham, N.J.: Chatham House.

——— 1988. *Business, Money, and the Rise of Corporate PACs in American Elections.* New York: Quorum.

Elster, Jon, and Aanund Hylland, eds. 1986. *Foundations of Social Choice Theory.* New York: Cambridge University Press.

Emerson, Richard M. 1962. "Power-dependence relations." *American Sociological Review* 27:32–41.

Epstein, Edwin M. 1979. "The emergence of political action committees." Pp. 159–198 in Herbert E. Alexander, ed., *Political Finance.* Beverly Hills: Sage.

——— 1984. "PACs and the modern political process." Pp. 399–504 in Betty Bock, Harvey J. Goldschmid, Ira M. Millstein, and F.M. Scherer, eds., *The Impact of the Modern Corporation.* New York: Columbia University Press.

Esping-Andersen, Gosta, Roger Friedland, and Erik Olin Wright. 1976. "Modes of class struggle and the capitalist state." *Kapitalistate* nos. 4–5:186–220.

Esty, Daniel C., and Richard E. Caves. 1983. "Market structure and political influence: New data on political expenditures, activity, and success." *Economic Inquiry* 21:24–38.

Etzioni, Amitai. 1984. *Capital Corruption: The New Attack on American Democracy.* New York: Harcourt Brace Jovanovich.

——— 1988. *The Moral Dimension.* New York: Free Press.

Fararo, Thomas J., and John Skvoretz. 1987. "Unification research programs: Integrating two structural theories." *American Journal of Sociology* 92:1183–1209.

Faust, Katherine and A. Kimball Romney. 1985. "Does STRUCTURE find structure? A critique of Burt's use of distance as a measure of structural equivalence." *Social Networks* 7:77–103.

Ferguson, Thomas, and Joel Rogers. 1986. *Right Turn: The Decline of the Democrats and the Future of American Politics*. New York: Hill and Wang.

Fienberg, Stephen E., Michael M. Meyer, and Stanley S. Wasserman. 1985. "Statistical analysis of multiple sociometric relations." *Journal of the American Statistical Association* 80:51–67.

Fireman, Bruce, and William Gamson. 1979. "Utilitarian logic in the resource mobilization perspective." Pp. 8–44 in Mayer N. Zald and John D. McCarthy, eds., *The Dynamics of Social Movements*. Cambridge, Mass.: Winthrop.

Flanigan, William H. 1972. *Political Behavior of the American Electorate*. Second Edition. Boston: Allyn and Bacon.

Fligstein, Neil. 1990. *The Transformation of Corporate Control*. Cambridge: Harvard University Press.

Freeman, Linton C. 1979. "Centrality in social networks: I. Conceptual clarification." *Social Networks* 1:215–239.

Friedkin, Noah E. 1984. "Structural cohesion and equivalence explanations of social homogeneity." *Sociological Methods and Research* 12:235–261.

Friedland, Roger, and Donald Palmer. 1984. "Park Place and Main Street: Business and the urban power structure." *Annual Review of Sociology* 10:393–416.

Galaskiewicz, Joseph. 1985. *Social Organization of an Urban Grants Economy*. Orlando, Fla.: Academic Press.

Galaskiewicz, Joseph, and Ronald S. Burt. 1991. "Interorganization contagion in corporate philanthropy." *Administrative Science Quarterly* 36:88–105.

Galaskiewicz, Joseph, Stanley Wasserman, Barbara Rauschenbach, Wolfgang Bielefeld, and Patti Mullaney. 1985. "The impact of corporate power, social status, and market position on corporate interlocks in a regional network." *Social Forces* 64:403–431.

Galbraith, John Kenneth. 1952. *American Capitalism*. Boston: Houghton Mifflin.

Giddens, Anthony. 1973. *Class Structure of the Advanced Societies*. New York: Harper & Row.

Glasberg, Davita Silfen. 1989. *The Power of Collective Purse Strings*. Berkeley: University of California Press.

Gopoian, J. David. 1984. "What makes PACs tick?: An analysis of the allocation patterns of economic interest groups." *American Journal of Political Science* 28:259–281.

Gramsci, Antonio. 1971. *Prison Notebooks*. New York: International Publishers.

Granovetter, Mark S. 1973. "The strength of weak ties." *American Journal of Sociology* 78:1360–1380.

——— 1985. "Economic action and social structure: The problem of embeddedness." *American Journal of Sociology* 91:481–510.

Green, Donald, and Jonathan Krasno. 1988. "Salvation for the spendthrift incumbent: Reestimating the effects of campaign spending in House elections." *American Journal of Political Science* 32:884–907.

——— 1990. "Rebuttal to Jacobson's 'New evidence for old arguments.'" *American Journal of Political Science* 34:363–372.

Green, Mark, and Andrew Buchsbaum. 1980. *The Corporate Lobbies: Political Profiles of the Business Roundtable and the Chamber of Commerce.* Washington: Public Citizen.

Grenzke, Janet M. 1989. "PACs and the congressional supermarket: The currency is complex." *American Journal of Political Science* 33:1–24.

Griffin, Larry J., Joel A. Devine, and Michael Wallace. 1982. "Monopoly capital, organized labor, and military expenditures in the United States, 1949–1976." *American Journal of Sociology* 88:S113-S153.

Hacker, Andrew. 1976. "What rules America?" Pp. 363–371 in Maurice Zeitlin, ed., *American Society, Inc.* Second Edition. Chicago: Rand McNally.

Handler, Edward, and John Mulkern. 1982. *Business in Politics.* Lexington, Mass.: Lexington Books.

Hannan, Michael T., and Alice A. Young. 1977. "Estimation in panel models: Results on pooling cross-sections and time series." Pp. 52–83 in David R. Heise, ed., *Sociological Methodology 1977.* San Francisco: Jossey-Bass.

Harary, Frank, Robert Norman, and Dorwin Cartwright. 1965. *Structural Models: An Introduction to the Theory of Directed Graphs.* New York: John Wiley and Sons.

Hechter, Michael. 1987. *Principles of Group Solidarity.* Berkeley: University of California Press.

Heckathorn, Douglas D. 1984. "Mathematical theory construction in sociology: Analytic power, scope, and descriptive accuracy as trade-offs." *Journal of Mathematical Sociology* 10:295–323.

Herman, Edward S. 1981. *Corporate Control, Corporate Power.* New York: Cambridge University Press.

Herndon, James F. 1982. "Access, record, and competition as influences on interest group contributions to Congressional campaigns." *Journal of Politics* 44:996–1019.

Hicks, Alexander. 1984. "Elections, Keynes, bureaucracy, and class: Explaining U.S. budget deficits, 1961–1978." *American Sociological Review* 49:165–182.

Hirschman, Albert O. 1970. *Exit, Voice, and Loyalty.* Cambridge: Harvard University Press.

Holland, Paul W., and Samuel Leinhardt. 1970. "A method for detecting structure in sociometric data." *American Journal of Sociology* 70:492–513.

Hopkins, Terence K. 1964. *The Exercise of Influence in Small Groups.* Totowa, N.J.: Bedminster.

Hubert, Lawrence J. 1987. *Assignment Methods in Combinatorial Data Analysis.* New York: Marcel Dekker.

Hunter, Floyd. 1953. *Community Power Structure*. Chapel Hill: University of North Carolina Press.

Jacobs, David. 1974. "Dependency and vulnerability: An exchange approach to the control of organizations." *Administrative Science Quarterly* 19:45–59.

——— 1987. "Business resources and taxation: A cross-sectional examination of the relationship between economic organization and public policy." *Sociological Quarterly* 28:437–454.

——— 1988. "Corporate economic power and the state: A longitudinal assessment of two explanations." *American Journal of Sociology* 93:852–881.

Jacobson, Gary C. 1980. *Money in Congressional Elections*. New Haven: Yale University Press.

——— 1984. "Money in the 1980 and 1982 Congressional elections." Pp. 38–69 in Michael J. Malbin, ed., *Money and Politics in the United States: Financing Elections in the 1980s*. Chatham, N.J.: Chatham House.

——— 1990. "The effects of campaign spending in House elections: New evidence for old arguments." *American Journal of Political Science* 34:334–362.

Jenkins, J. Craig. 1983. "Resource mobilization and the study of social movements." *Annual Review of Sociology* 9:527–553.

Jenkins, J. Craig, and Barbara Brents. 1991. "Capitalists and social security: What did they really want?" *American Sociological Review* 56:129–132.

Jensen, Michael, and William Meckling. 1976. "Theory of the firm: Managerial behavior, agency costs, and ownership structure." *Journal of Financial Economics* 3:305–360.

Jones, Woodrow, Jr., and K. Robert Keiser. 1987. "Issue visibility and the effects of PAC money." *Social Science Quarterly* 68:170–176.

Josephson, Matthew. 1934. *The Robber Barons*. New York: Harcourt, Brace, and Co.

——— 1972. *The Money Lords*. New York: New American Library.

Kadushin, Charles. 1968. "Power, influence, and social circles: A new methodology for studying opinion makers." *American Sociological Review* 33:685–698.

Kaysen, Carl, and Donald F. Turner. 1959. *Antitrust Policy*. Cambridge: Harvard University Press.

Keller, Suzanne. 1963. *Beyond the Ruling Class*. New York: Random House.

Keohane, Robert, and Joseph Nye. 1977. *Power and Interdependence: World Politics in Transition*. Boston: Little, Brown.

Key, V. O. 1955. "A theory of critical elections." *Journal of Politics* 17:3–18.

Kingdon, John W. 1984. *Agendas, Alternatives, and Public Policy*. Boston: Little, Brown.

Knoke, David. 1988. "Incentives in collective action organizations." *American Sociological Review* 53:311–329.

Knoke, David, and Ronald S. Burt. 1983. "Prominence." Pp. 195–222 in Ronald S. Burt, Michael J. Minor, and Associates, *Applied Network Analysis: A Methodological Introduction*. Beverly Hills: Sage.

Koenig, Thomas. 1979. "Interlocking directorates among the largest Ameri-

can corporations and their significance for corporate political activity."
Ph.D. dissertation, Department of Sociology, University of California,
Santa Barbara.

—— 1987. "Business support for disclosure of corporate campaign contributions: An instructive paradox." Pp. 82–96 in Michael Schwartz, ed.,
The Structure of Power in America. New York: Holmes & Meier.

Koenig, Thomas, and Robert Gogel. 1981. "Interlocking corporate directorates
as a social network." *American Journal of Economics and Sociology*
40:37–50.

Koenig, Thomas, Robert Gogel, and John Sonquist. 1979. "Models of the significance of interlocking corporate directorates." *American Journal of
Economics and Sociology* 38:173–186.

Kolko, Gabriel. 1963. *The Triumph of Conservatism*. New York: Free Press.

Kornhauser, William. 1968. "'Power elite' or 'veto groups'?" Pp. 37–59 in G.
William Domhoff and Hoyt Ballard, eds., *C. Wright Mills and the Power
Elite*. Boston: Beacon Press.

Kotz, David M. 1978. *Bank Control of Large Corporations in the United
States*. Berkeley: University of California Press.

Krackhardt, David. 1987. "QAP partialling as a test of spuriousness." *Social
Networks* 9:171–186.

—— 1988. "Predicting with networks: Nonparametric multiple regression
analysis of dyadic data." *Social Networks* 10:359–381.

—— 1990. "Network analysis with structurally autocorrelated data." Unpublished manuscript. Johnson Graduate School of Management, Cornell
University.

Laumann, Edward O. and David Knoke. 1987. *The Organizational State: Social Choice in National Policy Domains*. Madison: University of Wisconsin Press.

Laumann, Edward O., and Peter V. Marsden. 1979. "The analysis of oppositional structures in political elites: Identifying collective actors."
American Sociological Review 44:713–732.

—— 1982. "Microstructural analysis in interorganizational systems."
Social Networks 4:329–348.

Laumann, Edward O., and Franz U. Pappi. 1976. *Networks of Collective Action: A Perspective on Community Influence Systems*. New York: Academic Press.

Lawrence, Paul R. and Jay W. Lorsch. 1967. *Organization and Environment*.
Cambridge: Harvard University Press.

Lazarsfeld, Paul F., and Robert K. Merton. 1954. "Friendship as a social pro-
cess: A substantive and methodological analysis." Pp. 18–56 in Morroe
Berger, Theodore Abel, and Charles Page, eds., *Freedom and Control in
Modern Society*. New York: Van Nostrand Reinhold.

Lazarsfeld, Paul F., Bernard Berelson, and Hazel Gaudet. 1944. *The People's
Choice*. New York: Columbia University Press.

Leifer, Eric M., and Harrison C. White. 1987. "A structural approach to markets." Pp. 85–108 in Mark S. Mizruchi and Michael Schwartz, eds., *Intercorporate Relations: The Structural Analysis of Business*. New York:
Cambridge University Press.

Levine, Joel H. 1972. "The sphere of influence." *American Sociological Review* 37:14–27.

Lieberson, Stanley. 1971. "An empirical study of military-industrial linkages." *American Journal of Sociology* 76:562–584.

Liebert, Roland J., and Allen W. Imershein, eds. 1977. *Power, Paradigms, and Community Research.* Beverly Hills: Sage.

Lincoln, James R. 1984. "Analyzing relations in dyads." *Sociological Methods and Research* 13:45–76.

Lindblom, Charles E. 1977. *Politics and Markets.* New York: Basic Books.

Lindenberg, Siegwart. 1989. "Social production functions, deficits, and social revolutions: Prerevolutionary France and Russia." *Rationality and Society* 1:51–77.

Lipset, Seymour Martin. 1960. *Political Man.* Garden City, N.Y.: Doubleday.
——— 1962. "Introduction." Pp. 15–39 in Robert Michels, *Political Parties.* New York: Free Press.

Loftin, Colin and Sally K. Ward. 1983. "A spatial autocorrelation model of the effects of population density on fertility." *American Sociological Review* 48:121–128.

Logan, John R., and Harvey L. Molotch. 1987. *Urban Fortunes: The Political Economy of Place.* Berkeley: University of California Press.

Lorrain, Francois, and Harrison C. White. 1971. "Structural equivalence of individuals in social networks." *Journal of Mathematical Sociology* 1:49–80.

Lowi, Theodore J. 1969. *The End of Liberalism.* New York: W. W. Norton and Co.

Lukes, Steven. 1974. *Power: A Radical View.* New York: Macmillan.

Maitland, Ian H. and Cho-Kan Pak. 1987. "The political consequences of linkages between firms." Paper presented at the Annual Meeting of the Academy of Management. New Orleans.

Maitland, Ian H., and Dong Soo Park. 1985. "Campaign contribution strategies of corporate political action committees." Minneapolis: Strategic Management Research Center, University of Minnesota, discussion paper #29.

Malbin, Michael J. 1979. "Campaign financing and the 'special interests.' " *The Public Interest* 56:21–42.

Manley, John F. 1983. "A class analysis of pluralism I and pluralism II." *American Political Science Review* 77:368–383.

Mann, Michael. 1986. *The Sources of Social Power.* New York: Cambridge University Press.

Mantel, Nathan. 1967. "The detection of disease clustering and a general regression approach." *Cancer Research* 27:209–220.

Mariolis, Peter. 1975. "Interlocking directorates and control of corporations." *Social Science Quarterly* 56:425–439.

Markovsky, Barry, and Edward J. Lawler. 1988. "Emotions and group solidarity." Paper presented at the Annual Meeting of the American Sociological Association. Atlanta.

Marsden, Peter V. 1981. "Introducing influence processes into a system of collective decisions." *American Journal of Sociology* 86:1203–1235.

———— 1983. "Restricted access in networks and models of power." *American Journal of Sociology* 88:686–717.

Marx, Karl. [1932] 1972. "The German Ideology: Part I." Pp. 111–164 in Robert C. Tucker, ed., *The Marx-Engels Reader.* New York: W. W. Norton and Co.

Masters, Marick F., and Barry D. Baysinger. 1985. "The determinants of funds raised by corporate political action committees: An empirical examination." *Academy of Management Journal* 28:654–664.

Masters, Marick F., and Gerald D. Keim. 1985. "Determinants of PAC participation among large corporations." *Journal of Politics* 47:1158–1173.

Merton, Robert K. 1936. "The unanticipated consequences of purposive social action." *American Sociological Review* 1:894–904.

———— 1949. *Social Theory and Social Structure.* New York: Free Press.

Michels, Robert. [1911] 1962. *Political Parties.* New York: Free Press.

Miliband, Ralph. 1969. *The State in Capitalist Society.* New York: Basic Books.

Mills, C. Wright. 1956. *The Power Elite.* New York: Oxford University Press.

Milner, Helen V. 1988. *Resisting Protectionism: Global Industries and the Politics of International Trade.* Princeton: Princeton University Press.

Mintz, Beth, and Michael Schwartz. 1985. *The Power Structure of American Business.* Chicago: University of Chicago Press.

Mintz, Beth, Peter Freitag, Carol Hendricks, and Michael Schwartz. 1978. "Problems of proof in elite research." *Social Problems* 23:314–324.

Mizruchi, Mark S. 1982. *The American Corporate Network, 1904–1974.* Beverly Hills: Sage.

———— 1983a. "An interorganizational theory of social class: A synthesis of the resource dependence and social class models of intercorporate relations." Paper presented at the Annual Meeting of the American Sociological Association. Detroit.

———— 1983b. "Who controls whom? An examination of the relation between management and boards of directors in large American corporations." *Academy of Management Review* 8:126–135.

———— 1984. "Interlock groups, cliques, or interest groups? Comment on Allen." *Social Networks* 6:193–199.

———— 1987. "Why does business stick together? An interorganizational theory of class cohesion." Pp. 204–218 in G. William Domhoff and Thomas R. Dye, eds., *Power Elites and Organizations.* Beverly Hills: Sage.

———— 1989. "Similarity of political behavior among large American corporations." *American Journal of Sociology* 95:401–424.

———— 1990a. "Similarity of ideology and party preference among large American corporations: A study of political action committee contributions." *Sociological Forum* 5:213–240.

———— 1990b. "Determinants of political opposition among large American corporations." *Social Forces* 68:1065–1088.

———— 1990c. "Cohesion, equivalence, and similarity of behavior: A theoretical and empirical assessment." Paper presented at the Tenth Annual Sunbelt Social Network Conference. San Diego.

—— 1991. "Market relations, interlocks, and corporate political behavior." *Research in Political Sociology* 5:167–208.

Mizruchi, Mark S., and David Bunting. 1981. "Influence in corporate networks: An examination of four measures." *Administrative Science Quarterly* 26:475–489.

Mizruchi, Mark S., and Thomas Koenig. 1986. "Economic sources of corporate political consensus: An examination of interindustry relations." *American Sociological Review* 51:482–491.

—— 1988. "Economic concentration and corporate political behavior: A cross-industry comparison." *Social Science Research* 17:287–305.

Mizruchi, Mark S., Peter Mariolis, Michael Schwartz, and Beth Mintz. 1986. "Techniques for disaggregating centrality scores in social networks." Pp. 26–48 in Nancy B. Tuma, ed., *Sociological Methodology 1986*. Washington: American Sociological Association.

Mizruchi, Mark S., and Michael Schwartz. 1987. "The structural analysis of business: An emerging field." Pp. 3–21 in Mark S. Mizruchi and Michael Schwartz, eds., *Intercorporate Relations: The Structural Analysis of Business*. New York: Cambridge University Press.

Mizruchi, Mark S., and Linda Brewster Stearns. 1988. "A longitudinal study of the formation of interlocking directorates." *Administrative Science Quarterly* 33:194–210.

Moe, Terry M. 1980. *The Organization of Interests*. Chicago: University of Chicago Press.

Mollenkopf, John. 1989. "Who (or what) runs cities, and how?" *Sociological Forum* 4:119–137.

Molotch, Harvey L. 1976. "The city as growth machine: Toward a political economy of place." *American Journal of Sociology* 82:309–331.

Moore, Gwen. 1979. "The structure of a national elite network." *American Sociological Review* 44:673–692.

Moore, Gwen, and Richard D. Alba. 1982. "Class and prestige origins in the American elite." Pp. 39–60 in Peter V. Marsden and Nan Lin, eds., *Social Structure and Network Analysis*. Beverly Hills: Sage.

Neustadtl, Alan, and Dan Clawson. 1988. "Corporate political groupings: Does ideology unify business political behavior?" *American Sociological Review* 53:172–190.

Neustadtl, Alan, Denise Scott, and Dan Clawson. 1991. "Class struggle in campaign finance? Political action committee contributions in the 1984 elections." *Sociological Forum* 6:219–238.

O'Connor, James. 1973. *The Fiscal Crisis of the State*. New York: St. Martin's Press.

Offe, Claus. 1972. "Political activity and class structures—An analysis of late capitalist societies." *International Journal of Sociology* II:73–108.

Oliver, Pamela E., and Gerald Marwell. 1988. "The paradox of group size in collective action: A theory of the critical mass. II." *American Sociological Review* 53:1–8.

Olson, Mancur. 1965. *The Logic of Collective Action*. Cambridge: Harvard University Press.

Ord, Keith. 1975. "Estimation methods for models of spatial interaction." *Journal of the American Statistical Association* 70:120–126.

Ornstein, Michael D. 1980. "Assessing the meaning of corporate interlocks: Canadian evidence." *Social Science Research* 9:287–306.

——— 1984. "Interlocking directorates in Canada: Intercorporate or class alliance?" *Administrative Science Quarterly* 29:210–231.

Palmer, Donald. 1983. "Broken ties: Interlocking directorates, and intercorporate coordination." *Administrative Science Quarterly* 28:40–55.

Palmer, Donald, Roger Friedland, and Jitendra V. Singh. 1986. "The ties that bind: Organizational and class bases of stability in a corporate interlock network." *American Sociological Review* 51:781–796.

Parkin, Frank. 1979. *Marxism and Class Theory: A Bourgeois Critique.* New York: Columbia University Press.

Parsons, Talcott. 1951. *The Social System.* New York: Free Press.

——— 1960. *Structure and Process in Modern Societies.* New York: Free Press.

Parsons, Talcott, and Neil Smelser. 1957. *Economy and Society.* London: Routledge & Kegan Paul.

Pennings, Johannes M. 1980. *Interlocking Directorates.* San Francisco: Jossey-Bass.

Perrow, Charles. 1967. "A framework for comparative organizational analysis." *American Sociological Review* 32:194–208.

——— 1986. *Complex Organizations: A Critical Essay.* Third Edition. New York: Random House.

Perrucci, Robert, and Marc Pilisuk. 1970. "Leaders and ruling elites: The interorganizational bases of community power." *American Sociological Review* 35:1040–1056.

Petersen, Trond. 1985. "A comment on presenting results from logit and probit models." *American Sociological Review* 50:130–131.

Pfeffer, Jeffrey. 1972. "Size and composition of corporate boards of directors." *Administrative Science Quarterly* 17:218–228.

——— 1987. "A resource dependence perspective on intercorporate relations." Pp. 25–55 in Mark S. Mizruchi and Michael Schwartz, eds., *Intercorporate Relations: The Structural Analysis of Business.* New York: Cambridge University Press.

Pfeffer, Jeffrey, and Gerald R. Salancik. 1978. *The External Control of Organizations: A Resource Dependence Perspective.* New York: Harper & Row.

Polanyi, Karl. [1944] 1957. *The Great Transformation.* Boston: Beacon Press.

Polsby, Nelson. 1959. "Three problems in the analysis of community power." *American Sociological Review* 24:796–803.

——— 1970. "How to study community power: The pluralist alternative." Pp. 297–304 in Michael Aiken and Paul Mott, eds., *The Structure of Community Power.* New York: Random House.

Poulantzas, Nicos. 1972. "The problem of the capitalist state." Pp. 238–253 in Robin Blackburn, ed., *Ideology in the Social Sciences.* London: Fontana.

——— 1973. *Political Power and Social Classes.* London: New Left Books.

Quinn, Dennis P., and Robert Y. Shapiro. 1991. "Business political power: The case of taxation." *American Political Science Review* 85 (forthcoming).

Ratcliff, Richard E. 1980. "Banks and corporate lending: An analysis of the impact of the internal structure of the capitalist class on the lending behavior of banks." *American Sociological Review* 45: 553–570.

Ratcliff, Richard E., Mary Elizabeth Gallagher, and David Jaffee. 1980. "Political money and ideological clusters in the capitalist class." Paper presented at the Annual Meeting of the American Sociological Association, New York.

Ratcliff, Richard E., Mary Elizabeth Gallagher, and Kathryn Strother Ratcliff. 1979. "The civic involvement of bankers: An analysis of the influence of economic power and social prominence in the command of civic policy positions." *Social Problems* 26:298–313.

Richardson, R. Jack. 1987. "Directorship interlocks and corporate profitability." *Administrative Science Quarterly* 32:367–386.

Riesman, David. 1953. *The Lonely Crowd.* Garden City, N.Y.: Anchor.

Rose, Arnold M. 1967. *The Power Structure.* New York: Oxford University Press.

Roth, Guenther, and Wolfgang Schluchter. 1979. *Max Weber's Vision of History.* Berkeley: University of California Press.

Rothenberg, Stuart, and Richard R. Roldan. 1983. *Business PACs and Ideology.* Washington: Free Congress Research and Education Foundation.

Rousseau, Jean-Jacques. [1762] 1913. *The Social Contract.* New York: Dutton.

Roy, William G. 1983. "The unfolding of the interlocking directorate structure of the United States." *American Sociological Review* 48:248–257.

Sabato, Larry J. 1984. *PAC Power: Inside the World of Political Action Committees.* New York: W. W. Norton and Co.

Salamon, Lester M., and John J. Siegfried. 1977. "Economic power and political influence: The impact of industry structure on public policy." *American Political Science Review* 71:1026–1043.

Sale, Kirkpatrick. 1976. *Power Shift: The Rise of the Southern Rim and its Challenge to the Eastern Establishment.* New York: Random House.

Salisbury, Robert H. 1984. "Interest representation: The dominance of institutions." *American Political Science Review* 78:64–76.

Sallach, David L. 1974. "Class domination and ideological hegemony." *Sociological Quarterly* 15:38–50.

Sailer, Lee D. 1978. "Structural equivalence: Meaning and definition, computation and application." *Social Networks* 1:73–90.

Scherer, F. M. 1980. *Industrial Market Structure and Economic Performance.* Chicago: Rand McNally.

Schumpeter, Joseph. 1942. *Capitalism, Socialism, and Democracy.* New York: Harper & Row.

Sciulli, David. 1991. *Theory of Societal Constitutionalism: Foundations of a Non-Marxist Critical Theory.* New York: Cambridge University Press.

Scott, John. 1979. *Corporations, Classes, and Capitalism.* London: Hutchinson.

Selznick, Philip. 1949. *TVA and the Grass Roots.* New York: Harper & Row.

Simmel, Georg. [1922] 1955. *Conflict and The Web of Group Affiliations.* Translated by Reinhard Bendix. New York: Free Press.

——— [1917] 1950. "The Triad." Pp. 145–169 in Kurt H. Wolff, ed., *The Sociology of Georg Simmel.* New York: Free Press.

Sobel, Robert. 1965. *The Big Board.* New York: Free Press.

Sonquist, John, and Thomas Koenig. 1975. "Interlocking directorates in the top U.S. corporations: A graph theory approach." *Insurgent Sociologist* 5:196–230.

Sorauf, Frank J. 1984. *What Price PACs?: Report of the Twentieth Century Fund Task Force on Political Action Committees.* New York: Twentieth Century Fund.

Soref, Michael. 1976. "Social class and a division of labor within the corporate elite: A note on class, interlocking and executive committee membership of directors of U.S. industrial firms." *Sociological Quarterly* 17:360–368.

Soref, Michael, and Maurice Zeitlin. 1987. "Finance capital and the internal structure of the capitalist class in the United States." Pp. 56–84 in Mark S. Mizruchi and Michael Schwartz, eds., *Intercorporate Relations: The Structural Analysis of Business.* New York: Cambridge University Press.

Stearns, Linda Brewster, and Mark S. Mizruchi. 1986. "Broken-tie reconstitution and the functions of interorganizational interlocks: A reexamination." *Administrative Science Quarterly* 31:522–538.

Stein, Arthur A. 1976. "Conflict and cohesion: A review of the literature." *Journal of Conflict Resolution* 20:143–172.

Stokman, Frans N., Jelle van der Knoop, and Frans W. Wasseur. 1989. "Interlocks in the Netherlands: Stability and careers in the period 1960–1980." *Social Networks* 10:183–208.

Stokman, Frans N., Rolf Ziegler, and John Scott, eds. 1985. *Networks of Corporate Power: A Comparative Analysis of Ten Countries.* Cambridge, England: Polity Press.

Stone, Clarence N. 1984. "Civic politics and economic development: Political economy perspectives." *Journal of Politics* 46:286–298.

Sweezy, Paul M. 1970. "The American ruling class." Pp. 356–371 in Maurice Zeitlin, ed., *American Society, Inc.* Chicago: Markham.

Sylvan, David, and Barry Glassner. 1985. *A Rationalist Methodology for the Social Sciences.* Oxford: Basil Blackwell.

Thompson, James D. 1967. *Organizations in Action.* New York: McGraw-Hill.

Thompson, James D. and William J. McEwen. 1958. "Organizational goals and environment: Goal-setting as an interaction process." *American Sociological Review* 23:23–31.

Toqueville, Alexis de. [1835–1840] 1945. *Democracy in America.* 2 vols. New York: Vintage.

Truman, David B. 1951. *The Governmental Process.* New York: Alfred A. Knopf.

United States Bureau of the Census. 1986. *Statistical Abstract of the United States.* Washington: U.S. Government Printing Office.

Useem, Michael. 1978. "The inner group of the American capitalist class." *Social Problems* 25:225–240.

———— 1979. "The social organization of the business elite and participation of corporate directors in the governance of American institutions." *American Sociological Review* 44:553–572.

———— 1982. "Classwide rationality in the politics of managers and directors of large corporations in the United States and Great Britain." *Administrative Science Quarterly* 27:199–226.

———— 1984. *The Inner Circle.* New York: Oxford University Press.

———— 1989. "The revolt of the corporate owners and the demobilization of business political action." *Critical Sociology* 16, nos. 2–3:7–25.

Useem, Michael, and Jerome Karabel. 1986. "Pathways to top corporate management." *American Sociological Review* 51:184–200.

Vanneman, Reeve and Lynn Weber Cannon. 1987. *The American Perception of Class.* Philadelphia: Temple University Press.

Vogel, David. 1989. *Fluctuating Fortunes: The Political Power of Business in America.* New York: Basic Books.

Walker, Jack. 1983. "The origins and maintenance of interest groups in America." *American Political Science Review* 77:390–406.

Weber, Max. [1947] 1964. *The Theory of Social and Economic Organization.* New York: Free Press.

Weinstein, James. 1968. *The Corporate Ideal in the Liberal State, 1900–1918.* Boston: Beacon Press.

Wellman, Barry. 1988. "Network analysis: From method and metaphor to theory and substance." Pp. 19–61 in Wellman and S. D. Berkowitz, eds., *Social Structures: A Network Approach.* New York: Cambridge University Press.

White, Douglas R., and Karl P. Reitz. 1983. "Graph and semigroup homomorphisms on networks of relations." *Social Networks* 5:193–234.

White, Harrison C., Scott A. Boorman, and Ronald L. Breiger. 1976. "Social structure from multiple networks. I. Blockmodels of roles and positions." *American Journal of Sociology* 81:730–780.

Whitt, J. Allen. 1982. *Urban Elites and Mass Transportation.* Princeton: Princeton University Press.

Whitt, J. Allen, and Mark S. Mizruchi. 1986. "The local inner circle." *Journal of Political and Military Sociology* 14:115–125.

Williams, Robin M., Jr. 1970. *American Society: A Sociological Interpretation.* Third Edition. New York: Alfred A. Knopf.

Williamson, Oliver E. 1975. *Markets and Hierarchies: Analysis and Antitrust Implications.* New York: Free Press.

Winship, Christopher. 1988. "Thoughts about roles and relations: An old document revisited." *Social Networks* 10:209–231.

Wolfinger, Raymond E. 1960. "Reputation and reality in the study of 'community power.' " *American Sociological Review* 25:636–644.

Wright, Erik Olin. 1985. *Classes.* London: Verso.

Wright, John R. 1989. "PAC contributions, lobbying, and representation." *Journal of Politics* 51:713–729.

Wrong, Dennis. 1961. "The oversocialized conception of man in modern sociology." *American Sociological Review* 26:184–193.

———[1979] 1988. *Power: Its Forms, Bases, and Uses.* Chicago: University of Chicago Press.

Yuchtman, Ephraim, and Stanley E. Seashore. 1967. "A system resource approach to organizational effectiveness." *American Sociological Review* 32:891–903.

Zald, Mayer N. 1970. "Political economy: A framework for comparative analysis." Pp 221–261 in Zald, ed., *Power in Organizations.* Nashville, Tenn.: Vanderbilt University Press.

Zald, Mayer N., and John D. McCarthy, eds. 1979. *The Dynamics of Social Movements.* Cambridge, Mass.: Winthrop.

Zeitlin, Maurice. 1974. "Corporate ownership and control: The large corporation and the capitalist class." *American Journal of Sociology* 79:1073–1119.

——— 1976. "On class theory of the large corporation: Response to Allen." *American Journal of Sociology* 81:894–904.

Zeitlin, Maurice, and Richard E. Ratcliff. 1988. *Landlords and Capitalists: The Dominant Class of Chile.* Princeton: Princeton University Press.

Zeitlin, Maurice, Lynda Ann Ewen, and Richard E. Ratcliff. 1974. "New princes for old? The large corporation and the capitalist class in Chile." *American Journal of Sociology* 80:87–123.

Zelizer, Viviana A. 1988. "Beyond the polemics on the market: Establishing a theoretical and empirical agenda." *Sociological Forum* 3:614–634.

Ziegler, Rolf. 1987. "Market, power, and cooptation: A structural-individualistic explanation of the German intercorporate network." Paper presented at the Nags Head Conference on Corporate Interlocks. Kill Devil Hills, N.C.

Name Index

Subject Index

Mark S. Mizruchi is Professor of Sociology at the
University of Michigan. Among his previous
books is *The American Corporate Network,
1904–1974.*